D1275946

ManageFirst®
Nutrition
Competency Guide

Donated by
◈ Chef Michael Therriat ◈

PEARSON
Prentice
Hall

Upper Saddle River, New Jersey 07458

Disclaimer

Published by Pearson Prentice Hall, 1 Lake Street, Upper Saddle River, NJ 07458.

ISBN: 978-0-13-228386-1 (Competency Guide with Examination Answer Sheet)

Printed in the U.S.A.

10 9 8

Table of Contents

A Message from the National Restaurant Association

Founded in 1919, the National Restaurant Association is the leading business association for the restaurant industry. Together with the National Restaurant Association Educational Foundation (NRAEF) and National Restaurant Association Solutions (NRA Solutions) our goal is to lead America's restaurant industry into a new era of prosperity, prominence, and participation, enhancing the quality of life for all we serve.

As one of the nation's largest private-sector employers, the restaurant, hospitality and foodservice industry is the cornerstone of the American economy, of career-and-employment opportunities, and of local communities. The overall impact of the restaurant industry is astounding. The restaurant industry is expected to add 1.8 million jobs over the next decade, with employment reaching 14.8 million by 2019. At the National Restaurant Association, we are focused on enhancing this position by providing the valuable tools and resources needed to educate our current and future professionals.

For more information on the National Restaurant Association, please visit our Web site at www.restaurant.org.

What is the ManageFirst Program™?

The ManageFirst Program is a management-training certificate program that exemplifies our commitment to developing materials by the industry, for the industry. The program's most powerful strength is that it is based on a set of competencies defined by the restaurant, foodservice, and hospitality industry as critical for success. For more information on the ManageFirst Program, visit www.managefirst.restaurant.org.

ManageFirst Program Components

The ManageFirst Program includes a set of Competency Guides, exams, Instructor Resources, certificates, a credential, and support activities and services. By participating in the program, you are demonstrating your commitment to becoming a highly qualified professional preparing either to begin or to advance your career in the restaurant, hospitality, and foodservice industry.

The Competency Guides cover the range of topics listed in the chart at right.

Competency Guide/Exam Topics

ManageFirst Core Credential Topics

Controlling Foodservice Costs

Hospitality and Restaurant Management

Human Resources Management and Supervision

ServSafe® Food Safety

ManageFirst Elective Topics

Customer Service

Food Production

Inventory and Purchasing

Managerial Accounting

Menu Marketing and Management

Nutrition

Restaurant Marketing

ServSafe Alcohol® Responsible Alcohol Service

Within the guides, you will find the essential content for the topic as defined by industry, as well as learning activities, assessments, case studies, suggested field projects, professional profiles, and testimonials. You can also find an answer sheet or an online exam voucher for a NRA Solutions exam written specifically for each topic. The exam can be administered either online or in a paper and pencil format (see inside front cover for a listing of ISBNs), and it will be proctored. Upon successfully passing the exam, you will be issued a customized certificate from NRA Solutions. The certificate is a lasting recognition of your accomplishment and a signal to the industry that you have mastered the competency covered within the particular topic.

To earn the ManageFirst Professional™ (MFP™) credential, you will be required to pass four core exams and one elective exam (to be chosen from the remaining program topics) and to document your work experience in the restaurant and foodservice industry. Earning the MFP credential is a significant accomplishment.

We applaud you as you either begin or advance your career in the restaurant, hospitality, and foodservice industry. Visit *www.managefirst.restaurant.org* to learn about additional career-building resources offered through the National Restaurant Association, including scholarships for college students enrolled in relevant industry programs.

ManageFirst Program Ordering Information

Review copies or support materials:
FACULTY FIELD SERVICES
Tel: 800.526.0485

Domestic orders and inquiries:
PEARSON CUSTOMER SERVICE
Tel: 800.922.0579
www.prenhall.com

International orders and inquiries:
U.S. EXPORT SALES OFFICE
Pearson Education International Customer Service Group
200 Old Tappan Road
Old Tappan, NJ 07675 USA
Tel: 201.767.5021
Fax: 201.767.5625

For corporate, government, and special sales (consultants, corporations, training centers, VARs, and corporate resellers) orders and inquiries:
PEARSON CORPORATE SALES
Tel: 317.428.3411
Fax: 317.428.3343
Email: managefirst@prenhall.com

For additional information regarding other Prentice Hall publications, instructor and student support materials, locating your sales representative, and much more, please visit *www.prenhall.com/managefirst.*

Acknowledgements

The National Restaurant Association Educational Solutions is grateful for the significant contributions to this competency guide made by the following individuals.

Theresa Marie Gargano Adamski, MS, MBA

Jonathan Deustch, PhD

Holly Ruttan Maloney, RD, LDN

Patricia Plavcan, MS, RD, LDN

Renee Zonka, RD, CEC, MBA, CHE

In addition, we are pleased to thank our many other advisors, subject matter experts, reviewers, and contributors for their time, effort, and dedication to this program.

Ernest Boger	Thomas Kaltenecker	James Perry
Robert Bosselman	Ray Kavanaugh	William N. Reynolds
Jerald Chesser	John Kidwell	Rosenthal Group
Cynthia Deale	Carol Kizer	Mokie Steiskal
Fred DeMicco	Cynthia Mayo	Karl Titz
John Drysdale	Fred Mayo	Terry Umbreit
Gene Fritz	Patrick Moreo	David Wightman
John Gescheidle	Robert O'Halloran	Deanne Williams
Thomas Hamilton	Brian O'Malley	Mike Zema
John Hart	Terrence Pappas	

Features of the ManageFirst® Competency Guides

We have designed the ManageFirst competency guides to enhance your ability to learn and retain important information that is critical to this restaurant and foodservice industry function. Here are the key features you will find within this guide.

Beginning Each Guide

Tuning In to You

When you open a ManageFirst competency guide for the first time, you might ask yourself: Why do I need to know about this topic? Every topic of these guides involves key information you will need as you manage a restaurant or foodservice operation. Located in the front of each review guide, "Tuning In to You" is a brief synopsis that illustrates some of the reasons the information contained throughout that particular guide is important to you. It exemplifies real-life scenarios that you will face as a manager and how the concepts in the book will help you in your career.

Professional Profile

This is your opportunity to meet a professional who is currently working in the field associated with a competency guide's topic. This person's story will help you gain insight into the responsibilities related to his or her position, as well as the training and educational history linked to it. You will also see the daily and cumulative impact this position has on an operation, and receive advice from a person who has successfully met the challenges of being a manager.

Beginning Each Chapter

Inside This Chapter

Chapter content is organized under these major headings.

Learning Objectives

Learning objectives identify what you should be able to do after completing each chapter. These objectives are linked to the required tasks a manager must be able to perform in relation to the function discussed in the competency guide.

Test Your Knowledge

Each chapter begins with some True or False questions designed to test your prior knowledge of some of the concepts presented in the chapter. The answers to these questions, as well as the concepts behind them, can be found within the chapter—see the page reference after each question.

Key Terms

These terms are important for thorough understanding of the chapter's content. They are highlighted throughout the chapter, where they are explicitly defined or their meaning is made clear within the paragraphs in which they appear.

Throughout Each Chapter

Exhibits

Exhibits are placed throughout each chapter to visually reinforce the key concepts presented in the text. Types of exhibits include charts, tables, photographs, and illustrations.

Think About It...

These thought-provoking sidebars reveal supportive information about the section they appear beside.

Activities

Apply what you have learned throughout the chapter by completing the various activities in the text. The activities have been designed to give you additional practice and better understanding of the concepts addressed in the learning objectives. Types of activities include case study, role-play, and problem solving, among others.

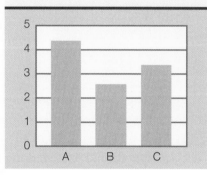

Exhibit

Exhibits are visuals that will help you learn about key concepts.

Think About It...

Consider these supplemental insights as you read through a chapter.

Activity

Activity

Types of activities you will complete include case study, role-play, and problem solving, among others.

At the End of Each Chapter

Review Your Learning

These multiple-choice or open- or close-ended questions or problems are designed to test your knowledge of the concepts presented in the chapter. These questions have been aligned with the objectives and should provide you with an opportunity to practice or apply the content that supports these objectives. If you have difficulty answering them, you should review the content further.

At the End of the Guide

Field Project

This real-world project gives you the valuable opportunity to apply many of the concepts you will learn in a competency guide. You will interact with industry practitioners, enhance your knowledge, and research, apply, analyze, evaluate, and report on your findings. It will provide you with an in-depth "reality check" of the policies and practices of this management function.

Tuning In to You

Knowledge of nutrition is a crucial part of providing food in a restaurant or foodservice operation. You are not just providing customer service; you are also playing a part in nourishing people's bodies and minds. The human body needs certain nutrients to grow, develop, and maintain health, and these nutrients must be obtained from a variety of food items in order to acquire all the ones that are needed.

Food is present at almost every contemporary social event, and people are turning more and more to restaurant and foodservice operations for their food. So, as a restaurant professional, you have an increasing impact on the nutritional intake of your guests and, therefore, on their health and happiness. Once you understand the importance of nutrition and the functions of nutrients in the body, it is a logical next step to want to provide nutritious meals to your customers.

Also, people are becoming more aware of nutrition and demanding that restaurant and foodservice operations provide healthy food choices. It is in your interest to pay attention to the nutritional demands of your guests; it is "good business" on your part, and just about every operation's menu has some healthy offerings, including fish and vegetarian items. But only a few healthy offerings isn't enough. Your menu should include a selection of healthy options to give people the choices they need.

As you probably already realize, the nutritional knowledge and skill demands of the restaurant and foodservice professional are increasing. Throughout your career, it is likely that you will work in many types of restaurant and foodservice operations that require varied areas of nutritional expertise. For example:

- Planning and preparing food in healthcare and other institutions
- Planning menus for a large restaurant chain with competition and profitability riding on your decisions
- Being a chef, recipe developer, and/or menu planner at an individual establishment
- Working in the dining-at-home segment of the food industry, helping people who no longer have time to prepare meals
- Working as a private chef

As you can see, having knowledge about nutrition is extremely valuable. It makes you marketable as professional and makes your foodservice establishment more desirable to consumers.

Professional Profile
Your opportunity to meet someone working in the field

Caren Messina-Hirsch

President
Food Performance, Inc.
Wheaton, IL

I fell in love with food at a very early age. It all began with the beautifully decorated cakes my parents bought to celebrate my birthdays. By the age of six, I was making my own small cakes in a play oven—the kind that used a light bulb as the heat source. I continued to be interested in food, and subsequently nutrition, throughout my elementary and high-school years.

Growing up in New Jersey, I was surrounded by peach orchards, strawberry and blueberry farms, fresh tomatoes, cucumbers, and other fresh fruit and vegetables from the local farmers' stands. At twelve, one of my school assignments was to write about what I wanted to be when I grew up. I picked dietetics for two reasons: the mother of a fellow classmate was a dietitian, and after talking with her I realized that dietetics was a good way to find out more about food and nutrition. Throughout high school, I was active in 4-H and FHA (Future Homemakers of America). I developed cooking skills and had great fun participating in many cooking contests and demonstrations.

When I graduated high school, I thought about going to culinary school, but these schools weren't as prestigious then as they are today, and there weren't many women attending them. Instead, to learn about nutrition and dietetics I attended Notre Dame of Ohio, a small Catholic college outside of Cleveland. I also worked all through college. By my senior year, I had worked in the campus foodservice kitchen, developed menus, and cooked for various retreats. During the summers, I worked for a local caterer but spent most of my days practicing dietetics and learning about food in a 3,000-bed state mental hospital. That facility had a butcher shop, bakery, large food-production facility, and many special diets. I worked with the dietitians and moved from one department to another, learning as much as I could. Because of this experience, I was offered a job immediately out of college, but I decided to continue my dietetic education by pursuing a master's degree.

I pursued a combination administrative/master's degree program at Oklahoma State University. Dietetic students worked in and supervised on-campus dining facilities and off-campus school foodservice and hospital facilities while also attending classes. There also was an on-campus central bakery that produced baked goods and made daily deliveries to the main campus. I managed this facility while completing my degree. (Although working in a bakery may not sound very nutritious, sweets in moderation are part of a balanced diet, and college students not only consume but burn lots of calories.)

After graduation, I longed to work in a test kitchen but didn't get the opportunity. Instead, I spent a year at Syracuse University as a dining-room manager. There, I looked after the welfare of 300 students with various nutritional issues, including a few vegetarians. I also continued to compete in a variety of food-related contests. After a year at Syracuse, I finally was offered a technical service/test-kitchen position with General Mills in Minneapolis, MN. GM's test-kitchen group is responsible for testing products and writing label directions. I also traveled throughout the country representing General Mills at various venues, including food shows and working with foodservice operators, and I worked closely with the well-established and respected General Mills Nutrition Department.

After seven years of working for a large food company and establishing a strong network, I decided to start my own food consulting business, Food Performance™. Having a dietetics background has been important for many projects related to my business, including developing low-fat/low-calorie menus for a large food manufacturer, managing a national sampling campaign of reduced-sodium products for the healthcare market, and developing foodservice recipes with specific nutritional criteria. I also had the opportunity to teach a nutrition course to the American Culinary Federation (ACF) members as part of the requirements for ACF certification.

I believe that, regardless of the occupation you choose, your skill levels need to be constantly improved. So, in spite of my many years in the kitchen, I recently decided to attend culinary school to sharpen my culinary skills. After completing the program's courses, I received a cooking certificate from Kendall College. Now I am able to merge sound cooking techniques and nutrition in my pursuit of dietary excellence.

In addition to Food Performance™, I was also a partner in Food Beat™, a menu database company. In this capacity, I saw how nutrition has influenced and will continue to influence the development of chain-restaurant menus. This only reinforces what I have seen over my entire career—that food and nutrition are incredibly interconnected. I believe that chefs and dietitians trained in preparing healthy food and understanding the nutritive values of food can and do have an enormous influence on the health of Americans.

Nutritional Cooking— Art and Science

Inside This Chapter

- What Is Nutrition?
- How We Got to This Point
- Achieving Nutritious Food Choices
- Markets for Nutritious Cooking Skills and Knowledge
- Applying Nutrition Principles to Cooking Is Both Art and Science

After completing this chapter, you should be able to:

- Explain the importance of nutrition in the restaurant and foodservice industry.
- Explain why achieving balanced nutrition is important.
- Explain why making food both nutritious and interesting is important.
- Explain how nutrition principles are dynamic and change as scientists learn more about food and metabolism.
- List the factors that affect people's food choices.
- Explain why restaurateurs are becoming more aware of the need to provide good nutrition in all menus.
- Explain how to obtain nutrition information for recipes and menus.
- Explain, in general, how making food both nutritious and interesting is a combination of art and science.

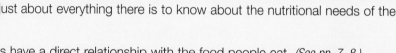

Key Terms

ACF-certified chef

Charque

Confit

Culinary arts

Food science

Home meal replacement

Jerked beef

Nutrients

Nutrition

Pastirma

Pemmican

Registered dietetic technician

Registered dietitian

Salt pork

Think About It...

Think of the last time you looked at a menu selection that sounded delicious. You visualized this colorful plate with its tantalizing textures. You couldn't wait to dive into it. After you ate, you savored the taste and wished for more. You remember, "What a phenomenal meal!" But was the meal actually healthy for you?

Introduction

You might be a chef, a recipe developer, a menu planner, a manager, or some other professional in a restaurant or foodservice operation, or studying to become one. You most likely are not planning to be a dietitian or a nutritionist. So you are probably asking why you should learn about nutrition. Nutrition is important for the health of everyone and of all ages, as shown in *Exhibit 1a.* Consequently, as a restaurant or foodservice professional, you are in the position to help your customers eat more nutritiously by making food both nutritious and delectable. In this chapter, you will learn that nutrition is becoming more important to restaurant and foodservice operations because many customers today are more aware and concerned about their own nutrition. You will learn that providing healthy, delicious food is not only necessary but possible. To accomplish this, you also will learn how easy it is to determine the nutritional content of various types of food.

Exhibit 1a

People of all ages and ethnicities need balanced nutrition.

What Is Nutrition?

Nutrition is the science of the nutrients in food and how they are ingested, digested, absorbed, transported, and utilized to build and maintain the body. Nutrition is involved with nutrients, the nutritional needs of the body, and bodily processes related to the acquisition and use of nutrients. Nutrients are the chemicals needed to support the body for daily metabolic functions of growth and development. Thus, nutrition also refers to the nutrient values of food and the amount of these nutrients being supplied to people's bodies.

Why Is Nutrition Important?

Food is needed to provide energy, build body structure, and enable the many chemical reactions that cause the human body to function. An insufficient quantity of nutrients or an improper balance of nutrients causes decreased energy, developmental problems, decreased focus, and increased fatigue. Everyone needs to receive the full supply of nutrients they need on a regular and continual basis. This is done almost totally through the food that people eat.

Ultimately, what people eat is their choice, although some individuals' choices may be limited by their economic situation. Nevertheless, everyone is dependent for some of their food on restaurant and foodservice operations. Therefore, as restaurant and foodservice professionals, you are involved in supplying some of the nutrients that people need. To do this well, you should understand what humans' nutritional needs are and how you can help people to follow a balanced, nutritious diet plan.

Why People Need Help with Nutrition

The concept that the body needs specific nutrients, in specific quantities, combined with the knowledge to choose food that supplies them should be enough for making consistent food choices for a healthy body, but this is not often true. In fact, expecting people to use all the principles of nutrition to make food selections is unrealistic for several reasons:

■ **Most people do not have the scientific knowledge to make these decisions.** They do not know enough details to make sound choices, though they have some knowledge gained from popular reports.

■ **People have learned other ways to select food.** In childhood and later, many people developed nonscientific ways to make food choices: through learned behavior, psychological needs, and social needs.

■ **Nutrition principles seem to keep changing.** Nutrition at the consumer level can be controversial and confusing. On a regular basis, the news media report on studies or claims that certain nutrients or types of food will make people healthier and live longer. Then later, a different study or expert rebuts the first report. Which study should be believed? As a consequence of this confusion, people often disregard nutrition principles and go on eating what they enjoy whether it is healthy or not.

The Present Situation

Today's restaurant and foodservice operations provide a wide variety of food based on people's demands. Recently, restaurants have expanded their menus to include a larger variety of options that fit into a healthy lifestyle. Some restaurants are marketing the sound nutrition or low caloric level of their meals. For example, one restaurant advertises that all meals have fewer than 475 calories. However, restaurants cannot force their customers to choose food wisely and balance their diets. Ultimately, the responsibility lies with each person to make smart food choices, and today's restaurant and foodservice operations make this possible.

How You Can Help

To have a healthy diet, people need to receive all the necessary nutrients in the proper proportions and quantities. This does not have to occur at each meal, just over a period of time like several days or a week. However, when dining out, customers want good taste and value. They want food that is aromatic, colorful, and full of flavor. This is because food is enjoyed through all the senses. First people see it, then they smell it, hear it cooking, and finally they taste it. Whether or not the food is nutritious is not sensed during dining, but it has an effect on the body. People need nutritious food, but they generally opt for food that tastes good.

People should not have to go without nutritious food to get good taste. Contrary to popular belief, healthy, nutritious food can be great tasting when the chef has an understanding of nutrition principles and uses it when developing recipes. Nutritious cooking sells well when the food is prepared and presented in an appetizing manner.

Foodservice professionals, like the ones shown in *Exhibit 1b,* who are educated in nutrition are needed to provide nutritious food for all modern dining situations. When you, as a restaurant or foodservice professional, understand the dynamics of combining nutrition science and culinary art, you will be able to provide food that meets the needs of the consumer for nutrition and sensory enjoyment. You will be able

Exhibit 1b

Foodservice professionals should understand how to prepare food that is both tasty and nutritious.

to make a positive contribution to the expanding market for consumption of food outside the home. In return, your restaurant or foodservice operation should grow larger and more successful.

How We Got to This Point

Exhibit 1c

Food in prehistoric times merely fueled the body.

Over millions of years, animals and humans developed the ability to store excess calories as fat. This was good because it also enabled humans to survive the cold, lean months of winter in northern climates. The body fat kept them alive until spring, when food was more plentiful. Humans, especially those in cold climates, adopted this type of eating. They ate a lot of food during the warmer months to fatten up for the harsh conditions ahead.

In the distant past, eating was a challenge. Before tools for cooking were available, fresh meat and fish were thrown on hot coals or stones, as shown in *Exhibit 1c*. As a result, the meat was covered with grit and ashes. During the winter months it was difficult to get meat, so salt was used to preserve it. Heavily salted meat and fish were eaten with some difficulty, but they kept people alive.

With the advancing technical sophistication that occurred during medieval times came the use of different cooking tools and techniques. Food was made more palatable and wholesome by cooking it on spits and using pots. When the salted meat and fish were cooked in water, they became easier to eat because the saltiness was diminished; a more desirable taste had been discovered. Salt became a valuable commodity. It was a bargaining tool used in trade for other items needed for survival.

Also throughout history, salt and fat were used to bind and preserve. For example:

■ **Pemmican** is dried meat that has been powdered or shredded and then mixed with fat to form a solid product. It was made by North American Indians, but it was quickly adopted by the settlers.

■ Egyptians discovered that melted animal fat put on top of cooked meat in a jar and allowed to harden could preserve meat; thus the process of **confit**—meat cooked and preserved in its own fat— was invented.

■ **Jerked beef** or **charque** is meat that has been salted, pressed, and dried. It can be kept for months because it resists insect and mold infestation.

- **Pastirma** is a highly seasoned, dried meat product found today in Turkey, Egypt, and Armenia that originally came from ancient Greece.

- **Salt pork** is the salted flesh of pig and is still eaten today.

For centuries, these dietary practices were considered safe. Modern-day concerns about high blood pressure, heart disease, and obesity associated with eating food containing too much fat and salt were nonexistent.

With the advancement of time and cooking techniques, enjoyment of food became an interest for some groups of people, who consumed food not only for sustenance and survival but also for appreciation of its taste. In other words, the **culinary arts**—the art of preparing food for sensory enjoyment as well as to meet dietary needs—had been invented. Wealthy societies ate to excess, gorging on meats, sauces, gravies, and unique-tasting food items. They placed emphasis on impressive flavors in addition to meeting nutritional needs. The introduction of additional spices and seasoning continued to increase people's curiosity and demand for great food. Chefs and cooks were hired to create dishes for royalty and the wealthy. Great chefs and skilled tradesmen increased in number and developed skills, to impress their customers and show off their talents, incorporating ever-advancing techniques of preparation and presentation. Today's food strives for excellence in both flavor and presentation, as shown in *Exhibit 1d*.

At the same time people began enjoying the sensual side of food, researchers started studying the effects of food on the body. In the nineteenth century, scientists knew that food kept the body alive. They thought that only one substance, as yet unidentified, nourished the body. At that time, three food groups were known: carbohydrates, proteins, and fats. Fruit and vegetables were not yet placed into any category; they were simply side dishes. In the early twentieth century, scientists began discovering other nutrients and assigning letters and numbers to these unknown items; they were later called vitamins.

Clearly, nutrition principles are dynamic, and they continue to change even today as scientists learn more about food and nutrition. Each advance has changed the way people look at food, not only for pleasure but for good health. It is often confusing and challenging for the public to follow advances in nutrition, but it is necessary. It is especially important for you, as a restaurant or foodservice professional, to understand and stay current on the latest nutrition principles, as you are in the position of helping change thousands of years of eating habits to fit the relatively few years of nutritional science now available.

Exhibit 1d

Modern food emphasizes taste and presentation.

Think About It…

Which food interests your senses the most? What is it about this food that stimulates your senses?

Achieving Nutritious Food Choices

Professionals and laypeople alike know that eating a balanced diet provides energy and focus for the day. It nourishes the mind and body. Adults thrive, and children grow and prosper with good nutritional habits; for example, studies have shown that test scores are higher when children have an adequate breakfast.

Earlier in this chapter it was stated that food choices are made based on learned behavior, psychological needs, and social needs. Actually, many factors, whether logical or perceived, influence food choices, some of which are listed below:

- **Personal preference**—Likes and dislikes from a variety of experiences

- **Traditions and habits**—The result of never having been introduced to a food or always having eaten a food

- **Philosophical and moral beliefs**—Value judgments on consuming certain food

- **Health concerns**—Food choices made to maximize health

- **Availability**—Food choices being provided at the moment

- **Income level**—Necessity of only buying food within one's means

- **Convenience**—Time and distance that can be spent to obtain and eat food

- **Parental influence**—A parent's impression of his or her likes and dislikes on a child

- **Nutritional "urban legends"**—Ideas that it is good to eat a certain food or that a certain food should be avoided

- **Allergies**—Inability by some people to eat certain types of food without experiencing unpleasant or life-threatening symptoms

- **Emotions**—Association of either positive or negative feelings with a certain food

- **Social influences**—What other people are eating or avoiding

All these factors influence a person's taste—what a person likes and dislikes. Taste is the primary reason for making choices about the types and amounts of food to eat; nutritional needs take a distant second. Appetites are stimulated by the senses in selecting food to eat. People see food in advertisements like the ones in *Exhibit 1e*, television commercials, pictures on menus, and on plates carried by servers to other guests in restaurants. The aroma of food triggers mouths to begin watering in the anticipation of eating. Also, hearing the sounds of food cooking might be part of the eating experience.

Exhibit 1e

Food advertisements are strong influencers of food choices.

Finally, feeling the texture of food on the tongue and tasting it on the palate is the culmination of eating and experiencing the food choice. All of these are important parts of enjoying food and, therefore, important reasons why people choose certain types of food. What is essential in restaurant and foodservice operations is that these aspects of food enjoyment and choice are congruent with balanced nutrition. Only restaurant and foodservice operators and their employees can make this happen in public dining situations.

Markets for Nutritious Cooking Skills and Knowledge

There is a growing market for cooks and foodservice personnel to have skills in preparing and serving nutritious food. At one point in time, nutritional cooking skills and knowledge were thought to be needed only in healthcare or school foodservice, but that is no longer true.

Increased Out-of-Home Eating

The restaurant industry has seen a continued increase in the number of people eating meals away from home. The average person eats four or five meals per week away from home, and many workers eat out for two meals per day during the workweek. The general restaurant public is becoming increasingly concerned about nutritional value. Many customers today want food that is lower in calories, cholesterol, sodium, and fat appears to be here to stay.

As a result, more stringent and comprehensive nutritional demands are being made of the restaurant industry:

- Interest is increasing in healthier items in general.
- Low-fat cooking methods—e.g., broiling, roasting, steaming, and poaching—are preferred to frying.
- Concern is growing about fat content and cholesterol.
- Demand is increasing for leaner meat, seafood, and poultry.
- Demand is increasing for heart-healthy menus and menu choices.
- Diabetics are seeking more complex carbohydrates.
- Overweight people are looking for lower calorie food.
- Demand for food items with less sodium is increasing.

Because of these customer-driven factors, chefs and servers are increasingly expected to become knowledgeable about nutrition and preparing healthy food. This increased demand for nutrition skills and knowledge is seen in:

■ Restaurant and foodservice markets

■ Career opportunities for food preparers, recipe developers, and menu planners

■ Food-products industry

Increasing Foodservice Markets

Breakfast is still the most commonly eaten meal at home, especially by those of younger families. Yet it is often the children who have eaten; the parents have not because they are caught up in the morning rush. Marketing to this group is an area that still has room to grow. The restaurant industry currently targets breakfast sales for "take and go" items. However, this market has considerable room for increased healthy options.

More and more of the family food dollar is being slated for dining away from home. It might be for quick-service dining, family dining, high-end dining, or home meal replacements. As a result, people are demanding wholesome food from these operations that is fresh, good quality, attractively presented, and of course, tasty.

The market for **home meal replacements**—food that has been made, cooked, chilled, and ready for simple reheating—is a fast-growing segment of the restaurant and foodservice industry. People are no longer willing to spend hours to prepare a meal.

The introduction of home meal replacements, like the one shown in *Exhibit 1f,* has added a new meaning to fast take-out food. Today, people can purchase home replacement meals in a variety of ways:

■ Expanded take-out areas at grocery stores that provide complete meals

■ Meals already prepared, ordered, and delivered to the home, which sometimes have dietary restrictions included

■ Meals assembled by the consumer in the provider's kitchen facilities to be brought home and then refrigerated or frozen for consumption at a later time

■ Special take-out services inside regular restaurants

Exhibit 1f

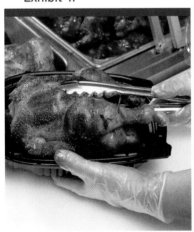

Home meal replacements are becoming a larger part of diets in the United States.

The Internet as a Food Market

The Internet has become a virtual food market. People use it for a variety of food functions previously supplied by businesses, friends, and themselves:

- Ideas for meal planning

- Recipes

- Nutrition information

- Food purchases that are delivered to the door

- Cooking demonstrations

- Cooking-equipment purchases

Changes in the Quick-Service Segment

The quick-service industry is now providing more food alternatives. Many diners want the convenience of eating quickly, and at the same time, want a healthy meal. The industry has responded well, as seen by all the new offerings of food products, including:

- Baked, broiled, roasted, and flame-grilled meat and poultry

- Roasted chicken

- Fresh fruit and vegetables

- Low-fat milk, milkshakes, and ice cream

- Rolled sandwiches, or "wraps," using low-fat tortillas

- Salads with low-fat dressing and with or without grilled meat and fresh fruit

- Alternatives to fried side dishes, such as applesauce or fruit cups

Changes in the Casual-Dining and Fine-Dining Segments

Casual-dining and fine-dining restaurants also have listened and responded to the requests of their customers. Independent restaurants as well as chains have changed some of their menu items and cooking techniques to incorporate healthier food choices.

Nutritious Cooking in Other Types of Dining Operations

Many foodservice dining operations, like the one shown in *Exhibit 1g,* have focused on healthier cooking for some time. These operations generally have a captive audience, meaning that people visit and dine in the operation almost daily for one reason or another. They include:

Exhibit 1g

School cafeterias have long been concerned about students' diets and nutrition.

- **School foodservice**—These operations provide lunches to students in kindergarten through twelfth grade. Special requirements for government-funded lunch programs must be followed in these operations.

- **College and university foodservice**—These operations provide food for college students, faculty, and staff. Menus are varied and might be elaborate.

- **Corporate dining**—Many office buildings and factories have cafeterias or vending services for their employees for breakfast and lunch; sometimes catering is used to achieve this.

- **Healthcare foodservice**—These services provide meals to patients, some with special dietary needs, as well as to employees. Also, they often cater special functions for doctors and members of the facility's board.

- **Senior living centers**—These provide varied dining services from typical restaurant fair to special dietary needs, depending on the residents' health and ages.

- **Correctional facilities**—Jail and prison cafeterias provide meals for inmates and employees. Special diets must be followed for some people.

Exhibit 1h

Nutrition-Related Jobs

College professor

Cook

Corporate chef

Culinologist

Diet technician

Foodservice manager

Food scientist

Food technologist

Freelance instructor

Menu planner

Nutrition scientist

Private chef

Recipe developer

Research chef

Restaurant manager

Service staff

Nutrition-Related Job Needs

Knowledge of nutrition and the ability to apply it to cooking can increase your marketability. There are many careers and positions in restaurant and foodservice operations in which knowledge of nutrition (which might include a college degree, licensing, and/or certification) is important; *Exhibit 1h* lists some of these. In addition, nutrition skills and knowledge are becoming increasingly important in several key career areas.

Some people are hiring private chefs to cook healthy meals either for their entire families or for family members with special dietary needs. Private chefs are also often hired by entertainers, sports figures, and celebrities; they know that healthy eating will give them the stamina and energy to perform at their best.

Spas and health clubs often will hire someone with nutritional cooking knowledge to satisfy the needs of guests, whether it is through meal preparation or cooking classes. These chefs and cooks must be very creative to provide great-tasting food with low calories. Portions are usually small, so they must understand how to incorporate flavor in the food with minimal ingredients.

In more and more restaurant and foodservice operations, it is important to be able to answer questions about basic nutrition. In restaurants, guests often have questions about the nutritional content of food on the menu. To prepare employees to answer these questions, dining-room managers should have training for service staff about the menu items, and chefs should train the cooks about the nutritional aspects of the food being prepared. These employees look to their leaders to provide the necessary information so they in turn can provide factual information to their guests.

Nutrition Professionals

To meet the demands for nutritional cuisine, restaurants, foodservice operations, and food companies should consider hiring or contracting with a third party for nutritional services when developing menus and recipes. A third-party consultant may be a registered dietitian (RD), a registered dietetic technician (DTR), or a chef certified by the American Culinary Federation (ACF). See *Exhibit 1i* for some facts about these three professions and their training. The RD and the DTR are trained to modify and nutritionally analyze recipes and menus. ACF-certified chefs can select and prepare nutritional ingredients to make healthy menus for different cuisines.

As the market for nutritional information has grown, many companies have realized they must strenuously review their products. Therefore, the need for qualified professionals with nutrition education is only increasing.

Exhibit 1i

Three Professions Concerned with Nutrition

Profession	Education/Training
Registered Dietitian	A registered dietitian (RD) must complete an approved American Dietetic Association four-year undergraduate program plus advanced training through an internship or master's degree. After completing advanced training, the person must pass a national exam. To maintain RD status, RDs must meet continuing-education course requirements.
Registered Dietetic Technician	A registered dietetic technician (DTR) must complete an approved American Dietetic Association two-year undergraduate program. A national exam is available to further certify knowledge. To maintain DTR status, DTRs must meet continuing-education course requirements.
ACF-Certified Chef	An ACF-certified chef must complete criteria of the American Culinary Federation that includes a certain number of points earned from education, experience, and awards. Three main education components must be met along with culinary work. Those components are thirty hours each of coursework in nutrition, sanitation and supervisory management. After meeting the point requirement, a national certification exam must be passed. To maintain certification status, continuing education must be completed.

Food-Products Industry

The food-products industry is a multibillion-dollar business. It supplies restaurant and foodservice operations as well as consumers with a wide variety of food products. Over the centuries, and more rapidly in recent years, food-product needs have changed. Products are continually being developed to assist in reducing labor and food costs in restaurant and foodservice operations. Many of these also are developed to facilitate healthy eating.

A skilled cook must know how to use these products to produce actual dishes and menus in real-world settings. He or she also must be able to determine the value of these products by comparing food labels for nutritional advantages and then modifying methods of cooking and recipes to best utilize these products, while keeping food costs under control.

Nutrition research continues to discover how the different nutrients affect metabolic processes in the body. Food manufacturing uses certain nutrients and processes for stabilization, binding, texture, and flavor enhancement. Over time, research has shown that some of these nutrients and processes may actually be adversely affecting the nutritional value of the food being processed. An example of this is the research on trans fats. The food-products industry welcomed the use of trans fats because of their ability to stabilize shortening, bind various components so they did not separate, and flavor certain desserts. Then researchers discovered that trans fats are harmful for consumption. As a result, food scientists and research chefs have redeveloped many products to take out trans fats and bring these products back to the market.

Exhibit 1j

Cooking is both an art and a science.

Applying Nutrition Principles to Cooking Is Both Art and Science

Combining nutritional principles with excellent cooking skills to produce delectable dishes is possible for every chef, recipe developer, and menu planner. However, implementing nutritional principles in actual recipes and menus is not a simple matter of adding food with the right nutrients in the right proportions. Nor is it a simple matter of eliminating or reducing certain ingredients and increasing or adding others. Doing such things mechanically results in recipes that may not work, do not taste good, and might not be eaten. That is why both the science of nutrition and the art of cooking must be combined in your recipes and menus. A nutritionally accomplished cook must be both an artist and a scientist, as shown in *Exhibit 1j*.

Nutritional Cooking Is an Art

The art of cooking is to understand the function of food ingredients and the aesthetic (flavor, texture, and aroma) profiles of food and then combine this knowledge to create dishes that are creative and delicious.

Nutritional cooking not only considers using healthy ingredients and cooking methods but also includes:

■ Purchasing, handling, and storing ingredients properly

■ Increasing amounts of fruit and vegetables

■ Using salt with care and purpose

■ Using fat only where it makes the best contribution to flavor

Knowing different cooking techniques that allow application of nutrition principles is key to optimizing healthy cooking. The nutritionally skilled cook should be able to modify a recipe to meet nutritional guidelines set forth by the needs of the diner and still maintain the essence of the dish being prepared. An example is preparing a low-fat meatloaf starting with a traditionally high-fat meatloaf recipe. The accomplished cook knows how to substitute ingredients, like changing the meat to a low-fat version, using egg whites instead of whole eggs, decreasing the salt, and increasing spices, while minimizing any change or loss of taste.

Nutritional Cooking Is a Science

Understanding food science—the study of the changes that occur in food with chemical and physical reactions—is key to the accomplished skilled cook. Nutrients in food are changed, diminished, or destroyed by improper storage, light, heat, acidity, and alkalinity. The skilled cook should know how to work with fresh, frozen, and canned ingredients using nutrition-preserving preparation and cooking methods to produce the maximum quality, highest yield, tastiest, and healthiest cuisine.

How to Do Nutritional Cooking

Later chapters of this guide will provide details on combining the art of cooking and the science of nutrition. At this point, you should realize that doing so is not only possible, but also not that difficult. You simply have to want to do it, along with learning about nutrition, nutrients, the nutrient content of different types of food, and the affects of purchasing, handling, storing, and cooking on nutrient contents. In fact, there are culinary courses that teach this; many culinary schools have courses entitled "Nutritional Cooking" to train chefs to combine these two skill areas.

Activity

Reviewing Menus for Healthy Selections

Visit at least three restaurants: a quick-service restaurant, an independent family restaurant, and a casual chain restaurant. Obtain permission to take a menu or menu copy from each restaurant; if the menu is only a wall sign, copy it by hand. Review all three menus for the presence of healthy selections, then answer the questions below on a separate sheet of paper.

1 Identify the healthy menu options on each menu.

2 Ask the manager or chef how each healthy food item was prepared to make it a healthy option.

3 Describe how the menu was written to indicate that the menu item was healthy; for example, the use of symbols, words, or proprietary names indicating a healthy menu selection.

4 Did any restaurant provide nutrient content on the menu or anywhere else?

Summary

Good nutrition is good for everyone. It leads to better health and stamina, and it leads to greater success in the restaurant and foodservice business. Restaurant and foodservice professionals educated in nutrition are needed to provide nutritious food for all modern dining situations. When you, as a professional, understand the dynamics of combining nutrition science and culinary art, you will be able to provide food that meets the needs of the consumer for nutrition and sensory enjoyment.

Although humanity has had thousands of years to develop nutritional needs and traditional ways to meet them, we have had only a few years of research to uncover the body's true nutritional needs and *better* ways to meet them. This knowledge continues to increase, resulting in progressive improvements in the principles of nutrition.

With a solid foundation of knowledge of nutrition, restaurant and foodservice professionals can develop or modify recipes and menus to give them more nutritional balance while maintaining the taste and other sensory appeals they have. Doing this involves a combination of cooking art and nutrition science.

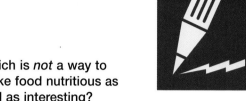

Review Your Learning

1 Most people's food choices are influenced by all of the following *except*

A. food allergies.

B. food availability.

C. traditions.

D. government dietary recommendations.

2 Achieving good nutrition in restaurant and foodservice menus and recipes is important because

A. many people in the United States are afflicted with malnutrition diseases.

B. menus then can be certified by the Food and Drug Administration.

C. customers' health, energy levels, and well-being depend on it.

D. nutritious food always tastes better than non-nutritious food.

3 Making food both nutritious and interesting is important for all of the following reasons *except*

A. both are required by the Dietary Guidelines for Americans.

B. most customers will not eat uninteresting food.

C. customers need to have nutrition in addition to taste.

D. people eat with all five senses.

4 Nutrition principles change over time for all of the following reasons *except*

A. cooks learn more and more about nutrition.

B. food scientists continually learn more about the body's use of food.

C. physiologists and other scientists continually learn more about the functioning of the body.

D. people's dietary needs change as we make technological advances.

5 Which is *not* a way to make food nutritious as well as interesting?

A. Substitute low-fat items for high-fat items.

B. Leave fats out of recipes.

C. Use leaner meat types or cuts.

D. Broil meat instead of frying it.

6 People have demanded that the restaurant and foodservice industry do all of the following *except*

A. provide healthier food choices.

B. provide selections with lower fat and cholesterol levels.

C. provide smaller portions.

D. provide heart-healthy menus.

7 Providing good nutrition is important to the restaurant industry because

A. it is required by law.

B. employers demand it.

C. customers demand it.

D. the American Dietetic Association requires it.

8 Fat and salt were important in the past for

A. preserving food for later consumption.

B. keeping pots clean.

C. trading.

D. having tasty dishes for royalty.

continued on next page

Review Your Learning *continued from previous page*

9 **Nutritional knowledge by restaurant and foodservice professionals**

A. is not really important for developing recipes.

B. increases their marketability.

C. is a waste of time because customers do not care about nutrition.

D. limits the type of jobs available to them.

10 **Nutritional cooking is an art that incorporates the knowledge of all of the following *except***

A. cooking techniques.

B. proper storage and handling of food.

C. proper use of salt and fat where appropriate.

D. the bases for people's food choices.

The Basic Nutrients— Their Importance in Health

2

Inside This Chapter

- Healthy Body Weight

- Nutrients—Substances That Nourish the Body

- Carbohydrate, Protein, and Lipid

- Vitamins and Minerals—The Regulators

- Water—The Most Important Nutrient

- Nutritional Value of Food

- Digestion, Absorption, and Transport of Nutrients

After completing this chapter, you should be able to:

- List the six basic types of nutrients found in food along with their characteristics.

- Describe the major functions of carbohydrates, proteins, and lipids in the body.

- Describe the roles of vitamins, minerals, and water.

- Explain the effect of alcohol consumption on the body.

- List reasons to decrease the consumption of empty-calorie food.

- Describe the digestion, absorption, and transport of nutrients.

- List the organs of the digestive system and the major function of each.

Test Your Knowledge

1. **True or False:** Carbohydrates provide more kilocalories per gram than protein or fat. *(See p. 24.)*

2. **True or False:** Water is refreshing and hydrating but not an essential nutrient. *(See p. 26.)*

3. **True or False:** Alcohol is a non-nutrient that provides seven kilocalories of energy per gram when metabolized by the body. *(See p. 26.)*

4. **True or False:** Nutrient density is the compactness of nutrients in a food. *(See p. 26.)*

5. **True or False:** Minerals are chemical elements that become part of the structure of the body. *(See p. 25.)*

Key Terms

Amino acid

Bolus

Carbohydrate

Chyme

Digestion

Digestive system

Digestive tract

Empty-calorie food

Fat

Kilocalorie

Kilogram

Lipid

Lipoprotein

Metabolism

Minerals

Mucosa

Nutrient dense

Oil

Phytochemical

Phytonutrient

Protein

Villus, villi

Vitamin

Exhibit 2a

Food is the primary source of nutrients.

Introduction

In Chapter 1, you learned that nutrition is important for health and should be a concern of everyone, including restaurant and foodservice professionals, since the source of nutrition is food like that shown in *Exhibit 2a*. The major topic in the area of nutrition is nutrients. This chapter gives an overview of nutrients; subsequent chapters provide more details.

There are six types of nutrients, and all are essential to health. You will learn what they are and what their major functions are in providing energy, providing building materials, and enabling the myriad chemical reactions that make bodies work. Along the way, you will learn about "empty calories," what they are, and why they should be avoided.

Think About It...

Experts say that people need to eat a variety of food types. Do you know what the different types are and why this is true?

The human body obtains the nutrients it needs by ingestion followed by digestion and absorption. As a restaurant or foodservice professional, you should have a basic understanding of the digestive process, since it is linked with your ability to provide useful nutrients to your customers. This information is covered generally in this chapter. Subsequent chapters provide more details on the digestion of the different types of nutrients.

Healthy Body Weight

The goal of nutrition is to nourish the body and help it remain healthy. The human body has evolved over time to have certain characteristics and certain needs. Some of these needs are for the proper nutrients to make the body work effectively. Although people differ somewhat in body characteristics, their nutritional needs are remarkably similar. There are only a few factors that influence the need for nutrients of a body that is not diseased:

- Age
- Gender
- Body size

Throughout this guide you will see tables that give nutrient requirements for people; these tables usually have separate requirements for different ages and genders, but not for body size. That is because these tables assume that the body being fed is a healthy body and neither overweight nor underweight. Later chapters will define overweight, underweight, and obesity, but for now, *Exhibit 2b* lists the range of body weights considered healthy for a person based on height.

Exhibit 2b

Healthy Body Weight

Height	Normal Body Weight (pounds)	Height	Normal Body Weight (pounds)
4'10"	91–118	5'8"	125–163
4'11"	94–123	5'9"	128–168
5'0"	97–127	5'10"	132–173
5'1"	100–131	5'11"	136–178
5'2"	104–137	6'0"	140–183
5'3"	107–140	6'1"	144–188
5'4"	110–144	6'2"	148–193
5'5"	114–149	6'3"	152–199
5'6"	118–154	6'4"	156–204
5'7"	121–158		

Based on the U.S. Centers for Disease Control and Prevention's BMI Index

Nutrients—Substances That Nourish the Body

Most people select food in response to their appetite and senses. Food may look appetizing, smell inviting, and taste good. Few people choose food only for the nutrients it contains. However, the nutritional needs of the body are fairly consistent, and supplying this nutrition is an important function of the food you eat. Humans need certain nutrients on a regular basis to maintain health and prevent disease. Once you learn which nutrients are needed daily, you can begin to plan menus and recipes that incorporate nutritional principles and meet your customers' expectations for cuisine that tastes good and is also nutritious.

A nutrient is a chemical substance that provides nourishment to the body. The roles of the different types of nutrients are varied; they include providing energy, adding structure to the body, and regulating body reactions. There are six basic categories of nutrients that are important to the body (see *Exhibit 2c*):

- Carbohydrates
- Proteins
- Lipids
- Vitamins
- Minerals
- Water

In addition to these nutrients, there are various other chemical substances called phytochemicals present in food. **Phytochemicals** (also known as **phytonutrients**) are technically any chemical or nutrient derived from a plant,

Exhibit 2c

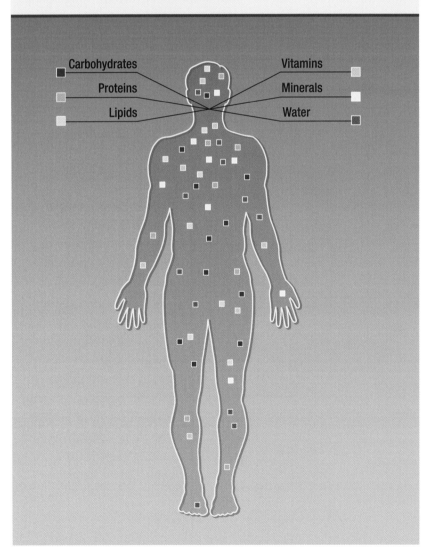

The Six Essential Nutrients

Carbohydrates

Proteins

Lipids

Vitamins

Minerals

Water

Nutrients nourish the body and are essential to its health and growth.

but the term "phytochemical" is commonly used to refer to chemicals that somehow aid the body in fighting or avoiding diseases.

Nutrients are found in food items in different amounts. There is no food that contains all the necessary nutrients needed by humans. People who want to be well nourished must eat a diet with a large variety of food items in order to obtain all the nutrients necessary. By making intelligent decisions about recipe and menu items with health in mind, you, as a restaurant or foodservice professional, can make a big difference in the number of beneficial nutrients you offer your customers.

Exhibit 2d

Carbohydrates are good for the body and should be part of your diet.

Carbohydrate, Protein, and Lipid

The two primary needs of the body are energy and building blocks. Three categories of nutrients help to meet these needs: carbohydrates, proteins, and lipids. Each has special functions in the body.

Carbohydrates

Carbohydrates are a class of nutrients that includes starches, sugar, and dietary fiber. Carbohydrates provide the body with four kilocalories of energy per gram of food eaten. Technically, a **kilocalorie** is the energy needed to heat one **kilogram** (about 2.2 pounds) of water by approximately 2°F (1°C). In nutrition, the unit of measurement for energy is the kilocalorie, which is one thousand calories, and this term will be used throughout this guide when a specific amount of energy is presented. In common usage when discussing nutrition, dieting, and food, kilocalories usually are simply called calories, even though this word technically refers to an energy unit one thousand times smaller.

It was originally thought that carbohydrates were made of carbon and water, thus the name stems from the fact that carbohydrate contains the elements carbon, hydrogen, and oxygen. Examples of food items that provide abundant carbohydrate are pasta, rice, tortillas, cereal, baked potato, honey, and table sugar to name a few. (See *Exhibit 2d*.) Carbohydrate food items add not only calories but vitamins, minerals, and fiber to the diet.

Unfortunately, in recent years, carbohydrates have become nutrients of contention because many people think that eating carbohydrates will make them gain weight. This is not true. It is true that the primary role of carbohydrate in the diet is to supply energy. If a person expends all the calories eaten, it is unlikely that person will gain weight even when eating normal amounts of carbohydrate. Thus, most people need not fear carbohydrate as a food category because, in truth, it is excess calories from all nutrient sources and lack of exercise that are the actual culprits in weight gain.

The energy provided by carbohydrates helps people utilize dietary protein for other purposes by sparing it from being used as an energy source. Because of this, the U.S. government recommends that 45 to 65 percent of calories per day come from carbohydrate food items. More details about carbohydrates will be covered in Chapter 4.

Proteins

Proteins are another class of nutrients that can supply energy to the body, although this is not their primary function. Rather, proteins provide the building blocks, in the form of amino acids, the body uses for a variety of things, including muscles, tissues, enzymes, and hormones. Proteins are large complex molecules that contain long chains of amino acids. If used for energy, proteins can provide four kilocalories of energy per gram to the body.

Amino acids are chemical compounds that have special functions in the body. One of the primary functions of amino acids is to supply nitrogen for growth and maintenance. In addition to their role in growth, amino acids maintain fluids, keep the body from getting too acidic or basic, and act as transporters as **lipoproteins** (molecules combining a lipid and a protein), and more. Twenty amino acids can be found in food; however, only nine of them must be obtained from food each day, while the others can be made by the body.

Proteins can be found in abundance in meat, eggs, cheese, beans, nuts, legumes, and milk, as shown in *Exhibit 2e.* Vegetables and grains also contain protein. Your vegetarian customers may want diets that draw mostly or solely from these vegetables and grains.

The U.S. government recommends that people consume from 10 to 35 percent of their calories from protein food items. More details about proteins are provided in Chapter 5.

Lipids

The last category of the energy-yielding nutrients is lipids. **Lipids** are a class of nutrients that contain triglycerides, cholesterol, and phospholipids. Triglycerides are the fats and oils in the food people eat as well as those used in the body. **Fat** is usually defined as a lipid that is solid at room temperature and **oil** as a lipid that is liquid at room temperature. Food items high in lipids include butter, lard, vegetable oil, nuts, sour cream, and cream cheese. (See *Exhibit 2f.*) Lipids provide abundant energy, with each gram containing nine kilocalories per gram, over twice the amount yielded by carbohydrate or protein.

Exhibit 2e

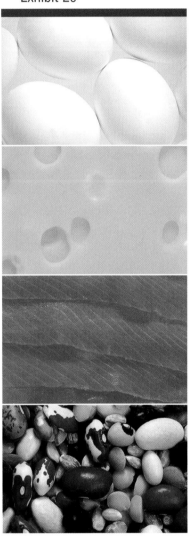

Proteins are the building blocks used by the body for developing muscles, tissues, enzymes, and hormones.

The U.S. government recommends that people consume 20 to 35 percent of their kilocalories from lipids.

Lipids provide more than twice the amount of energy of carbohydrates or protein.

People's perception of the amount of lipids that should be in their diet may be somewhat skewed. Some people believe their diets should be lipid free. This is incorrect and harmful, since the absence of essential lipids will cause fatty acid deficiency diseases. Also, diets low in lipids are suspected of lowering the amount of high-density lipoproteins produced by the body, which protect the cardiovascular system by lowering cholesterol. On the other hand, some people may not have taken seriously warnings to reduce the amount of saturated fats in their diets, keeping heart disease the number one cause of death in the United States. Knowing how lipids affect health will allow you to alter recipes and menus to meet the needs of your customers. (The details will be covered in Chapter 6.)

Food should be people's primary source of vitamins and minerals in most circumstances.

Vitamins and Minerals— The Regulators

Vitamins are organic compounds, while **minerals** are inorganic elements. Both are needed in relatively small amounts by the body for regulation of metabolic processes. Except for vitamin D, neither vitamins nor minerals can be made by the body and must be derived from the diet, through food like that shown in *Exhibit 2g*. Vitamins and minerals participate in growth, reproduction, and the operation and maintenance of the body. In addition, some minerals, calcium for example, serve as structural components of the body.

In the absence of adequate amounts of vitamins and minerals, people may become deficient and can develop deficiency diseases. Nutrition experts encourage people to get most of their vitamins and minerals from food. If this not possible, a vitamin-mineral supplement may be helpful. However, since food provides other substances that promote health and prevent disease, like fiber and phytochemicals, food should be the primary source for obtaining vitamins and minerals.

Exhibit 2h

Offering a glass of water to your guests is more than a courtesy; you are providing them the key to hydration.

Water—
The Most Important Nutrient

Water is the most important of the six classes of nutrients, although it is often overlooked because of its familiarity. Water is essential to all forms of life and is the most universal solvent. It enables a tremendous number of chemical reactions, among which are most of the chemical reactions that make the human body work. Without water, life as humans know it would not exist.

Water is a perfect medium for the metabolic processes of the body. About 50 to 70 percent of the body is water by weight. It has many important roles in the body, including metabolic reactions, temperature regulation, removal of wastes, and hydration. Offering customers a cold glass or bottle of water, as shown in *Exhibit 2h,* is more than just a courtesy; it is important for their health.

Nutritional Value of Food

Food items containing large amounts of nutrients and few calories are said to be **nutrient dense.** Food items like whole grains, fruit, vegetables, lean meat, fish, poultry, and low-fat dairy products are nutrient dense. Cookies, candy, and sweetened beverages are considered **empty-calorie food** because they are high in calories but have few other nutrients. These types of food items have little or no beneficial effect on the body or its metabolism. When planning recipes and menus for good nutrition, it is important to ensure that nutrient-dense food items are the focus of the plate.

Alcohol, a familiar accompaniment to many meals, has mixed effects on the body. Alcohol provides seven kilocalories of energy per gram when metabolized by the body but provides no other nutrients; thus, it is considered empty calories. Some research has focused on alcohol's ability when used in moderation to reduce the risk of cardiovascular events, including strokes, and to decrease diabetes and dementia. Moderation is defined in the *Dietary Guidelines for Americans 2005* as consumption of up to one drink per day for women and up to two drinks per day for men. A single drink is defined as 12 fluid ounces of regular beer, 5 fluid ounces of wine, or 1.5 fluid ounces of eighty-proof distilled spirits. It should be noted, however, that an excessive amount of alcohol in the diet has many risks, including cancers of the digestive system such as oral, esophageal, pancreatic, liver, colon, and rectal. An excessive amount is more than the moderate amounts just defined.

Activity

What Is in Your Food?

Food items can be generally classified by the energy-yielding nutrients they contain. Some food items are merely empty calories while others are nutrient-dense. See how well you can do at distinguishing them. Indicate with a checkmark the major nutrient contributions of each of these food items. Also indicate whether each is high or low in nutrient density. (All the food items listed in the table contain vitamins and minerals in varying levels.)

Food	Carbohydrate	Protein	Lipid	High or low nutrient density
Bacon				
Baked beans				
Cookies				
Corn				
Cream cheese				
Eggs				
Grapefruit juice				
Grapes				
Green beans				
Ham				
Jelly beans				
Nonfat milk				
Pasta				
Rice cereal				
Salmon				
Sirloin steak				
Sour cream				
Tofu				
Waffles				

Digestion, Absorption, and Transport of Nutrients

The phrase "you are what you eat" reminds people that what they eat is important to their health. Each day the food you eat is broken down through digestion and absorbed into your body. What food you choose to eat, along with your genetics, daily habits, and living environment, determine your health. (See *Exhibit 2i.*)

Exhibit 2i

Factors That Affect the Body's Health

Genetics   Exercise   Environment

Digestion is the process of breaking food down to the simplest or most elemental parts to be absorbed and used by the body. Digestion is much more than just the physical and chemical breakdown of food; it also includes the senses. As a restaurant or foodservice professional, you know the importance of creating ambiance for diners. This helps to engage the customer in the enjoyment of food, and the anticipation of food begins the digestion process.

The Digestive System

Digestion is carried out by the **digestive system,** which is the hollow tube from mouth to anus, also called the **digestive tract.** It is composed of the oral cavity, pharynx, esophagus, stomach, small intestine, large intestine, rectum, and anus. In addition to this hollow muscular tube, the liver, pancreas, and gall bladder participate by secreting fluids into the digestive track. (See *Exhibit 2j.*)

The digestive tract has an inside lining called the **mucosa,** a mucous membrane that protects the lining of the tract and provides secretions from underlying tissue, a submucosa with connective tissue and blood vessels, a muscular layer, and the serosa, which lines the abdominal cavity and provides a passage for blood vessels, nerves, and the lymphatic system. Throughout the process of digestion there is an involuntary wave of contraction called peristalsis that propels food down the digestive tract. In the small intestine, there is also segmentation that further mixes the food fragments until they are completely mixed with intestinal secretions. All of the digestive process is under hormonal and enzymatic control.

The Digestive System

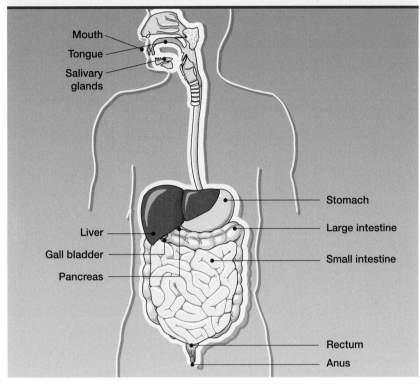

Food is broken down and absorbed by the digestive system.

Oral Cavity— Mouth, Tongue, and Salivary Glands

The mouth accepts the food and starts the mechanical and chemical digestion of food. The teeth masticate (chew) the food, grinding it into smaller pieces and mixing it with saliva. As food touches the tongue, the tastes of food are revealed through the taste buds; these sensory receptors translate the tastes and send an electrical impulse to the brain. The sense of smell also plays an important role in taste.

There are three sets of salivary glands in the mouth. They produce approximately 1.0 to 1.5 liters of fluid each day to keep food and the tissue in the mouth moist. The parotid salivary gland is responsible for secreting salivary amylase, which starts the digestion of starch. The tongue then positions the masticated food to be swallowed, which passes the masticated food through the pharynx to the esophagus on its way to the stomach. When the food enters the mouth it is called food; when it leaves the mouth, it is considered a wet, soft **bolus** of food.

Stomach, Small Intestine, and Large Intestine

The bolus of food is pushed down the esophagus to the stomach where the lower esophageal sphincter opens to allow the entry of the bolus. Normally, the sphincters, which are powerful muscles, only allow a one-way trip for the food and close once the food has been passed on to the next phase of digestion.

The function of the stomach is to temporarily store food, mechanically mix food, continue some chemical digestion, initiate other chemical digestion, and produce a chemical called intrinsic factor. The food is then exposed to powerful hydrochloric acid and pepsin, an enzyme that digests protein. All of this mixing and the addition of acid and enzymes produces a thin semiliquid fluid called **chyme.**

Alcohol can be absorbed from the stomach and small intestine. When absorbed, it immediately enters the blood, where it is distributed throughout the body. When food is present, more alcohol ends up in the small intestine. Thus, it is absorbed later than when food is not present.

Exhibit 2k

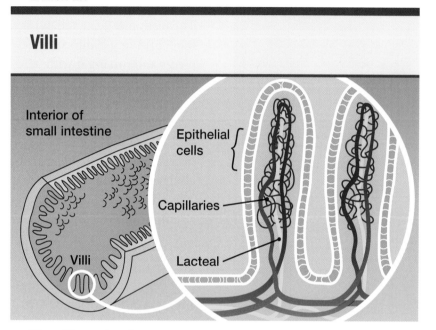

Villi

Interior of small intestine

Epithelial cells

Capillaries

Villi

Lacteal

The villi are tiny fingerlike projections that absorb nutrients and pass them into the bloodstream.

Liver, Gall Bladder, and Pancreas

The chyme passes through the pyloric sphincter to move from the stomach to the small intestine, which is about twenty feet long. The small intestine has fingerlike projections called **villi** (plural of **villus**) that increase the surface area, and thus the absorptive capacity, of the small intestine. On each villus are epithelial cells that also have microvilli. The villi are the location of the capillaries—tiny blood vessels—and lacteals—lymphatic vessels that absorb dietary fats, as shown in *Exhibit 2k*.

In the small intestine, the chyme is digested completely and nutrients are absorbed. First the pancreas secretes additional enzymes for carbohydrate, protein, and lipid digestion. In addition, bicarbonate flows from the pancreas into the small intestine. The gall bladder secretes bile, which was produced by the liver and then stored in the gall bladder until needed, into the small intestine. The bile emulsifies fats, allowing enzymes to reduce the fats to fatty acids and glycerol. Other digestion processes are happening in the small intestine, including the final breakdown of starch to glucose and the breakdown of disaccharides to monosaccharides so they can be absorbed.

When digestion is completed, starches and sugars have been broken down to monosaccharides, and lipids have been disassembled into glycerol, fatty acids, and monoglycerides. The long-chain fats enter the lymphatic system. The monosacharides and short-chain fatty acids are sent to the liver for use in **metabolism**—the process by which living organisms and cells break down complex chemicals into their components and reassemble the components into larger molecules needed by the body. Proteins are broken down into amino acids and then absorbed.

Large Intestine

The large intestine is approximately five feet long. It contains the cecum, the ascending, descending, transverse colon, the rectum, and the anus. The ileocecal valve is the sphincter that controls the entry of liquid wastes of digestion from the small intestine to the large intestine. The major role of the large intestine is to reabsorb water, vitamins, minerals, and bile salts. Insoluble fiber is not broken down, so intestinal bacteria now metabolize any fiber into fatty acids and gas.

The final stage of the digestive process is the movement of material from the colon to the rectum and then out through the anus, or anal sphincter, at the time of elimination.

This overview of the digestive system and digestion has shown that:

- Several stages of mechanical and chemical processing are required to digest food.

- The different types of nutrients are digested at different times and with different chemicals.

- The different types of nutrients are absorbed at different points in the digestive system.

Also, it is hoped that the working of the digestive system is now clearer and that misinformation about the digestive process and the absorption of nutrients has been reduced. After all, the absorption of nutrients needed by the body is really what nutrition is about.

Summary

Nutrients are chemical substances that provide nourishment to the body. There are six basic classes of nutrients important to the body that are found in food. They are: carbohydrates, proteins, lipids, vitamins, minerals, and water. In addition to the six basic classes of nutrients, there are phytonutrients, or phytochemicals, found in some food that helps to prevent disease. Carbohydrate and protein provide four kilocalories of energy per gram, and lipid provides nine kilocalories of energy per gram. Although proteins can supply energy, they are not normally used this way but, instead, are used to provide building blocks in the form of amino acids. Alcohol is a non-nutrient that provides seven kilocalories of energy per gram. Digestion and absorption are complicated processes that separate nutrients and incorporate them into the body.

Activity

Match the Organ to the Function

Now that you have learned about the digestive system, match the organ on the left with its function on the right.

	Component of the Digestive System	Function
	Mouth, teeth, tongue, and salivary glands	A. Mixes chyme with bile and pancreatic juices to ensure complete digestion. Products of digestion are absorbed here.
	Pharynx	B. Muscular sphincter that releases waste.
	Esophagus	C. Performs metabolic regulation and produces bile.
	Stomach	D. Stores and concentrates bile.
	Small intestine	E. Secretes enzymes and bicarbonate to digest starches, proteins, and fats.
	Large intestine	F. Common passage for swallowing food.
	Rectum	G. Reabsorbs water and bile. Compacts waste.
	Anus	H. Receives the bolus of food and mixes into a liquid. Adds acids and pepsin to digest proteins.
	Liver	I. Stores wastes until they can be eliminated.
	Gall bladder	J. Shreds and tears the food into smaller pieces and mixes it with saliva.
	Pancreas	K. Transports the bolus of food to the stomach.

Review Your Learning

1 Oils and fats are part of a class of nutrients called

   A. amino acids.

   B. protein.

   C. lipids.

   D. starches.

2 Carbohydrate and protein food items yield _____ kilocalories per gram.

   A. four

   B. seven

   C. nine

   D. eleven

3 Proteins are complex compounds formed of long chains of

   A. cholesterol.

   B. starch.

   C. amino acids.

   D. phospholipids.

4 In health studies, moderate consumption of alcohol shows

   A. it has some beneficial effects on health.

   B. it has some detrimental effects on health.

   C. it has no known value as a nutrient.

   D. All of the above

5 The three energy-yielding nutrients are

   A. proteins, vitamins, and lipids.

   B. proteins, carbohydrates, and minerals.

   C. carbohydrates, lipids, and vitamins.

   D. carbohydrates, proteins, and lipids.

6 The most important nutrient to the body is

   A. protein.

   B. water.

   C. carbohydrate.

   D. lipid.

7 Which does *not* help in the regulation of the metabolic processes?

   A. Vitamins

   B. Alcohol

   C. Minerals

   D. Water

8 Cookies, candies, and sweetened beverages are considered what type of food?

   A. Empty-calorie

   B. Fast

   C. Nutrient dense

   D. None of the above

9 Sugars are absorbed in the

   A. stomach.

   B. small intestine.

   C. large intestine.

   D. liver.

10 Bile is produced in the liver and stored in the

   A. small intestine.

   B. pancreas.

   C. gall bladder.

   D. large intestine.

Notes

Understanding Nutritional Standards and Guidelines

3

Inside This Chapter

- A Healthy Diet
- Dietary Reference Intakes
- *Dietary Guidelines for Americans 2005*
- MyPyramid
- Nutrition Labeling—Implementation and Interpretation

After completing this chapter, you should be able to:

- Explain and use Dietary Reference Intakes, *Dietary Guidelines for Americans 2005*, MyPyramid, Daily Values, and food labels to assess the adequacy of a diet or set of menu choices.
- Use the USDA's MyPyramid to evaluate the food groups and portion sizes of a diet or set of menu choices.
- Assess the adequacy of portions in menu development.
- Describe food-labeling requirements.
- Summarize the Nutritional Labeling and Education Act of 1990 (NLEA) as it relates to restaurant and foodservice operations.
- State the FDA requirements for a food to be labeled "healthy."

Test Your Knowledge

1 **True or False:** Most restaurant and foodservice operators use standard serving sizes when plating food. *(See p. 47.)*

2 **True or False:** The correct use of the Recommended Dietary Allowances and Adequate Intake values is to plan nutritious meals for people who are ill. *(See p. 39.)*

3 **True or False:** A food label must include information on the amount of trans fatty acids. *(See p. 53.)*

4 **True or False:** Dietary Reference Intakes represent a revision of the Recommended Dietary Allowances. *(See p. 37.)*

5 **True or False:** Vendors at ball parks must provide nutrition information for their hot dogs. *(See p. 51.)*

6 **True or False:** Restaurant and foodservice operations that make health claims on menus must provide nutrition information. *(See p. 52.)*

7 **True or False:** Physical activity is a component of MyPyramid. *(See pp. 43–44.)*

8 **True or False:** Restaurants and foodservice operations must use the Nutrition Facts panel format to communicate nutrition information for menu items that contain a health claim. *(See p. 52.)*

Key Terms

Acceptable Macronutrient Distribution Range (AMDR)

Adequate Intake (AI)

Allergen

Daily Values (DVs)

Dietary Guidelines for Americans 2005

Dietary Reference Intakes (DRI)

Estimated Average Requirement (EAR)

Estimated Energy Requirement (EER)

Food label

Healthy

MyPyramid

Nutrition Facts panel

Nutrition Labeling and Education Act of 1990 (NLEA)

Recommended Dietary Allowance (RDA)

Resting metabolic rate (RMR)

Thermic effect of food

Tolerable Upper Intake Level (UL)

USDA Organic

Introduction

In the United States, nutrition professionals use standards and guidelines to teach balanced nutrition to consumers and help them achieve a healthy diet. When people are motivated to change their dietary intake to improve their health, they look to the restaurant and foodservice industry for menu choices that are tasty and nutritious. Restaurant and foodservice operators who understand nutrition are more likely to benefit by catering to interest in healthful food as well as tasty food. Fortunately, many of the current standards for nutrition and tools for applying the standards are easily accessible to restaurant and foodservice operators and can easily be applied to menus to provide healthful food choices. In this chapter you will learn about these standards and recommendations.

Another part of the U.S. government's method of helping consumers make informed choices about what they eat is requiring that certain food be labeled with relevant nutritional information. These requirements always apply to packaged food items in grocery stores. In this chapter, you will learn what the requirements are, and when and how they apply to restaurant and foodservice operations.

Exhibit 3a

RDAs can be used to determine the adequacy of this population's diet.

A Healthy Diet

In 1997, the Food and Nutrition Board of the Institute of Medicine, which is part of the National Academy of Sciences, changed the way nutrition professionals evaluate the diets of healthy people. Previously, the Recommended Dietary Allowances (RDAs)—the average daily dietary intake levels sufficient to meet the nutrient requirements for almost all healthy individuals—were used to evaluate and plan menus. Also, RDAs served as resources in interpreting dietary intake records of populations (see *Exhibit 3a*), establishing standards for food assistance programs, and establishing nutrition-labeling guidelines.

The goal of using RDAs was to prevent diseases caused by nutrient deficiencies. However, in developed countries such as the United States, diseases caused by nutrient deficiencies are now rare. The current focus of nutrition is much more on the connection between health and nutrition. In response to this change in focus, in 1997 the Food and Nutrition Board developed the **Dietary Reference Intakes (DRIs)**, a set of daily nutrient and energy intake amounts for healthy people of a particular age range and gender.

Dietary Reference Intakes

While the DRIs still identify the amounts of nutrients needed to prevent deficiency, they also identify the intake adequate for reducing the risk of chronic disease in healthy people.

DRIs for most nutrients consist of three of the following four values:

■ **Estimated Average Requirement (EAR)**—Estimated average daily dietary intake level to meet the nutritional requirements of half of the healthy people of a particular age range and gender.

■ **Recommended Dietary Allowance (RDA)**—Average daily dietary nutrient intake sufficient to meet the nutrient requirement of nearly all (97 to 98 percent) healthy individuals of a particular age and gender group.

■ **Adequate Intake (AI)**—Daily dietary intake level of healthy people assumed to be adequate when there is insufficient evidence to set an RDA.

■ **Tolerable Upper Intake Level (UL)**—Highest level of daily nutrient intake that poses no risk of adverse health effects to almost all individuals of a certain age range.

In addition to the values for nutrients, the DRIs also include two values for energy:

■ **Estimated Energy Requirement (EER)**—Dietary energy intake believed to maintain energy balance in a healthy adult of a certain age, gender, weight, height, and level of activity.

■ **Acceptable Macronutrient Distribution Range (AMDR)**— A range of intakes for a particular energy source, such as fats, that refers to a reduced risk of disease while providing enough essential nutrients. AMDR shown in *Exhibit 3b* is for adults. It is expressed as a percentage of total energy intake, because its requirement does not depend on other energy sources or an individual's caloric needs.

How DRIs Are Determined

The Food and Nutrition Board conducts reviews of the scientific literature, then analyzes findings and develops recommendations. The process includes at least one public meeting for input from other organizations, experts, and the public. The results of this study are written into the DRIs. The current DRIs are available through the United States Department of Agriculture (USDA) at *www.nal.usda.gov/fnic*.

Exhibit 3b

Acceptable Macronutrient Distribution Range (AMDR)

Nutrient	Percent
Carbohydrates	45 to 65 percent
Proteins	10 to 35 percent
Lipids	20 to 35 percent

Reprinted with permission from *Dietary Reference Intakes for Energy, Carbohydrate, Fiber, Fat, Fatty Acids, Cholesterol, Protein, and Amino Acids (Macronutrients)*. ©2005 by the National Academy of Sciences, courtesy of the National Academies Press, Washington, DC.

The Role of DRIs in Meal and Menu Planning

Dietary planning, whether for an individual or a group, involves developing a diet that is nutritionally adequate without being excessive. The goal for individuals is to achieve recommended and adequate nutrient intakes. A restaurant or foodservice operation can help its customers achieve an adequate nutrient intake by using DRIs in its menu planning.

As stated earlier in this chapter, DRIs consist of several different types of reference values. RDAs, AIs, and ULs are the DRIs most commonly used for meal planning. RDAs and AIs provide the nutrient recommendations for adequate intake for the majority of healthy individuals. For example, by referencing the RDA for calcium, a menu planner can determine that the RDA for calcium for adults aged nineteen to fifty is 1,000 milligrams per day. AIs provide the recommendations for those nutrients that do not have an RDA. ULs provide the upper intake limits that individuals should not exceed of a given nutrient. RDAs and AIs can be used to ensure that meals meet nutrient requirements; ULs can be used to ensure that meals do not exceed the recommended intake.

In a restaurant setting there are two steps in using DRIs for menu planning:

1. Use RDAs and AIs to identify goals for nutrients in meals. For example, a menu planner might determine that at least some menu items should provide at least half the recommendation for calcium.

2. Use a nutrient-based food guidance system, such as MyPyramid (discussed later in this chapter), to select food for menu items and to determine portion sizes.

For existing menus, DRIs can be used to evaluate the potential of each existing menu item to supply nutrients that meet the RDAs and AIs. For those menu items that do not supply sufficient nutrients, the restaurant or foodservice professional must determine whether there are ways to change the menu items to increase the likelihood of providing adequate nutrients.

Meal planning for institutional settings, such as the school shown in *Exhibit 3c*, requires a meal planner to first evaluate the nutritional requirements of the group for which meals are provided. The RDAs and AIs are then used to plan meals that meet the nutrient requirements for that group. In foodservice settings that provide all daily meals, meal planners must ensure that nutrient requirements are met each day, or for school lunch or breakfast programs, must meet one-third of the daily requirements.

Exhibit 3c

The meals provided in this school have been planned to provide part of the children's nutritional requirements.

Dietary Guidelines for Americans 2005

The *Dietary Guidelines for Americans 2005* is a document published jointly by the Department of Health and Human Services and the USDA. This report offers science-based advice for healthy people over the age of two about food choices to promote health and reduce risk for major chronic diseases. Like the RDAs, these dietary guidelines apply to diets eaten over several days, not to single food items or meals. These guidelines are updated every five years to reflect the latest Dietary Reference Intakes and other research. They also form the basis for federal food and nutrition programs. The *Dietary Guidelines for Americans 2005* contains nine focus areas; each one contains one or more key recommendations, which are summarized in *Exhibit 3e* on pages 41–42.

Applying *Dietary Guidelines for Americans 2005* in a Restaurant or Foodservice Setting

Restaurant and foodservice operations can help their customers meet dietary guidelines by providing menu items that focus on the kinds of food mentioned in the guidelines:

- Fresh fruit
- Vegetables from each of the vegetable subgroups of dark green, orange, legumes, starchy vegetables, and other vegetables (see *Exhibit 3d*)
- Whole grains
- Lean meat and fish
- Fat-free or low-fat milk and dairy products

Exhibit 3d

A variety of dark green, orange, and starchy vegetables is part of a healthy diet.

The way in which menu items are prepared can also contribute to following the dietary guidelines. As recommended by the guidelines, be aware of how much fat, sugar, and sodium that food-preparation techniques add, and minimize the use of these ingredients. When planning and preparing menu items, it is important to remember that there are no bad food items. If a variety of nutritious food is on the menu, customers will be able to select menu items that comprise a good diet.

Exhibit 3e

Dietary Guidelines Focus Areas

Focus Area	Key Recommendations
Adequate Nutrients within Calorie Needs	■ Consume a variety of nutrient-dense food and beverages within and among the basic food groups while limiting the intake of saturated fats, trans fats, cholesterol, added sugars, salt, and alcohol. ■ Meet recommended intakes within energy needs by adopting a balanced eating pattern, such as MyPyramid.
Weight Management	■ Balance calories from food and beverages with calories expended to maintain body weight in a healthy range. ■ To prevent gradual weight gain over time, make small decreases in food and beverage calories and increase physical activity.
Physical Activity	■ Engage in regular physical activity and reduce sedentary activities to promote health, psychological well being, and a healthy body weight. ■ Achieve physical fitness by including cardiovascular conditioning, stretching exercises for flexibility, and resistance exercises or calisthenics for muscle strength and endurance.
Food Groups to Encourage	■ Consume a sufficient amount of fruit and vegetables while staying within energy needs. Two cups of fruit and 2½ cups of vegetables per day are recommended for a 2,000-calorie intake, with higher or lower amounts depending on the calorie level. ■ Choose a variety of fruit and vegetables each day. In particular, select from all five vegetable subgroups (dark green, orange, legumes, starchy vegetables, and other vegetables) several times a week. ■ Consume three or more ounces of whole-grain products per day (or the equivalent), with the rest of the recommended grains coming from enriched or whole-grain products. In general, at least half the grains should come from whole grains. ■ Consume three cups per day of fat-free or low-fat milk or equivalent milk products.
Carbohydrates	■ Choose fiber-rich fruit, vegetables, and whole grains often. ■ Choose and prepare food and beverages with little added sugars or caloric sweeteners, such as amounts suggested by MyPyramid and the DASH Eating Plan. ■ Reduce the incidence of dental caries by practicing good oral hygiene and consuming sugar- and starch-containing food and beverages less frequently.

MyPyramid.gov
STEPS TO A HEALTHIER YOU

continued on next page

U.S. Department of Health and Human Services and U.S. Department of Agriculture, *Dietary Guidelines for Americans 2005*

continued from previous page

Focus Area	Key Recommendations
Fats	■ Consume less than 10 percent of calories from saturated fatty acids and less than 300 mg/day of cholesterol, and keep trans fatty acid consumption as low as possible. ■ Keep total fat intake between 20 to 35 percent of calories, with most fats coming from sources of polyunsaturated and monounsaturated fatty acids, such as fish, nuts, and vegetable oils. ■ When selecting and preparing meat, poultry, dry beans, and milk or milk products, make choices that are lean, low fat, or fat free. ■ Limit intake of fats and oils high in saturated and/or trans fatty acids, and choose products low in such fats and oils.
Sodium and Potassium	■ Consume less than 2,300 mg (approximately one teaspoon of salt) of sodium per day. ■ Choose and prepare food with little salt. At the same time, consume potassium-rich food, such as fruit and vegetables.
Alcoholic Beverages	■ Those who choose to drink alcoholic beverages should do so sensibly and in moderation—up to one drink per day for women and up to two drinks per day for men. ■ Alcoholic beverages should not be consumed by some individuals, including those who cannot restrict their alcohol intake, women who are trying to become pregnant, pregnant and lactating women, children and adolescents, individuals taking medications that can interact with alcohol, and those with specific medical conditions. ■ Alcoholic beverages should be avoided by individuals engaging in activities that require attention, skill, or coordination, such as driving or operating machinery.
Food Safety*	To avoid microbial foodborne illness: ■ Clean hands, food-contact surfaces, and fruit and vegetables. Meat and poultry should not be washed or rinsed. ■ Separate raw, cooked, and ready-to-eat food while shopping, preparing, or storing food. ■ Cook food to a safe temperature to kill microorganisms. ■ Chill (refrigerate) perishable food promptly and defrost food properly. ■ Avoid raw (unpasteurized) milk and any products made from unpasteurized milk, raw and partially cooked eggs and food containing raw eggs, raw and undercooked meat and poultry, unpasteurized juices, and raw sprouts.

*These are consumer-based guidelines. For more specific restaurant and foodservice information, see *ServSafe Coursebook*.

Food Selection Tools

The USDA's MyPyramid food guide and the Nutrition Facts panel serve as tools to put dietary guidelines into practice. MyPyramid translates the RDAs and dietary guidelines into the kinds and amounts of food to eat each day. Nutrition Facts panels help people select the appropriate packaged food products to meet their nutritional needs. Both of these tools are discussed in more detail.

MyPyramid

People's needs regarding food combinations and portions vary based on their age, activity level, and gender. **MyPyramid** is a tool developed by the USDA. It has two educational purposes and teaches people:

- How to eat a balanced diet from a variety of food groups without counting calories
- How to include physical activity in their daily lives and adjust food intake for the amount of activity

MyPyramid gives people a quick estimate of what and how much to eat; it also replaces the 1992 Food Guide Pyramid and incorporates the recommendations of the *Dietary Guidelines for Americans 2005*. The food groups represented in MyPyramid are:

- Grains
- Milk and dairy products
- Vegetables
- Meat and beans
- Fruit

Fats and oils contain essential fatty acids and are also shown on MyPyramid but are not considered a food group. There are calories allocated for these oils that are not part of the discretionary calorie allowance in MyPyramid.

MyPyramid Symbol

The MyPyramid symbol shown in *Exhibit 3f* on the next page emphasizes six key themes:

1. Proportionality
2. Variety
3. Activity
4. Moderation
5. Gradual improvement
6. Personalization

Exhibit 3f

MyPyramid.gov
STEPS TO A HEALTHIER YOU

MyPyramid symbolizes the importance of engaging in physical activity and of eating a variety of food in the proper proportions.

Courtesy of U.S. Department of Agriculture. USDA does not endorse any products, services, or organizations.

Proportionality

The width of each colored band on the pyramid suggests how much food a person should choose from each food category. For example, the green band, which represents vegetables, is wider than the red band, which represents fruit. This suggests that people should include more servings of vegetables than fruit in their daily diets. Since the widths are just a general guide, an individual wanting to know the specific number of servings recommended for his or her age, gender, and activity level must check *www.MyPyramid.gov* for more information.

Variety

The color bands differentiate the six food categories representing the five food groups—grains, vegetables, fruit, milk, meat and beans— plus fats and oils. This illustrates that food from all food groups is needed each day for good health. *Exhibit 3g* shows the food category represented by each color and gives examples of daily recommendations for female and male adults ages nineteen to thirty.

Specific recommendations for people of a specific age range, gender, and physical activity level can be found at *www.MyPyramid.gov*.

Activity Level

In MyPyramid, a person's activity level is represented by the steps and the person climbing them; this is a reminder of the importance of daily physical activity. Nearly all Americans should be more active because physical activity helps to maintain health. Specific recommendations for people of different physical activity levels can be found at *www.MyPyramid.gov*.

Exhibit 3g

MyPyramid Food Categories

Grains	Vegetables	Fruits	Oils	Milk	Meat and Beans
Examples of Food					
Bread Cereal Rice Pasta	Dark green vegetables Orange vegetables Starchy vegetables Dry beans and peas Other vegetables	Apricots Apples Bananas Grapes Raisins	Vegetable oil Animal fats Nuts Olives Avocados	Milk Cheese Yogurt Ice cream Cottage cheese	Meat Fish Fowl Eggs Dry beans and peas Nuts and seeds
Daily Recommendations for females (F) and males (M), ages 19 to 30					
F 6 ounces **M** 8 ounces At least one-half of the servings should be whole grain.	**F** 2½ cups **M** 3 cups Eat more dark green and orange vegetables and dry beans and peas.	**F** 2 cups **M** 2 cups Eat a variety. Choose fresh, frozen, canned, or dried fruit. Limit daily intake of fruit juices.	**F** 6 teaspoons **M** 7 teaspoons Make most of fat sources from fish, nuts, and vegetable oils. Select fats with zero trans fat. Limit solid fats.	**F** 3 cups **M** 3 cups Choose low-fat or fat-free milk products.	**F** 5½ ounces **M** 6½ ounces Select lean or low-fat meat and poultry. Select fish high in omega-3 fatty acids more often.
Serving Equivalents					
One ounce equivalent: 1 slice bread 1 cup cereal ½ cup cooked rice or pasta	**One cup equivalent:** 1 cup cooked or raw vegetables 2 cups leafy greens	**One cup equivalent:** 1 cup fruit ½ cup dried fruit	**One teaspoon equivalent:** 1 teaspoon oil, liquid or solid Some food, such as peanut butter, counts toward oil servings. Refer to the MyPyramid Web site on how to count oils.	**One cup equivalent:** 1 cup milk or yogurt 1½ ounces natural cheese 2 ounces processed cheese	**One ounce equivalent:** 1 ounce meat, fish, or poultry ½ cup cooked dry beans or peas 1 egg 1 tablespoon peanut butter ½ ounce nuts or seeds

Adapted from the U.S. Department of Agriculture's MyPyramid

Moderation

The narrowing of each food group from the bottom to the top represents moderation. The wider base represents food with little or no solid fats or added sugar. The USDA recommends choosing these food items more often. The narrower top represents food containing more added sugar and fat. The more active a person is, the more often these food items will fit his or her diet.

Gradual Improvement

The MyPyramid slogan of "Steps to a Healthier You" suggests that people can benefit from taking small steps to improve their diet and lifestyle.

Personalization

The slogan, the person on the steps, and the Web site all suggest personalization of food intake. Caloric needs vary by age and activity level. Most older adults need less food, in part due to decreased activity. Individuals who are trying to lose weight and eat smaller amounts of food may need to select more nutrient-dense food to meet their nutrient needs. The *www.MyPyramid.gov* Web site provides a way for an individual to determine the kinds and amounts of food to eat each day.

Exhibit 3h

This six-ounce steak, served as one portion in a restaurant, is double the meat recommendation of MyPyramid for an entire day.

Standard Food Choices and Special Groups

Individuals approach the subject of eating with different needs. This is why the MyPyramid Web site reflects varying choices for different populations, such as children or the elderly. Many factors affect food choices, including age, habit, environment, and economic factors. MyPyramid is a useful tool in helping consumers comparison shop for nutrients so they can make informed choices.

Standard Serving Sizes versus Serving Portions

The standard serving sizes used in MyPyramid were developed by the USDA based on national surveys. These recommended serving sizes are often smaller than people realize and much smaller than the portions provided in packaged food or food served in most restaurant or foodservice operations. (See *Exhibit 3h*.) The daily recommendation of five to eight standard servings of grain might seem like a lot until the serving size of one ounce is taken into consideration. For example, one standard serving of pasta according to MyPyramid is one-half cup. However, many people eat a cup or more of pasta in a meal, thus consuming two or more standard servings.

Meals at a restaurant or foodservice establishment sometimes provide a customer with half or more of the customer's daily allotment of calories. This is because historically, restaurant and foodservice operators have used their competition, their customer's demands, and their operation's serving-portion size as a guide when plating food. In general, an operation's serving portions are larger than the standard serving size used in MyPyramid, sometimes significantly larger. Some operations even offer a way to upgrade to a larger portion size for a little added cost, adding more calories to the customer's order.

Restaurants and foodservice operations can help their customers stay within their daily calorie allotment by implementing the following tactics:

- Provide several portion sizes of a given menu item.

- Provide an easy way for a customer to eat a portion of the food at the restaurant and take the rest of the food home.

- Provide an easy way for customers to split an entrée with others in their dining party.

Energy Balance and Calories

Both the *Dietary Guidelines for Americans 2005* and MyPyramid draw attention to the importance of balancing energy needs with energy consumption. This balance is maintained by managing energy (caloric) intake through food selection to match the energy expended.

Three factors influence an individual's daily energy needs:

- **Resting metabolic rate (RMR)**—Amount of energy (number of calories) needed for body functioning at complete rest. Each person's RMR varies based on gender, stage of life, genetics, and percentage of lean body mass. The RMR accounts for approximately 65 percent of total daily calorie needs.

- **Thermic effect of food**—Number of calories needed to digest, absorb, transport, and store nutrients in the body. Each time a person eats food, his or her RMR increases slightly and stays elevated for about five hours to fuel the use of food. The thermic effect of food accounts for 5 to 10 percent of daily calorie needs.

- **Physical activity**—Includes normal daily activities, such as walking from room to room, brushing teeth, and washing dishes, as well as purposeful exercise, such as running, hiking, and swimming. The number of calories expended through physical exercise varies widely depending on an individual's size, fitness level, and activity intensity. Physical activity accounts for 25 to 35 percent of daily calorie needs.

An individual's energy needs are met by the food the individual eats. Carbohydrates, fats, and proteins supply energy, measured in calories, in varying amounts.

Not every nutrient contributes the same number of kilocalories per gram. Carbohydrates and proteins provide about four kilocalories per gram. Fat contributes more than twice as much, about nine kilocalories per gram. Therefore, food items that are high in fat are also high in calories. However, many low-fat or nonfat food items may also be high in calories because they contain a lot of carbohydrates, especially sugars.

Of the factors that impact energy balance, only physical activity and food selection are within an individual's control. Therefore, to maintain a balance in energy intake and expenditure, an individual can decrease food intake, increase physical activity, or do both.

Using MyPyramid for Menu Planning

Many of the suggestions for applying the dietary guidelines to menu planning also apply to using MyPyramid. However, there are three ways in which restaurant and foodservice professionals can use MyPyramid for specific guidance.

- **As a guide to the appropriate serving sizes for the various food groups**—Proportion the serving sizes as the pyramid is proportioned: very little oil, smaller meat items, and more vegetables, fruit, and whole grains.

- **To determine portion sizes**—Evaluate the portion sizes offered by your operation in the light of the serving sizes and number; revise them as needed or expand current menu offerings with additional portion sizes.

- **To provide a more balanced menu**—Use MyPyramid as a quick guide to what constitutes a healthful diet, and plan menus that help customers get the most nutrition for their calories when eating at your establishment.

Since a restaurant or foodservice operation meal is probably not the only meal your customer will eat during the day, your operation might consider gearing its portions to a percentage of the recommended servings of each food group. For example, the MyPyramid recommendation is for a daily intake of five to six and one-half ounces of meat. If you currently offer eight-ounce steaks, you might consider changing the portion size to four or five ounces or to also offer a four- or five-ounce steak.

Since MyPyramid breaks down its recommendations by gender and age, you can use it as a guide when planning menu items for specific customer groups. For example, if your operation targets people over the age of fifty-one, you might consider gearing portions to reflect MyPyramid recommendations for this age group or add a menu section for them.

Restaurant and foodservice professionals can offer a variety of food items to cover all food groups, select lean meat, and reduce the amount of fats and oils used in cooking. By doing this, your operation can offer a wide variety of healthful meals that your customers can enjoy in good conscience.

Activity

Assessing Menu Items

In this activity, you will assess the adequacy of portions on a restaurant or foodservice operation's menu for one segment of the establishment's customer base.

1 With the manager's permission, obtain a copy of a restaurant or foodservice operation's menu.

2 Select a customer group; for example, men ages nineteen to thirty.

3 Determine the recommended servings and serving sizes for each food group for the selected customer group using the MyPyramid Web site at: *www.MyPyramid.gov* and use the "Inside the Pyramid" link.

4 Complete the table below with this information.

Customer Group:	
Food Group	**Serving Recommendations**
Grains	
Vegetables	
Fruit	
Milk	
Meat and Beans	

5 Select two to three menu items from each menu category such as appetizers, salads, sandwiches, entrées, and desserts.

6 Determine which food groups the menu item contains and the approximate portion size for the food group. For example, a grilled grouper sandwich might include four servings of grain, three servings of meat and beans, and one serving of vegetables.

7 Create a table like the one on the next page to capture your information.

continued on next page

Assessing Menu Items *continued from previous page*

Menu Item Name	Food Groups Covered	Number of Servings in Portion

8 Evaluate the menu items to determine which items fit within the recommended servings.

9 On a separate sheet of paper, answer the following questions:

☐ How does the portion size for each selected menu item compare to the number of servings recommended on MyPyramid?

☐ Which menu items should a customer choose to stay within the guidelines?

☐ If you were the restaurant or foodservice operation owner, manager, or chef, which menu items would you change to bring them closer to the recommended servings?

☐ How might you change them?

☐ What have you learned about restaurant and foodservice operation portion sizes versus standard servings from this activity?

Nutrition Labeling— Implementation and Interpretation

Another tool that helps people implement the DRIs and the dietary guidelines is the food label, a label on packaged food that lists the nutrients included and their amounts. The food label takes the guesswork out of good nutrition. Nutrition labeling is now nearly universal on packaged food. In the United States, the Nutrition Labeling and Education Act of 1990 (NLEA) an amendment to the Food, Drug, and Cosmetic Act of 1938, went into effect in 1994. It made major changes to the content and scope of the nutrition label and to other elements of food labels.

The NLEA provides the Food and Drug Administration (FDA) with specific authority to require nutrition labeling of most food products regulated by the agency. The NLEA specifies which food products require labels, provides details of what must be included on a food label, and describes the companies and/or food products that are exempt from providing complete nutrition information. In addition, the NLEA requires that all nutrient-content claims, such as "high fiber" and "low fat," and health claims be consistent with agency regulations.

Food Items Exempt from Nutrition Labeling

Under NLEA, some food items are exempt from nutrition labeling:

- Food served for immediate consumption, in such locations as hospital cafeterias, airplanes, mall cookie counters, sidewalk vendors, and vending machines

- Ready-to-eat food that is not for immediate consumption but is primarily prepared on site; for example, bakery, deli, and candy store items

- Food shipped in bulk, as long as it is not for sale in that form

- Medical food, such as that used to provide special patient needs

- Plain coffee and tea, some spices, and other food items that contain no significant amounts of any nutrients

In addition to the food listed above, fresh fish and meat and poultry products regulated by the USDA are not covered by the NLEA. The NLEA also allows nutritional information about game meat, such as deer, bison, and quail, to be provided on counter cards or other point-of-purchase materials rather than on individual packages. In addition, food produced by small businesses may also be exempt from nutrition labeling. Finally, nutrition labels are voluntary for many raw food items, such as fruit and vegetables.

Nutrition Information Required for Restaurant and Foodservice Operation Food Items

As previously noted, the FDA does not require ready-to-eat food products to be labeled with nutrition information. However, the FDA does require nutrition information for food products about which an operation makes a health or nutrient-content claim on its menus, signs, or other forms of advertising. In these situations, operations must provide a reasonable basis for making the claim. For example, if the claim "heart healthy" appears on a restaurant or foodservice operation's menu, the owner must be able to demonstrate that there is a reasonable basis for believing that the food qualifies to bear the claim.

Restaurants and foodservice operations have some flexibility in demonstrating the reasonable basis, such as using recipes endorsed by medical or dietary groups, cookbooks, nutrient databases, and other reasonable means to provide assurance that the food meets the nutrient value for the claim. Presentation of nutritional information does not need to take the form of the Nutrition Facts panel. The nutritional information can be stated by any reasonable means—signs, posters, brochures, or notebooks—as long as the information is available to customers upon request.

The Nutrition Facts Panel

The **Nutrition Facts panel** is the part of the food label that contains the nutrition information required by the FDA; an example is shown in *Exhibit 3i*. The Nutrition Facts panel can be a useful tool in helping design a balanced, varied, and healthful diet and to select food items for a diet that will meet the dietary guidelines. In addition,

Exhibit 3i

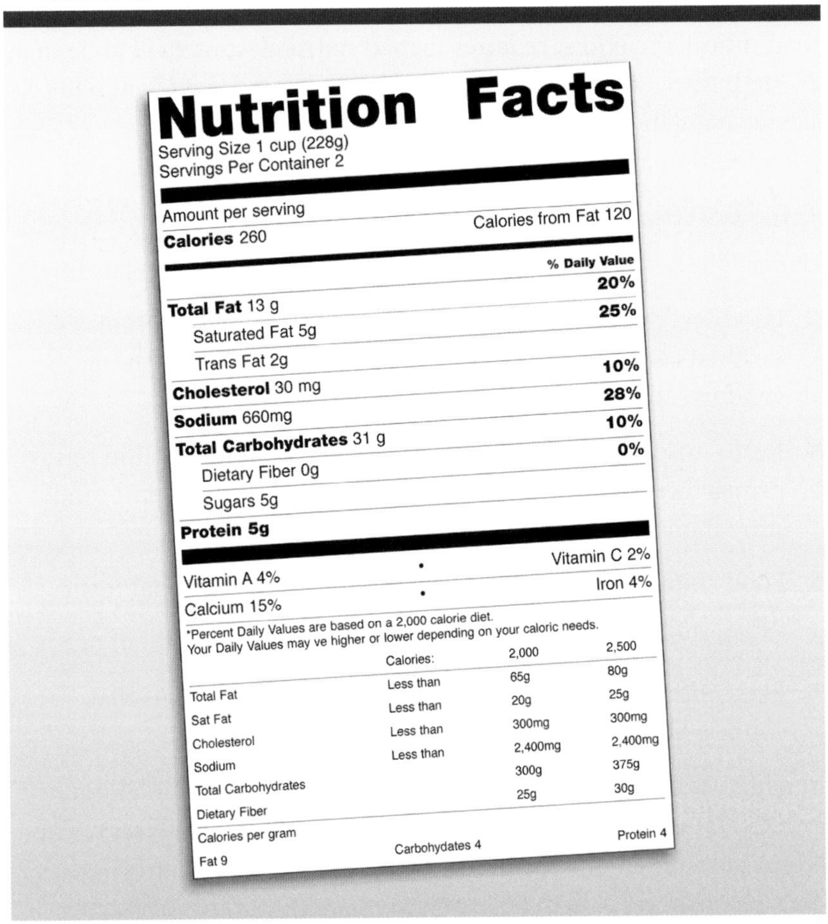

This format of the Nutrition Facts panel, which shows trans fat content, became mandatory on January 1, 2006.

U.S. Food and Drug Administration

learning how to read and use nutrition information can help people to:

- Avoid food allergens

- Plan special diets

- Cut back on fat, sodium, cholesterol, or calories

It is important to remember that, since there is no bad food, people can use the nutritional information listed on food labels to make healthy diet choices.

Mandatory Components of a Nutrition Facts Panel

The USDA requires a Nutrition Facts panel to have certain components about nutrients, which is required because these nutrients address current health concerns. The order in which the nutrients must appear reflects the current priority of dietary recommendations. The mandatory components are:

- **Serving size and servings per container**—The serving size is the basis for reporting each food's nutrient content and is defined as the amount of food customarily eaten at one time for each food category, based on the USDA's food-consumption surveys. To report the serving size, the FDA allows the use of common household measures, such as cup, tablespoon, teaspoon, piece, slice, parts (such as "⅛ pizza"), and common household containers used to package food products (such as a jar). Ounces may be used, but only if a common household unit does not apply. Standard serving size is followed by the metric amount, e.g., the number of grams. The servings per container reflect how many servings are contained within the package. The size of the serving on the food package influences the number of calories and all the nutrient amounts listed on the top part of the label.

- **Total calories and calories from fat**—Caloric content of one serving, as well as the number of calories from fat in a single serving.

- **Total fat and saturated fat**—Total grams of fat in one serving and the number of grams of saturated fat in one serving (included in grams of total fat per serving).

- **Trans fat**—As of January 1, 2006, all labels must list grams of trans fatty acid, also called trans fat, which has been shown to have a negative effect on cholesterol and heart health. Like the other fats, the amount of trans fat is listed as the number of grams in one serving.

Exhibit 3j

Order for Listing Optional Vitamins and Minerals

Vitamin D

Vitamin E

Thiamin

Riboflavin

Niacin

Vitamin B$_6$

Folate

Vitamin B$_{12}$

Biotin

Pantothenic acid

Phosphorus

Iodine

Magnesium

Zinc

Copper

Note: These vitamins and minerals must be listed when added to a food as a nutrient supplement or when used as the basis of a health claim.

- **Cholesterol**—Cholesterol is listed in milligrams and the percentage of daily values is based not on calories, but on a daily recommendation of three hundred milligrams or less.

- **Sodium**—Sodium is listed in milligrams with a percentage of daily values based on a daily recommendation of 2,400 milligrams or less. The National Academy of Sciences now recommends limiting sodium to 1,500 milligrams or less daily.

- **Total carbohydrate, dietary fiber, and sugars**—Dietary fiber and sugars are included in a food's total carbohydrate content. Dietary fiber has been associated with decreasing cholesterol and aiding in food transportation through the digestive tract.

- **Protein**—Total grams of protein in one serving.

- **Vitamin A, vitamin C, calcium, and iron**—The FDA requires the label to list the vitamins A and C and the minerals calcium and iron because of their connection to health conditions like osteoporosis and anemia. *Exhibit 3j* shows the allowable optional vitamins and minerals.

There are some variations in the format of the Nutrition Facts panel. For example, labels of food items for children under two years of age must not carry information about saturated fat, polyunsaturated fat, monounsaturated fat, cholesterol, calories from fat, or calories from saturated fat. This is to prevent parents from incorrectly assuming that infants and young children must restrict fat intake. Fat is important during these years to ensure adequate growth and development.

Daily Values (DVs)

Each nutrient on the Nutrition Facts panel is reported as a percentage of the **Daily Values (DVs)**, which are food-label reference values determined from the FDA's Reference Dietary Intakes (RDIs) and Daily Reference Values (DRVs). Providing daily values on the Nutrition Facts panel helps people see how different types of food contribute to their overall daily diet. Although there is no bad food, it is important that the percentages of daily values of the nutritional components are listed so that food products can be assembled into a healthful diet.

The DVs are provided in percentages based on a 2,000-calorie diet to which a single serving of a food item contributes. For example, a food that has thirteen grams of total fat would show a percent Daily Value (%DV) of 20 percent, which means that a serving of that food contributes 20 percent of the total daily fat grams an individual should consume in a 2,000-calorie diet. Since calorie needs vary from one person to the next, the %DV can be tailored to meet individual needs or used as a guide to the relative amount of certain nutrients in a serving of a given food.

Ingredient Labeling

Ingredients must be declared on all food items with more than one ingredient. Ingredients must be listed in order by their weight contained in the product, with the ingredient of greatest quantity listed first.

Food Additives

Because some people may be allergic to certain additives, the ingredient list must include:

- FDA-certified color additives, such as FD&C Blue No. 1, by name
- Sources of protein hydrolysates, which are used in food as flavors and flavor enhancers (e.g., MSG)
- Caseinate as a milk derivative for food that claims to be nondairy, such as coffee whiteners

Juices

The NLEA requires beverages that claim to contain juice to declare the total percentage of juice. In addition, the FDA has established criteria for naming juice beverages. The label of a multijuice beverage whose predominate juice is present in small amounts must state that the product is flavored with that juice or state the amount of the juice in a 5-percent range. For example, a product with a small amount of cranberry juice must use the phrases "cranberry-flavored juice blend" or "juice blend with 2 to 7 percent cranberry juice."

Allergens

Effective January 1, 2006, food labels must disclose that a food contains one or more of the eight major food allergens—substances that can cause an allergic reaction for some people:

- Milk
- Eggs
- Peanuts
- Tree nuts
- Fish
- Shellfish
- Soy
- Wheat

Next to the ingredient list, the label must say either "contains" (e.g., peanuts) or list the source of the ingredient. (See *Exhibit 3k*.)

Exhibit 3k

INGREDIENTS: BROCCOLI SPEARS IN SAUCE CONTAINING WATER, ENZYME MODIFIED BUTTER, SUGAR, SALT, MODIFIED CORN STARCH, XANTHAN GUM, SODIUM STEAROYL LACTYLATE, ARTIFICIAL COLOR.
CONTAINS MILK INGREDIENTS.

DISTRIBUTED BY **Ouska Sales, Inc.**
GENERAL OFFICES **NEWTON IA 50208 USA**

PRODUCT OF MEXICO

The ingredient list for this food product points out that it contains milk, a major food allergen.

Labeling Terms

Prior to the NLEA of 1990, food manufacturers had no restrictions on using terms such as *lite* or *low-calorie*. The term *light*, or *lite*, could mean anything from fewer calories or less fat to the color of the food. To protect consumers from misleading advertising, regulators defined the terms to be used to describe the level of a nutrient in a food. *Exhibit 3l* lists some of the key terms and their definitions.

Exhibit 3l

Health-Related Labeling Terms

Term	Definition (amount per serving)
Calorie-free	Less than 5 calories
Sugar-free, fat-free	Less than 0.5 grams
Low fat	3 grams or less total fat
Low saturated fat	1 gram or less
Low sodium	Less than 140 milligrams
Very low sodium	Less than 35 milligrams
Cholesterol-free	Less than 2 milligrams of cholesterol and 2 grams or less of saturated fat
Low cholesterol	Less than 20 milligrams
Low calorie	Less than 40 calories
High fiber	5 grams or more fiber
High in (nutrient)	20 percent or more of the DV for the nutrient
Good source of (nutrient)	10–19 percent of DV for the nutrient
Reduced	25 percent or less of a nutrient or calories than the regular product
Less	25 percent less of a nutrient or calories than a reference food
Light/lite	Either:
	■ ⅓ less calories or ½ the fat of reference food
	■ 50 percent less sodium content in an already low-calorie, low-fat food

U.S. Food and Drug Administration

Labeling Food as Healthy

According to the FDA, a food must meet all the following requirements to be labeled "**healthy.**" (Exempt from this rule are some raw, canned, and frozen fruit and vegetables and certain cereal-grain products, which can be labeled "healthy" as long as they do not contain ingredients that change the nutritional profile.)

■ Low in fat and saturated fat

■ Limited amounts of cholesterol and sodium

■ Single-item food must provide at least 10 percent of one or more of:

    ☐ Vitamin A

    ☐ Vitamin C

    ☐ Iron

    ☐ Calcium

    ☐ Protein

    ☐ Fiber

■ Meal-type products, such as frozen entrées, must provide 10 percent of two or three of the nutrients named above, in addition to meeting the other criteria. The sodium content cannot exceed 360 milligrams per serving for individual food items and 480 milligrams per serving for meal-type products.

Labeling Organic Food

Food labeled with the USDA Organic seal means that the product is at least 95 percent organic and meets USDA organic standards. These standards include the use of renewable resources and the conservation of soil and water in growing food. In addition, organic food is grown without the use of conventional pesticides, fertilizers made with synthetic ingredients or sewage sludge, bioengineering, or ionizing radiation. Animals are given no antibiotics or growth hormones. The word organic may appear on packages of meat, cartons of milk or eggs, cheese, and other single-ingredient food items. Truthful claims, such as free-range, hormone-free, and natural, may also appear on food labels; however, these terms and organic are not interchangeable.

Misperceptions about Label Terms

Although the NLEA has placed restrictions on the use of certain terms on food labels to protect consumers from misleading advertising, some people have misperceptions about food labeled as organic, fat free, or high fiber, among others. For example, some people have the perception that low-fat food is always better for them than regular food or that a person can eat as much as he or she wants of organic food because it does not contain harmful ingredients. These and other misperceptions might cause people to take actions that are contrary to those recommended by MyPyramid and other nutrition standards. As a restaurant or foodservice manager, you must be aware of common misperceptions customers may have about nutrition so you can avoid creating additional misperceptions and can educate customers about the nutritional content of the offerings at your establishment. *Exhibit 3m* on the next page lists some common misperceptions and why they are incorrect.

Think About It...

What common misperceptions have you heard about organic, low-fat, or high-fiber food?

Exhibit 3m

Common Misperceptions Regarding Food Label Terms

Misperception	Why the Statement Is a Misperception
"You can eat as much as you want of organic food items because they do not contain harmful ingredients."	All food, whether organic or nonorganic, contains calories. Any food, including organic food, should be selected based on its ability to meet an individual's nutritional and energy needs.
"Organic food items always have low environmental impact and are less harmful to the environment than food items grown with traditional methods, because organic methods involve less chemical and hormone use."	There is no guarantee that food items labeled as organic are actually grown and processed in organic methods. There are also questions concerning whether the "organic" label includes technologies such as genetic engineering and irradiation.
"Organic food helps keep small farmers in business because these are the farmers who use organic methods."	Farms of any size can and do use organic farming methods. It is the use of methods specified by the USDA that constitutes an organic farm.
"Organic food is always more healthy than nonorganic food because food without chemicals and hormones is healthier than food with these additives."	All food items contain nutrients needed for health. The USDA makes no claims that organically produced food is healthier than nonorganic food. Organic food differs from nonorganic food in the way it is grown, handled, and processed.
"Low-fat food is always better for you than regular food."	Low-fat food may contain higher amounts of other nutrients, such as sodium or sugar, that make the low-fat food a less desirable choice.
"High-fiber food is always better for you than regular food."	All grains are good sources of complex carbohydrates. Grains that have not been refined (whole grains) are better sources of fiber and other important nutrients, such as selenium, potassium, and magnesium. Each person has an individual tolerance for fiber. Not everyone can tolerate high fiber diets, therefore lower fiber food is needed.

Health Claims

Claims for relationships between a food, nutrient, and the risk of a health-related condition are allowed and can be made in several ways (see *Exhibit 3n*):

■ Third-party references, such as the National Cancer Institute

■ Symbols, such as a heart

■ Descriptions

Exhibit 3n

This food product claims to be heart healthy. Note the use of symbols and descriptions.

The claim cannot state the degree of risk reduction and can only use "may" or "might" in discussing the nutrient or food-disease relationship. Claims also must state that other factors play a role in that disease, and must be phrased so that the relationship between the nutrient and the disease is understood.

Examples of such rules are:

- **Calcium and osteoporosis**—To carry a claim relating calcium and osteoporosis, a food must contain 20 percent or more of the daily value for calcium (200 milligrams) per serving, have a calcium content that equals or exceeds the food's content of phosphorus, and contain a form of calcium that can be readily absorbed in the body. The claim must name the target group most in need of adequate calcium intakes as well as the need for exercise and a healthy diet. A product that contains 40 percent or more of the daily value for calcium must state that a total dietary intake greater than 200 percent of the daily value for calcium (that is, 2,000 milligrams or more) has no additional (known) benefit.

- **Fat and cancer**—To carry a claim relating fat and cancer, a food must meet the nutrient-content claim requirements for "low fat."

- **Saturated fat and cholesterol and coronary heart disease**— A claim relating saturated fat and cholesterol and coronary heart disease may be used if the food meets the definitions for the nutrient-content claim "low saturated fat," "low cholesterol," and "low fat," or, if fish and game meat, for "extra lean."

- **Fiber-containing grain products, fruit, and vegetables and cancer**—To carry a claim relating fiber and cancer, a food must be or contain a grain product, fruit, or vegetable and meet the nutrient-content claim requirements for "low fat," and, without fortification, be a "good source" of dietary fiber.

- **Fruit, vegetables, and grain products that contain fiber and risk of coronary heart disease**—To carry a claim relating fiber and coronary heart disease, a food must be or contain fruit, vegetables, or grain products and meet the nutrient claim requirements for "low saturated fat," "low cholesterol," and "low fat" and contain, without fortification, at least 0.6 g soluble fiber per serving.

- **Sodium and hypertension (high blood pressure)**—To carry a claim relating sodium and hypertension, a food must meet the nutrient-content claim requirements for "low sodium."

- **Fruit and vegetables and cancer**—A claim regarding cancer may be made for fruit and vegetables that meet the nutrient-content claim requirements for "low fat" and, without fortification, for a "good source" of one or more of dietary fiber, vitamin A, or vitamin C.

Exhibit 3o

Servers who serve this salad to customers must know that it contains tree nuts, a food allergen for some people.

■ **Folic acid and neural tube defects**—A claim relating folic acid and neural tube defects is allowed on dietary supplements that contain sufficient folate and on conventional food items that are naturally good sources of folate, as long as they do not provide more than 100 percent of the Daily Value for vitamin A as retinol or preformed vitamin A or vitamin D. For example, "Healthful diets with adequate folate may reduce a woman's risk of having a child with a spinal cord defect."

■ **Dietary sugar alcohols and dental caries (cavities)**—A claim relating dietary sugar alcohols and dental caries applies to food products, such as candy or gum, containing sugar alcohols (xylitol, sorbitol, mannitol, maltitol, isomalt, lactitol), hydrogenated starch hydrolysates, or hydrogenated glucose syrups, alone or in combination.

■ **Soluble fiber from certain types of food, such as whole oats and psyllium seed husk, and heart disease**—To carry a claim relating soluble fiber and heart disease, the label must state that fiber must be part of a diet low in saturated fat and cholesterol, and the food must provide soluble fiber. The amount of soluble fiber in a serving of the food must be listed on the Nutrition Facts panel.

Using the Food Label in a Restaurant or Foodservice Setting

Since food labels are primarily on packaged food, a restaurant or foodservice operation's opportunity to use the food label will depend on the amount of packaged food used by the operation. For operations that use packaged food, menu planners and chefs can use the food label in the following ways:

■ **To determine the serving size and number of servings in a container**—This information can help in specifying the number of packages of the packaged food needed in a standardized recipe.

■ **To refer to the nutrient listing and %DVs**—This is done to compare food and to select food low (5 percent or less) in fat, sodium, and sugar, and high (20 percent or more) in vitamin A, vitamin C, and calcium.

■ **To scan the ingredient list for allergens**—This information can be included on the menu and/or can be provided to servers. (See *Exhibit 3o.*)

In addition, staff responsible for receiving deliveries can review the label to ensure the food product received matches the food ordered. This is especially important if a specific type of product, such as a salt-free, organic, or whole-grain product, was ordered.

Activity

Calories per Serving

Contact a local food-products company to request a short interview with a quality assurance specialist. In the interview, focus on the Nutrition Facts panel for one of the company's products, and ask the QA specialist to describe the process by which the calories per serving was determined.

Summary

Healthful diets contain the amounts of essential nutrients and calories needed to prevent nutritional deficiencies and excesses. Healthful diets, along with physical activity, also provide the right balance of nutrients and healthy lifestyle habits to reduce risks of disease.

Dietary planning, whether for an individual or a group, involves offering menu choices that are nutritionally adequate, with the help of tools such as the Food Guide Pyramid. Food choices are the result of history, culture, and environment, as well as energy and nutrient needs. People also eat food for enjoyment. Family, friends, and beliefs play a major role in the ways people select food and plan meals.

Many genetic, environmental, behavioral, and cultural factors can affect health. Understanding their own family histories of disease or risk factors can help consumers make informed food choices. Healthful diets help people of all ages to have the energy they need to work productively and feel their best. Food choices also can help reduce the risk of disease.

Review Your Learning

1 **All of the following food items are exempt from nutrition labeling** *except*

   A. snacks offered in airplanes.

   B. entrées in hospital cafeterias.

   C. cookies sold in kiosks at shopping malls.

   D. a box of instant breakfast drinks at the local grocery store.

2 **The food groups in MyPyramid are**

   A. grains, vegetables, milk, meat, oils.

   B. vegetables, fruit, milk, meat.

   C. grains, vegetables, fruit, milk, meat.

   D. grains, vegetables, fruit, milk, meat, oils.

3 **The goal of the** *Dietary Guidelines for Americans 2005* **is to**

   A. help Americans choose diets that meet daily nutrient requirements.

   B. help Americans choose diets that promote health and reduce chronic disease.

   C. help Americans who are ill to manage their diets.

   D. help Americans determine the amount of physical activity they need each day.

4 **Which food item is** *not* **one of the eight major allergens?**

   A. Wheat

   B. Milk

   C. Chicken

   D. Fish

5 **All of the following are requirements for a restaurant or foodservice operation relative to nutrition information** *except*

   A. an operation can use any reasonable means, such as signs, posters, or brochures, to present nutrition information to customers.

   B. if an operation makes a health claim about a menu item, the operation must have a reasonable basis for the claim.

   C. if an operation makes a health claim about a menu item, the nutritional information for the menu item must be available to customers.

   D. if an operation makes a health claim about a menu item, the nutritional information for the item must be on the menu.

6 **Which is** *not* **required on the Nutrition Facts panel on a food label?**

   A. Dietary fiber

   B. Trans fat grams

   C. Calories from protein

   D. % Daily Value of vitamin C

7 **The % Daily Values are found in**

   A. the Nutrition Facts panel.

   B. *Dietary Guidelines for Americans 2005*.

   C. MyPyramid.

   D. Dietary Reference Intakes.

8 **To be labeled "healthy," a food must meet the following requirements** *except*

   A. the food must be low in fat and saturated fat.

   B. the food must contain fewer than 150 calories per serving.

   C. the food must contain limited amounts of cholesterol and sodium.

   D. the food must contain less than 360 milligrams of sodium per serving.

9 **All of the following are requirements for labeling food ingredients *except***

    A. allergens must be identified with the word *allergen*.

    B. ingredients must be declared on food items with more than one ingredient.

    C. ingredients must be listed in order by their weight contribution.

    D. color additives must be listed by name.

10 **Which are food label reference values?**

    A. Dietary Reference Intakes

    B. Recommended Dietary Allowances

    C. Daily Values

    D. *Dietary Guidelines for Americans 2005*

Notes

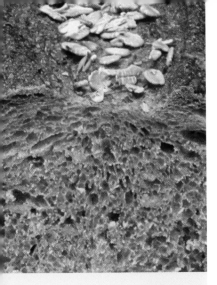

Carbohydrates

Inside This Chapter

- Carbohydrate Basics
- Simple Carbohydrates: The Sugars
- Complex Carbohydrates: Polysaccharides
- Dietary Fiber
- Digestion, Absorption, and Metabolism of Carbohydrates
- Carbohydrates and Health Problems

After completing this chapter, you should be able to:

- Define the term carbohydrate.
- State the recommended dietary allowances (RDA) for carbohydrate.
- Name the types of carbohydrates and their food sources.
- Describe the importance of carbohydrates in the diet.
- State the types of dietary fiber and their importance to health.
- List types of food that are good sources of dietary fiber.
- Explain how the body metabolizes and stores carbohydrate.
- Explain diabetes and its causes and effects.

Test Your Knowledge

1 **True or False:** Food containing a source of carbohydrate is found in each of the five food groups—grains, vegetables, fruit, milk, and meat and beans. *(See p. 68.)*

2 **True or False:** The best weight-reduction diets are low-carbohydrate diets. *(See p. 68.)*

3 **True or False:** The largest storage area for carbohydrate in the body is the liver. *(See p. 76.)*

4 **True or False:** Soluble fiber included in the diet assists the body in keeping blood cholesterol levels low. *(See p. 73.)*

5 **True or False:** Recommendations for dietary fiber intake are higher for men over fifty years of age than for men under fifty years of age. *(See p. 73.)*

Key Terms

Adipose tissue

Bran

CHO

Complex carbohydrate

Dental caries

Dextrose

Diabetes

Dietary fiber

Disaccharide

Endosperm

Enriched

Folate

Folic acid

Fructose

Galactose

Germ

Glucagon

Glucose

Glycogen

Hyperglycemia

Hypoglycemia

Insoluble fiber

Insulin

Ketoacidosis

Ketone bodies

Lactose

Laxation

Maltose

Monosaccharide

Photosynthesis

Polysaccharide

Raffinose

Refined

Simple carbohydrate

Soluble fiber

Stachyose

Starch

Stone ground

Sucrose

Sugar

Whole grain

Whole wheat

Introduction

As a restaurant or foodservice professional, you should understand carbohydrates so you can develop nutritious and tasty recipes and menus for your customers. Doing this involves understanding the proportions of nutrient types people should have in their diets as well as how to make food that tastes good. Being a professional means being good at both of these things.

In Chapter 2 you learned that carbohydrates are a class of nutrients that includes sugar, starch, and fiber. In this chapter you will learn more about carbohydrates and why they are an important part of everyone's diet. Carbohydrates can be classified as either simple carbohydrates or complex carbohydrates. You will learn their differences and how each type affects the human body. This chapter also discusses recommended daily allowances and other dietary recommendations for carbohydrates. Knowing these dietary recommendations will help you to make balanced meals for your customers.

Carbohydrate Basics

A carbohydrate is an organic chemical that consists only of carbon, hydrogen, and oxygen atoms in various numbers and arrangements. An organic chemical is one consisting of chains or rings of carbon atoms along with other atoms. Since a carbon atom is designated by the letter *C*, a hydrogen atom by an *H*, and an oxygen atom by an *O*, carbohydrates can be designated as CHO. (This abbreviation is sometimes found in books and articles about nutrition.) Carbohydrates contain hydrogen atoms and oxygen atoms in a two-to-one ratio, just like the water molecule, H_2O.

Carbohydrate provides four kilocalories of energy per gram of food. This is the same as protein but about half the kilocalories per gram of fat, which has nine kilocalories per gram. Although some people choose to follow a low-carbohydrate diet as a lifestyle choice, most people get half of their caloric requirements each day from food abundant in carbohydrate as part of a healthy diet.

The National Academy of Sciences has set the Recommended Dietary Allowance (RDA) for carbohydrate at 130 grams per day for adults. The age-related recommendations are shown in *Exhibit 4a*. In addition, the academy has designated the range of caloric intake (in kilocalories) that should come from various nutrients; this is called the Acceptable Macronutrient Distribution Range (AMDR).

Think About It...

How much fiber does the typical person need to eat each day?

Exhibit 4a

Dietary Reference Intake for Carbohydrates per Day

Age (years)	Carbohydrates (grams)
0–0.5	60
0.5–1.0	95
Over 1	130

Reprinted with permission from *Dietary Reference Intakes for Energy, Carbohydrate, Fiber, Fat, Fatty Acids, Cholesterol, Protein, and Amino Acids (Macronutrients).* ©2005 by the National Academy of Sciences, courtesy of the National Academies Press, Washington, DC.

Exhibit 4b

Nutritious and tasty meals should be between 45 to 65 percent carbohydrate.

Carbohydrate intake for each individual fluctuates each day depending on the food chosen. Although most people choose approximately 50 percent of their kilocalories from carbohydrate, many people have individual needs, such as athletes who eat high-carbohydrate diets during training and competition. The Food and Nutrition Board's recommendation for carbohydrate provides for differences in carbohydrate intake by setting the range at 45 to 65 percent of daily caloric intake like the meal shown in *Exhibit 4b*. The AMDR is a helpful guideline when planning and assessing menus for use by the public.

The *Dietary Guidelines for Americans 2005* also put an emphasis on **whole grains**—using the entire grain. This called public attention to the importance of carbohydrates and good health. This has helped the public welcome breads and cereals back to their plates after years of shunning them during the recent fad to avoid carbohydrates. It also has given restaurant and foodservice operations more latitude in developing recipes and menus.

Carbohydrates are the body's preferred source of fuel and are a relatively inexpensive source of calories as well. In addition to their value as a fuel, carbohydrates provide an abundance of nutrients. For example, most of the grains people eat are **enriched**—have vitamins and minerals added after grinding into flour—and provide the vitamins thiamin, riboflavin, niacin, and folic acid and the mineral iron. Eating whole grains also provides the body with increased amounts of fiber and trace minerals like zinc. Fruit and vegetable groups offer a wide range of vitamins, especially vitamins A and C. In the protein group (now known as the meat and bean group), legumes and beans provide both insoluble and soluble fiber along with protein. The amount of carbohydrate contained in some common food items is shown in *Exhibit 4c*.

Carbohydrates are classified as either simple or complex. **Simple carbohydrates** are sugars, which consist of monosaccharides and disaccharides; they are called "simple" because they are single carbohydrate units—the building blocks of more complex carbohydrates. **Complex carbohydrates** are so named because they contain more numerous combinations of saccharides, like oligosaccharides and polysaccharides.

Exhibit 4c

Carbohydrate in Some Common Food Items

Food	Carbohydrates (grams)
Romaine lettuce, three ounces	3.3
Zucchini squash, one small	3.4
Applesauce, sweetened, half cup	10.0
Pasta with marinara sauce, half cup	11.3
Navel orange	12.5
Vanilla ice cream, half cup	23.6
Hash brown potatoes, one patty	25.4
Buttermilk pancake, six inches in diameter	28.7
Glazed doughnut	50.8
Barbecue potato chips, one ounce	52.8
Egg bagel, medium size	53.0

U.S. Department of Agriculture

Exhibit 4d

Honey is simply collected from honey combs and filtered; table sugar is refined from sugar beets or sugar cane.

Simple Carbohydrates: The Sugars

The first group of carbohydrates to discuss is sugars; in fact, **sugars** are the simplest carbohydrates. Sugars in food consist of naturally occurring and refined sugars. Honey, shown in *Exhibit 4d,* is an example of a natural sugar since it is used as found in nature. Table sugar is a **refined** sugar because it has been extracted from sap and purified; it is a product of either cane or beet sugar.

Monosaccharides

Most sugars are classified as monosaccharides or disaccharides. A **monosaccharide** is a molecule consisting of a single sugar unit that can be digested no further. The monosaccharides are glucose, galactose, and fructose, as described in *Exhibit 4e* on the next page. Notice that the names all end in "ose." "Ose" is the chemical ending for "sugar."

Glucose is the most important of the monosaccharides because it is the body's blood sugar. Glucose is not used alone in cooking, but it may be found in processed food or food products. However, honey and corn syrup are routinely used in cooking. Both honey and corn syrup contain glucose in a mixture with other sugars. The natural form of glucose is known as **dextrose.**

Fructose is referred to as fruit sugar. It is found in fruit and honey and is the sweetest of the sugars. It can be found in sweetened beverages as high-fructose corn syrup.

Exhibit 4e

Monosaccharides

Name	Found In
Glucose	Honey and corn syrup. Also results from breaking down carbohydrates and is synthesized in the liver and kidneys.
Fructose	Honey, tree fruit, berries, melons, and some root vegetables, such as beets, sweet potatoes, parsnips, and onions
Galactose	Not present in significant quantities in food. Is part of the disaccharide lactose.

U.S. Department of Agriculture

The third of the monosaccharides is **galactose.** It is not found in food alone but is bound with glucose as part of lactose, a disaccharide. Galactose is considered a nutritive sweetener because it has food energy, but it is less sweet than glucose and not very water soluble.

All carbohydrates must eventually be broken down to monosaccharides because only these can be absorbed. Monosaccharides can cross the intestinal cells of the small intestine and are transported to the liver. Glucose crosses in a form that the body can use directly. Fructose and galactose can be used for energy or converted to **glycogen**—a long, branched-chain organic molecule related to glucose and used for energy storage in the liver or muscle.

Disaccharides

Disaccharides are molecules consisting of two units of monosaccharides. These double-sugars are present in countless types of food and food products. The disaccharides are sucrose, lactose, and maltose. (See *Exhibit 4f.*)

Exhibit 4f

Disaccharides

Name	Found In
Sucrose (table sugar)	Sap of many plants. Usually extracted from the sap of sugar cane or sugar beets, but also from sorghum and sugar maple.
Lactose (milk sugar)	Milk
Maltose (malt sugar)	Grains. Also produced by breakdown of starch.

U.S. Department of Agriculture

Sucrose, the combination of fructose and glucose molecules, is referred to as table sugar. It is found in kitchens in many forms, such as plain sugar, brown sugar, and confectioners' sugar. Sucrose is ideal for cooking and baking. It is the second-sweetest sugar next to fructose, and it has many properties that allow it to be versatile in the kitchen, including its solubility and viscosity. However, sucrose is a big contributor to **dental caries** (tooth decay), because the bacteria that live in the mouth can rapidly utilize sucrose.

Lactose, the combination of galactose and glucose, is called milk sugar. Lactose is known mostly for the problems many people encounter when they have lactose intolerance and cannot break down this sugar during digestion. However, there are many lactose-intolerant people who can digest the amount of lactose in a glass of milk if it is taken with a meal. People with lactose intolerance also may tolerate yogurt and aged cheese. Lactose intolerance is very individual. People with lactose intolerance may tolerate some dairy products if they take enzymes at the time they consume lactose to help them digest it. There also are special low-lactose or lactose-free dairy products that many people prefer; others may choose to drink soy milk to avoid problems with lactose. Restaurant and foodservice operations would help these customers if such products were made available.

Maltose (malt sugar) is glucose bonded to another glucose molecule. It is found in grains and as a byproduct of the breakdown of starch.

Exhibit 4g

Refined sugar is used to make caramel.

Sugars in Cooking

The sugars discussed in previous sections are available for use in cooking in the following products:

- Confectioners' sugar (powdered sugar)
- Caramel (see *Exhibit 4g*)
- Corn syrup
- Dextrose
- Fructose
- Fruit juices and reductions of fruit
- Glucose
- High-fructose corn syrup
- Honey
- Invert sugar
- Lactose
- Maple syrup
- Maltose
- Malt syrup
- Molasses
- Polydextrose
- Sucrose, or table sugar
- Syrups
- Turbinado sugar

Complex Carbohydrates: Polysaccharides

Photosynthesis is the process by which plants store energy. Plants harness the energy from the sun and utilize water, carbon dioxide, and soil nutrients to produce long chains of glucose bonded together as **starch,** a **polysaccharide** (molecule comprised of twenty to thousands of sugar units.) These strands of starch may be straight chains or branched chains of glucose molecules. Types of food that contain good sources of complex carbohydrate as starch are pasta, rice, breads, beans, legumes, and vegetables. Starch is considered complex because it is made from combinations of the simple carbohydrates (sugars). Additionally, the body takes much longer to digest starches than it does sugars.

Oligosaccharides: Small Chains of Starch

Oligosaccharides are smaller complex carbohydrates composed of three to ten sugar molecules. Two oligosaccharides of note are **raffinose** and **stachyose.** The enzymes in the small intestine cannot break down these molecules as they can the polysaccharides, so raffinose and stachyose pass into the large intestine where intestinal bacteria can metabolize them. This produces gas. Some extremely nutritious food items, including lima beans, dried peas, and soybeans, contain raffinose and stachyose. Many people who consume beans on a regular basis have experienced intestinal discomfort and gas. There are enzymes that can be purchased and taken at the time these types of food are consumed that will enable breakdown in the small intestine and alleviate the gas symptoms.

As you will see in the next section, beans and legumes also provide good amounts of fiber. Beans contain both soluble and insoluble fibers that, in addition to their protein content, make them very desirable food in the diet.

Dietary Fiber

Dietary fiber is another type of carbohydrate that has glucose molecules bonded to each other in long strands, but it is different from starch because it cannot be broken down or digested by human digestive enzymes. In the stomach it provides a feeling of fullness or satiety. Since it is slow to leave the stomach, a person feels full for a period of time. Because of this effect, it helps with weight control. Fiber passes through the small intestine intact, or undigested. In the large intestine, some types of fiber can be broken down by bacterial enzymes, and this produces fatty acids and gas.

One of the health benefits of fiber is that it resists digestion and maintains its bulk. Diets that contain adequate fiber support regularity and **laxation**—looseness of the bowels. Having adequate fiber in the diet may decrease the incidence of hemorrhoids,

Exhibit 4h

Sources of Dietary Fiber

Soluble	Insoluble
■ Legumes (peas, soybeans, and other beans)	■ Whole-grain food
■ Oats	■ Bran
■ Some fruit (especially apples, bananas, and berries)	■ Nuts and seeds
■ Some nonroot vegetables (especially broccoli and carrots)	■ Vegetables such as green beans, cauliflower, zucchini, celery
■ Most root vegetables (especially potatoes and yams, but the skins are insoluble fiber)	■ Skins of some fruit, including tomatoes
	■ Skins of potatoes and yams

Exhibit 4i

Adequate Intake of Fiber

Age (years)	Males	Females
	(grams per day)	
1–3	19	19
4–8	25	25
9–13	31	26
14–18	38	26
19–30	38	25
31–50	38	25
51–70	30	21
70+	30	21

Reprinted with permission from *Dietary Reference Intakes for Energy, Carbohydrate, Fiber, Fat, Fatty Acids, Cholesterol, Protein, and Amino Acids (Macronutrients)*. ©2005 by the National Academy of Sciences, courtesy of the National Academies Press, Washington, DC.

diverticular disease of the colon, and cardiovascular disease. There is question about whether increasing fiber will help to prevent colon cancer; however, populations with high fiber intakes also have lower rates of colon cancer. Alternatively, this may be from the phytochemicals (also known as phytonutrients) contained in high-fiber food items such as whole grains, nuts, and vegetables. Technically, a phytochemical is any chemical or nutrient derived from a plant, but commonly, *phytochemical* is used to refer to non-nutrient chemicals that somehow reduce diseases.

Dietary fiber can be classified as soluble or insoluble. **Insoluble fiber** does not dissolve in water, and it simply passes through the digestive tract. **Soluble fiber** dissolves in water to form a soft gel that connects to bile salts and reduces cholesterol in the blood. It also may inhibit glucose absorption and thus smooth excessive swings of blood sugar.

Fiber is best obtained by eating high-fiber food because the bulk and nutrients of these types of food contribute to the diet. Good sources of soluble and insoluble fiber are provided in *Exhibit 4h*.

Adequate Intake

The Food and Nutrition Board has established recommended fiber intake per day, called the adequate intake, for Americans. (See *Exhibit 4i*.) This represents the minimum recommended level, not the maximum.

Whole Grains: An Opportunity to Meet Customer Needs

Whole grains or food made from them contain all the nutritionally essential parts of the grain: the bran, endosperm, and germ. (See *Exhibit 4j* on the next page.) The **bran** is the outer layer, which contains the highest percentage of fiber and nutrients. It is the same part of the grain that is in bran cereal. The **endosperm** is the starchy

Exhibit 4j

Whole-Grain Components

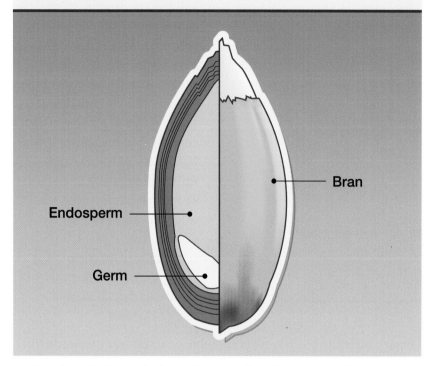

Food made from whole grains contains all the essential parts of the grain: bran, endosperm, and germ.

layer, which is the largest part of the grain and provides flour for white bread and pastries. The **germ** is a small, nutrient-rich inner layer. Wheat germ is sold separately for cooking and baking. When the grain is processed by crushing, cracking or pearling, or by some other process (including cooking), the whole-grain product should have about the same ratio of nutrients that are found in the original grain or seed.

Whole grains include:

- Barley
- Brown rice
- Corn and popcorn
- Millet
- Oats
- Rye
- Sorghum
- Teff
- Triticale (a cross between wheat and rye)
- Wheat—all varieties (e.g., spelt, kamut, emmer, and einkorn)

Also included as whole grains for nutritional and cooking purposes are these pseudo-cereals:

- Amaranth
- Quinoa
- Buckwheat
- Wild rice
- Flax

Think About It...

Have you ever eaten a whole-grain food such as whole-grain bread or pasta? How did it differ in taste from the nonwhole-grain item?

Why Whole Grains?

Whole-grain food has many health benefits. In health studies the consumption of whole grains has been linked to a decrease in the incidence of cardiovascular disease, improved function and decreased cancer of the large intestine, and improved blood-glucose control in people with diabetes. Whole grains have increased levels of antioxidants and increased amounts of minerals, including magnesium. The benefits of whole grains are just now being fully appreciated.

Exhibit 4k

Whole grains should be a part of a healthy diet, either as grains or ground into flour.

The Food and Drug Administration (FDA) allows the following health claim for whole-grain products that contain 51 percent or more of whole grain by weight: "Diets rich in whole-grain food and other plant food, and low in total fat, saturated fat and cholesterol, may reduce the risk of heart disease and certain cancers."[1]

The *Dietary Guidelines for Americans 2005* emphasize that all Americans should have at least one half of their dietary intakes of grain as whole grains. (See *Exhibit 4k.*) For a daily intake of 2,000 kilocalories, a person would be expected to eat about six ounces of grains each day. This translates to eating at least three ounces of whole grains each day.

Currently, there is a concerted effort among nutrition professionals to teach the public about whole grains, including what food to eat when eating out. Customers who want whole-grain food do not usually request it outright. Rather, they order something else or simply go to a different establishment next time. Including whole-grain items on the menu should not be overly difficult because whole grains are versatile and can be part of main dishes, side dishes, salads, soups, bakery items, and desserts. As a restaurant or foodservice manager, you can cater to your customers' requests and needs by including as many whole-grain items as possible in your menus and recipes.

Reading the Label

Since 1942, flour has been **enriched** with thiamine, riboflavin, niacin, and iron as part of the U.S. government's grain enrichment program, created in response to the devastation caused by pellagra—a disease caused by a lack of niacin and protein in the diet—during the Great Depression. In 1996, the grain enrichment program was amended to include **folate**—a form of folic acid—to try to decrease the incidence of spina bifida, a birth defect connected with insufficient levels of **folic acid,** a water-soluble B vitamin. Enriching a food replaces the above-named nutrients that were removed during the processing of a whole grain into a refined product. Although the enrichment program mandated that manufacturers return specific nutrients to processed grains, not all nutrients get replaced to the level they were in the original grain. In particular, fiber and trace elements like magnesium and zinc are not replaced.

The color of a bread is not an indication of whether it is made with whole grains; the color may be due to food coloring. The label should state that it has whole grains or **whole wheat**—made from the whole grain of wheat—and it should be the first ingredient listed. In addition, words like **"stone ground"**—ground into flour with stones rather than modern metal grinders–or "wheat" do not necessarily indicate the product is whole grain. Since customers in a restaurant or foodservice

---

[1] *Notification for a Health Claim Based on an Authoritative Statement: Whole Grain Foods and Heart Disease,* Food and Drug Administration, 11/25/03.

75

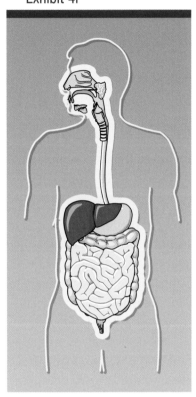

The digestion system processes carbohydrates into blood sugar through several stages.

operation cannot see the nutrition labels on the components of the food they order, you, as the manager or chef, should make this information available in some other way, such as with menu descriptions that indicate when whole grains are being used.

Digestion, Absorption, and Metabolism of Carbohydrates

Carbohydrates other than fiber are easily digested by the body. (See *Exhibit 4l.*) This results in the rapid insertion of glucose into the bloodstream and a consequent immediate increase in blood sugar.

Carbohydrate digestion begins in the mouth as the salivary glands supply salivary amylase, an enzyme that begins the breakdown of starch to polysaccharides and maltose. The body cannot break down the sugars in the mouth, so the digestion of these is completed later in the small intestine. However, although bodies do not digest sugars in the mouth, bacteria can use the sugar as fuel. This produces acids that damage and erode tooth enamel, causing dental caries.

After starches and sugars have been thoroughly chewed and immersed in saliva, they make their way down the esophagus to the stomach, where salivary amylase may continue or be inactivated depending on the acidity of the stomach's contents. In the stomach, the food is mixed into a semifluid liquid called chyme, which travels to the small intestine. In the small intestine, starch is further broken down by pancreatic amylase to dextrins and maltose. Disaccharides are further digested into monosaccharides. Monosaccharides are able to cross the intestinal wall to the portal vein and then be directed by the liver in response to body needs.

The liver and the muscle tissue both store blood glucose as glycogen. Glycogen is the form in which the body stores carbohydrate. The liver will store about 75 to 100 grams of carbohydrate, or 300 to 400 kilocalories. Muscle tissue has a much larger storage capacity of glycogen, at 300 to 400 grams, or 1,200 to 1,600 kilocalories. The liver will supply the muscles with energy, filling them up when they are depleted. However, once glucose is stored in the muscle, it must be used there, so the need for carbohydrate is continuous.

Glucose is a very versatile and important molecule to the body. The red blood cells, the brain, and the nervous system all use glucose as fuel. All other cells can use it, and the body keeps blood-glucose levels within a narrow range under tight hormonal control. The hormones **insulin** and **glucagon** are important in blood-sugar metabolism. Insulin is secreted by the pancreas and circulates in the blood. Its role is to help glucose enter the cell, thus reducing blood-sugar levels. Glucagon has the opposite effect; it promotes the release and production of glucose by the liver. Glucagon is a hormone to counteract insulin and bring up low blood-sugar levels.

Carbohydrates and Health Problems

Carbohydrates are an important part of a balanced diet. When they are overabundant or insufficient, health problems can occur.

Carbohydrates and Weight Gain

Do carbohydrates make a person gain weight? Actually, populations that predominantly eat large amounts of carbohydrates in their diet tend to be thinner. If the body's calorie requirements have not been exceeded, eating carbohydrate-rich food will not cause weight gain. This is because carbohydrates are used primarily for energy before they are stored.

However, if a person has eaten too much food and has excess, unused calories, the body will store the blood sugars as fat. The amount of glucose stored as fat is very small. The weight gain seen because of excess calories is due to the fat-sparing effect of carbohydrate. When carbohydrate is being expended as energy, the body stores dietary lipids in **adipose tissue** (body fat). This is because many more metabolic steps are required to convert sugar to dietary lipids than to convert dietary lipids to adipose tissue. Thus, increased body weight is due to low levels of exercise combined with excess calories from all energy-yielding nutrients and alcohol.

Sugary food, like those in *Exhibit 4m,* and alcoholic beverages are rich in calories but not in many other nutrients. When people consume these types of food, they are adding calories but not supplying the nutrients that the body needs. As in many things, small amounts of sugar and alcohol are not harmful, but excessive amounts are.

Ketosis: Glucose in Short Supply

When carbohydrates are not found in the diet or are present in an extremely low supply, there may be metabolic changes that can be unpleasant. Each cell requires a small amount of carbohydrate in the form of glucose to completely metabolize the lipids eaten or lipids resulting from weight reduction. When glucose is insufficient, the lipids being metabolized cannot be fully broken down by the liver. As a result, **ketone bodies,** incompletely metabolized products of

Exhibit 4m

For optimal nutrition, do not consume excessive amounts of food that supplies calories with little other nutrient value.

fatty-acid metabolism, build up in the blood. This causes ketosis. People who have limited their carbohydrate intake and thereby induce ketosis report effects such as constipation, headache, bad breath, and dry mouth. Those that follow extreme low-carbohydrate diets may risk other complications if ketosis is severe.

Hypoglycemia

Hypoglycemia is a low blood-glucose level caused by high insulin levels. In this case, dietary carbohydrate is in adequate supply, but the body is secreting too much insulin, driving too much glucose into the cells. The result is decreased blood glucose. Blood glucose is reduced to a point that an individual with this condition may become hungry and irritable and have other symptoms like feeling weak about an hour after eating food with abundant carbohydrates. Proper diagnosis is important because hypoglycemia has different treatments depending on the exact problem. For most people, hypoglycemia can be treated with smaller, more frequent meals and by choosing complex carbohydrates instead of simple carbohydrates and by including protein and fat with carbohydrates in meals to delay blood-sugar increases.

Diabetes: A Disease with Complications

Diabetes is a disease characterized by high blood-sugar levels (**hyperglycemia**). It occurs because of metabolic, genetic, and other conditions, such as pregnancy. Type 1 diabetes occurs when there is no insulin available to allow blood glucose to enter the cells and tissues. Without insulin, large amounts of glucose build up in the blood and overload the ability of the body to metabolize it. In addition to high levels of glucose in the blood, glucose spills into the urine. Common symptoms of diabetes include hunger, thirst, and frequent urination. Insulin must be taken each day to supply the insulin that the body does not naturally make. Ketone bodies result from the incomplete breakdown of fat that is mobilized in the absence of insulin. Not controlling the balance of insulin and blood sugar can lead to diabetic **ketoacidosis,** a life-threatening complication with symptoms including hyperglycemia and the buildup of ketone bodies in blood. The buildup of these ketone bodies can cause coma and death. Treatment for type 1 diabetes includes providing adequate calories, maintaining weight, encouraging regular exercise, eating controlled amounts of carbohydrate, and eating less saturated fat and trans fat, as well as regular doses of insulin.

If there are high insulin levels in the blood but the insulin does not seem to be recognized by the cells, this is referred to as insulin resistance or type 2 diabetes. Type 2 diabetes tends to reveal itself as people age. Obesity is another cause of it. If obesity is present, initial treatment is to get blood sugar under control with medication, then to encourage weight loss with diet and exercise. Type 2 diabetes is treated with many different medications, including insulin when necessary.

Although both types of diabetes have increased recently in the United States, most of the increase has been seen in type 2 diabetes. Part of the increase is being seen in children; this was not the case even a decade ago. Scientists and medical professionals have learned through studies that the increase in the disease is because of an increase in adipose tissue, which has been linked to a combination of inactivity and poor dietary intake, including an abundance of calories from both carbohydrates and fats.

Diabetes is considered a chronic disease with many different metabolic consequences. Individuals who develop diabetes must take good care of their health. No matter what kind of diabetes a person has, part of the treatment is adherence to a healthy diet, good medical care, and regular exercise. Complications like blindness, amputation, and cardiovascular disease are all too common in people with diabetes.

It is important to keep blood sugar within the range actually needed by the body. One part of doing this is having a nutritious and balanced diet without excesses of fats and carbohydrates. (See *Exhibit 4n.*) As a restaurant or foodservice professional, you have a role in helping your customers meet this goal by developing and using recipes, menus, and portions that fit these needs.

Exhibit 4n

Overconsumption of carbohydrates, especially sweets, is harmful to diabetics, who must regularly monitor their blood-sugar levels and, sometimes, inject themselves with insulin.

Activity

Carbohydrate Contributions of Common Food Items

The USDA has a special Web site where the public can find the nutrient values of food at *www.nal.usda.gov/fnic/foodcomp/search/*. To give you practice at using this Web site, look up the amount of carbohydrate in these food items and their calories for the food amount indicated.

Food	Carbohydrate Content (grams per serving)	Calories per Serving
Medium apple		
Large baked potato		
Half cup broccoli		
Half cup brown rice		
Four ounces of chocolate pudding, ready to eat		
Twelve ounces of cola		
One-eighth frosted chocolate cake		
Large French fries		
Multigrain hamburger roll		
One ounce of peanuts		
Eight ounces of nonfat milk		
Tofu, half cup		
One serving of watermelon		

Summary

Carbohydrates include sugars, starches, fiber, and oxygen and yield four kilocalories of energy per gram of food. They are abundant in pasta, rice, bread, tortillas, vegetables, fruit, and beans, among others. They fuel the body, spare protein for important purposes, and become part of the body's structure. The Dietary Reference Intakes provide a Recommended Dietary Allowance for intakes of carbohydrates and adequate intakes for fiber, which vary by a person's age, gender, and activity level. About half of a person's caloric intake should come from carbohydrates. If overall caloric intake is in line with bodily needs, eating carbohydrates will not cause weight gain.

Both type 1 and type 2 diabetes are increasing in the United States, the greatest change being the increased incidence of type 2, especially in children. In addition, medical professionals believe most of it may be preventable because it is the result of obesity.

Review Your Learning

1 All of the following are true about carbohydrates *except*

   A. a carbohydrate is an organic chemical containing carbon, hydrogen, and oxygen.

   B. carbohydrates cause obesity.

   C. 50 percent of calories should come from carbohydrates.

   D. diabetics must avoid excessive carbohydrates in their diets.

2 The recommended dietary allowance for carbohydrate for an adult is

   A. 20 grams of carbohydrate per day.

   B. 100 grams of carbohydrate per day.

   C. 130 grams of carbohydrate per day.

   D. There is no recommended dietary allowance for carbohydrate.

3 What are the types of carbohydrate?

   A. Monosaccharides and disaccharides

   B. Sugars and starches

   C. Soluble and insoluble

   D. Simple and complex

4 Dietary fiber is important to one's health because of all of the following *except*

   A. dietary fiber resists digestion and maintains its bulk.

   B. dietary fiber supports regularity and laxation.

   C. dietary fiber increases constipation.

   D. dietary fiber contains phytochemicals.

5 Which food items are *not* high in dietary fiber?

   A. Lean beef and turkey

   B. Whole grains and bran

   C. Fruit and vegetables

   D. Skins of potatoes and tomatoes

6 When carbohydrates are digested, which chemical is transferred to the bloodstream?

   A. Glycogen   C. Sucrose

   B. Glucose   D. Maltose

7 Which food item is *not* high in carbohydrate?

   A. Egg bagels   C. Potato chips

   B. Romaine lettuce   D. Glazed doughnuts

8 Carbohydrates are an important part of the diet for all the following reasons *except*

   A. carbohydrates are a relatively inexpensive source of calories.

   B. carbohydrates are the body's preferred source of fuel.

   C. since most carbohydrates are enriched, they provide the vitamins thiamin, riboflavin, niacin, and folic acid and the mineral iron.

   D. carbohydrates, especially pasta, help prevent obesity.

9 What are the two types of dietary fiber?

   A. Monosaccharides and disaccharides

   B. Soluble and insoluble

   C. Sugars and starches

   D. Simple and complex

10 All of the following are complications of diabetes *except*

   A. blindness.

   B. amputation of the legs.

   C. cardiovascular disease.

   D. increased dependence on simple carbohydrates.

Notes

Proteins

5

Inside This Chapter

- Protein Basics
- Proteins and Nutrition
- Nutritional Properties of Proteins
- Protein Changes during Cooking
- Excessive and Insufficient Protein in the Diet
- Dietary Requirements for Protein

After completing this chapter, you should be able to:

- Describe the makeup and characteristics of protein.
- List the functions of protein in the body.
- Explain essential amino acids and complete proteins.
- Explain how complementary incomplete proteins combined can equal complete proteins.
- Explain the effects of excessive and insufficient protein intake.
- State the recommended protein intake for humans.
- List good sources of protein in the diet.

Test Your Knowledge

1 True or False: A vegetarian diet always lacks adequate protein. *(See p. 91.)*

2 True or False: Consuming more protein than required by a person's body makes muscles larger. *(See p. 89.)*

3 True or False: There are twenty amino acids that must be obtained from food. *(See p. 85.)*

4 True or False: Eating hummus and bread together makes a complete high-quality protein. *(See p. 91.)*

5 True or False: People need about 225 grams (five ounces) of protein daily. *(See p. 96.)*

Key Terms

Amine group

Antibodies

Collagen

Complementary protein

Complete protein

Conditionally essential amino acid

Denaturation

Edamame

Enzyme

Essential amino acid

High-quality protein

Hormones

Incomplete protein

Isoflavone

Kwashiorkor

Marasmus

Miso

Negative nitrogen balance

Nitrogen balance

Organic acid group

Positive nitrogen balance

Protein balance

Protein deficiency

Protein energy malnutrition (PEM)

Protein turnover

Side chain

Soy

Soy milk

Tempeh

Textured soy protein

Textured vegetable protein (TVP)

Tofu

Introduction

Protein is an exciting macronutrient to learn about, not only because of the many important functions it serves in the human body, but also because of its key use in the culinary world, as shown in *Exhibit 5a*. In Chapter 2, you learned that protein is a class of nutrients that is made up of amino acids. In this chapter you will learn more of the specifics about protein and why it is important in everyone's diet.

Some of the important roles protein plays in the body are as enzymes, as hormones, as a defense against foreign invaders, to regulate the acidity of blood, and to support growth, maintenance,

Exhibit 5a

Protein sources are very important in cuisine.

Think About It...

Many people enjoy protein-rich food like meat and fish. If a person doesn't eat these types of food, how can he or she make sure to receive adequate protein?

and repair of body tissues. This chapter will explain these things as well as the essential and non-essential amino acids and how they help define a complete high-quality protein.

This chapter also will explain the simple ways to ensure that enough protein is consumed each day, although the typical intake for protein is well above the established RDA for healthy Americans. Both the potential problems caused by excessive and insufficient protein intake will also be discussed, along with a review of the potential health benefits regarding soy-protein consumption and examples of soy products.

Protein Basics

Before beginning an explanation of proteins in nutrition, you should know a few basic facts about them.

Makeup of Proteins

Proteins are a class of macronutrients that contribute four kilocalories per gram, the same as carbohydrates and half as much as fat. Proteins are organic chemicals that are composed of amino acids connected together with peptide bonds into long, complicated chains, as shown in *Exhibit 5b* on the next page. There are thousands of combinations possible.

What Are Amino Acids

Amino acids are organic molecules made of carbon (C), hydrogen (H), oxygen (O), and nitrogen (N) atoms combined in specific ways. There are twenty amino acids that can be synthesized by the genetic codes of plants and animals; they are used in human bodies and also by plants and animals.

Exhibit 5b

Amino Acids and Proteins

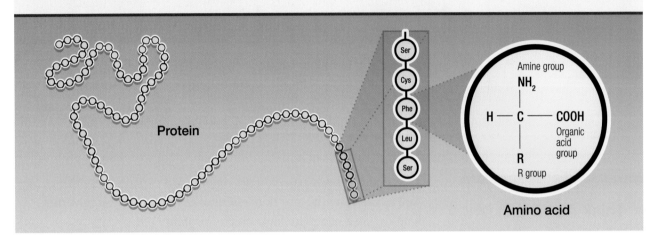

Proteins are made up of amino acids in various combinations, such as chains (shown), rings, and more complex structures.

Each amino acid has an identical unit (NH_2-CH-COOH) and a unique **side chain**—organic chains or rings of many types. The NH_2 group of atoms is called an **amine group.** The nitrogen contained in the amine group (NH_2) differentiates protein from the other macronutrients like fats and carbohydrates. The COOH group is called an **organic acid group.** Organic molecules composed of amines and organic acid groups are thus called amino acids. The CH is the carbon (and its hydrogen) to which the remaining carbon and hydrogen atoms are connected in the so-called side chain. The side "chain" can be a straight chain, a partial ring, a complete ring, or a more complex structure of carbon and hydrogen atoms. It is the nature of the side chain that defines each specific amino acid.

Protein Structure

Proteins come in four types of structures. *Exhibit 5b* shows the first or primary structure, which is the simplest, with each type of structure increasing in complexity. The primary structure is a straight chain of amino acids linked together by peptide bonds. As protein molecules become more complex, the amino acids in them start to attract each other like a magnet does to metal, and because of this, the protein structure starts to coil and bend. These are the secondary, tertiary, and quaternary structures of protein. The complexity of the protein structure is what makes it able to carry out specific functions.

Protein Digestion and Metabolism

Unlike carbohydrate digestion, protein digestion does not start in the mouth, but in the stomach. There, pepsinogen is activated by hydrochloric acid to become pepsin, which starts to break down the peptide bonds. Then the partially digested protein moves onto the small intestine, where the peptide bonds break down even more by digestive enzymes specific to protein. Finally, the proteins are broken down into separate amino acids so they can go through the small intestine into the bloodstream. Now the body can use them where they are needed.

Proteins and Nutrition

Proteins and amino acids generally are not used for energy like carbohydrates and fats. Although protein contains fuel in the form of kilocalories, these calories are not used as energy unless a person is in a physical state of starvation or has depleted his or her store of carbohydrates; the body's preferred sources of energy are carbohydrates and then fat. Protein's more important functions in the body are explained in the next section.

Major Functions of Protein in the Body

Protein is important because it is part of your muscles, skin, and even hair and nails. There are many important functions of protein in your body, including the growth and maintenance of cells. Also enzymes, hormones, and antibodies contain protein, and it plays an important role in regulating fluid and acid-base balance.

- **Antibodies**—When a virus enters the body, antibodies attack these unwanted foreign substances and deactivate them. Think of antibodies as an army of proteins that attack unwanted illnesses to keep the body well.

- **Enzymes**—Enzymes are the body's catalysts—molecules that enhance or retard chemical reactions. Enzymes exist to build or break down substances essential for life. Protein is part of some of the enzymes in your body and is therefore a necessary component of important body reactions that take place on a daily basis.

- **Fluid and acid-based regulators**—Fluid and acidity balance is regulated by protein in the body.

- **Hormones**—Some hormones are proteins. Hormones are the body's messenger molecules; they deliver or carry out important functions. For example, insulin is a hormone that regulates blood sugar in the body by transporting glucose into cells.

■ **Transportation**—Another one of proteins' jobs is to transport vitamins, minerals, and even lipids through the body so they can get to the areas where they are needed.

■ **Growth and maintenance**—Amino acids are needed in the body on a daily basis to support growth and maintenance of cells and tissue. Skeletal muscle, bone, skin, **collagen** (the primary protein of animal and human connective tissue), cartilage, red blood cells, nails, hair, and even the heart, liver, and kidney are made of protein.

■ **Energy**—As a last resort, proteins are broken down by the body to obtain energy. Although protein contains four kilocalories per gram, these calories are undesirable energy sources because the important functions for which protein is normally used will not occur if protein is used for energy. However, when sources of carbohydrate and fat are scarce, protein is used as an energy source to sustain life.

Exhibit 5c

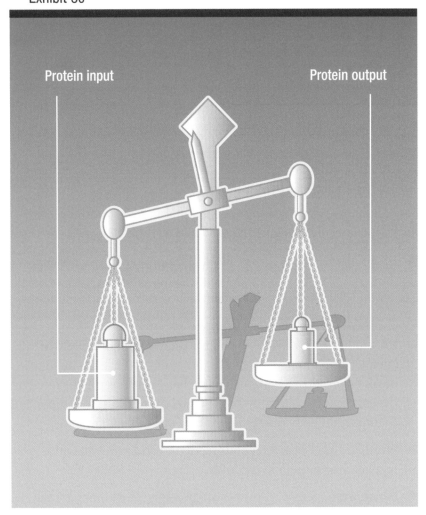

The comparison of protein input to protein output is called the body's protein balance.

Protein and Nitrogen Balances

Protein turnover, how protein is used and then synthesized (combined to form a new product), is an important function of protein metabolism. When a person's protein intake and protein usage are equal, the person is in a state of **protein balance.** (See *Exhibit 5c.*) The body's protein balance is closely related to its **nitrogen balance,** because nitrogen is a part of protein. The advantage of this is that nitrogen can be more easily measured in the body than protein.

Usually, people are in a normal state of nitrogen balance. However, during times of growth or development, like pregnancy, a person holds on to the protein and its nitrogen; this results in a state of **positive nitrogen balance** because there is more nitrogen being taken in than excreted. In the same way, when a person suffers from a chronic illness or is starving, that person is in a **negative nitrogen balance**—excreting more nitrogen than he or she is taking in as protein.

Keep in mind that consuming more protein than required does not make muscles larger. The only way to increase muscle mass is to exercise the muscles. When a person consumes more protein than needed, the body simply stores it as fat.

Nutritional Properties of Proteins

Remember that proteins are composed of amino acids and are broken down by the body into constituent amino acids. Then the body reassembles these amino acids into the thousands of proteins that keep it functioning. For this reason, a major part of the properties of proteins, from the nutritional viewpoint, is focused on the properties of the amino acids.

Exhibit 5d

Amino Acids by Essentiality to Humans

Essential	Non-essential	Conditionally essential
Must be obtained from the diet (RDI in milligrams for 150-pound human)	Can be made in the body	Can become essential
Histidine (unknown)	Alanine	Cysteine
Isoleucine (10 mg)	Arginine	Tyrosine
Leucine (14 mg)	Asparagine	
Lysine (12 mg)	Aspartic acid	
Methionine (13 mg)	Cysteine	
Phenylalanine (14 mg)	Glutamic acid	
Therionine (7 mg)	Glutamine	
Tryptophan (3.5 mg)	Glycine	
Valine (10 mg)	Proline	
	Serine	
	Tyrosine	

Amino Acids and Nutrition

As previously discussed, proteins are made up of long chains of amino acids, and twenty of them are used in the human body. (See *Exhibit 5d.*) The human body is able to make eleven of the twenty; however, the remaining nine either cannot be made or the body does not make them in large enough quantities. From a nutrition viewpoint, these nine amino acids are considered **essential amino acids** because people must obtain them from food.

Occasionally a non-essential amino acid becomes essential. A **conditionally essential amino acid** is one that may become essential under special circumstances and, therefore, needs to be obtained through food in the same way as essential amino acids. An example of this is cysteine, which ordinarily is a non-essential amino acid, and one of the sulphur-containing amino acids. When there is enough methionine and vitamin B_6 in the diet, the sulphur-containing amino acids will be produced without any problems. If either are lacking, the diet must include cysteine, which then makes it an essential amino acid.

When the body does not have enough of the amino acids required, the body cannot form the proteins it needs to function as hormones, enzymes, or antibodies or for transportation, maintenance, and growth.

Some Amino Acids of Note

Several amino acids are more noticeable because their presence or absence is quickly felt by the body.

- Many people feel tired after consuming a large meal that includes turkey; this is because of the amino acid tryptophan—an amino acid found in turkey and dairy products. Tryptophan in the body is used to produce the B vitamin niacin, which is used to produce serotonin, a neurotransmitter that exerts a calming effect and regulates sleep. It is actually the high carbohydrate intake at such meals that is the real cause of the problem because, through a series of steps, carbohydrates cause an increase in tryptophan levels in the blood, leading to the production of excess serotonin. For those affected by tryptophan-induced sleepiness, avoiding dairy products and poultry or even sleeping after a meal might be required.

- Food items that contain phenylalanine list this amino acid on the warning label because some children are born with a genetic malfunction called phenylketonuria (PKU for short), and cannot metabolize phenylalanine. Ingesting phenylalanine causes the body to build it up to dangerous levels, leading to brain damage and mental retardation. PKU should be caught and treated within two weeks of birth by a PKU screening. However, if PKU screening is not done or fails to detect this condition, PKU may not be diagnosed until three to six months of age, after the damage has been done. For this reason, all parents should check the food product labels of food given to the baby to ensure that their newborn does not ingest phenylalanine.

High-Quality and Complete Proteins

A food that contains all of the essential amino acids is considered a **high-quality protein** (also known as a **complete protein**). *Exhibit 5e* shows some food items with complete proteins. On the other hand, a food that is missing one or more essential amino acids is

44444

444444444444

considered an **incomplete protein** and is therefore not high quality. It is important for people to consume all of the essential amino acids by eating a varied diet to ensure they are present when needed by the body.

People who consume animal sources of protein on a regular basis have little need for worry because these sources are always complete in the essential amino acids. However, those who consume mostly vegetarian sources of protein may be lacking in essential amino acids because these are usually incomplete, with a few exceptions.

- Soy and quinoa have all nine essential amino acids; amaranth is almost as complete. If sufficient quantities of these food items are consumed, the body will have the essential amino acids it needs.

- Those who consume mainly vegetarian proteins should be sure to include complementary sources of protein in their meals. **Complementary protein** sources are food items that combined provide all nine essential amino acids, thus equaling a complete protein source. A good example of complementary protein food items served together to make a complete protein is beans and rice; some others are shown in *Exhibit 5e*. Separately, both are lacking at least one amino acid, but when consumed together, they contain all of the essential amino acids and form a complete protein.

To avoid a protein deficiency, people should obtain all nine essential amino acids within a twenty-four hour period,

Exhibit 5e

Examples of Complete and Complementary Protein Food Items

Complete Protein Food Items	Vegetarian Food Items with Naturally Complete Proteins	Complementary Protein Food Items
Beef	Soy	Beans and rice
Chicken	Quinoa	Whole-grain bread and peanut butter
Turkey		Hummus and bread
Pork		Corn and lima beans
Lamb		
Eggs		
Fish		
Shellfish		
Dairy products		

not necessarily at each meal. Whether or not a person is a vegetarian, consuming a variety of food containing high-quality protein or combinations of incomplete or complementary proteins assures adequate intake of amino acids.

Soy for Protein in the Diet

Soy, also called soybean, soya, or soya bean, is a legume that is native to eastern Asia but now is grown throughout the world. The beans from soy (shown in *Exhibit 5f*) are highly valued because soy is an inexpensive and high-quality vegetarian protein source. Soy consumption is currently more common in the United States than it was twenty years ago, but Asian countries, including China and Japan, have consumed soy as a staple protein source for centuries. The fact that soy is a major source of protein in these countries probably is one reason for lower rates of heart disease, stroke, and cancer in those areas.

Soy is a very good source of nutrients. Some benefits are:

■ It contains isoflavones—chemicals found almost exclusively in legumes and thought to be helpful in reducing cholesterol and cancer.

■ It has high amounts of polyunsaturated fat, vitamins, minerals, and fiber.

■ It has lower levels of saturated fat than meat.

The health benefits of soy are great enough that the Food and Drug Administration has authorized a health claim for food labels. This claim states, "25 grams of soy protein per day, as part of a diet low in saturated fat and cholesterol, may reduce the risk of heart disease." In order for this claim to be on a product including soy protein, it must have at least 6.25 grams of soy protein per serving.

Health Benefits of Soy

Possible health benefits from soy consumption are a very active area of research in the nutrition world. These benefits include:

■ **Cholesterol lowering effects**—Soy may lower LDL (bad cholesterol) and increase HDL (good cholesterol), thus decreasing coronary artery disease.

■ **Cancer fighting properties**—The isoflavones in soy may help decrease the chances of getting cancer.

■ **Prostate cancer**—Soy consumption may decrease prostate cancer risk.

■ **Bone health**—Soy may help decrease bone loss.

Exhibit 5f

Soybeans

Soybeans are an outstanding vegetable source of protein.

■ **Menopause**—Soy decreases menopausal symptoms.

On the other hand, although research is conflicting, there is some concern about those with breast cancer or at risk for breast cancer consuming large amounts of soy (i.e., more than fifty grams per day).

Food Sources of Soy

Examples of soy products include:

■ **Soybeans or** edamame—The least processed form of soy.

■ **Tofu, or bean curd**—Made from cooked and puréed soybeans.

■ **Soy milk**—Made by grinding dehulled soybeans mixed with water to become a milk-like beverage.

■ **Soy flour**—Roasted soybeans ground up into a flour texture.

■ **Textured soy protein**—Made from soy flour that has been defatted and sometimes called **textured vegetable protein (TVP)**. It is used not only as a vegetarian protein source in items like veggie burgers but also as a meat extender in meatloaf.

■ **Tempeh**—Made from whole, cooked soybeans that are formed into a cake.

■ **Miso**—Fermented soybean paste usually used for seasoning or in soup.

■ **Soy burgers, sausage, hot dogs, cheese, and cold cuts**—All contain soy as a meatless or vegetarian protein source to increase food choices for vegetarians. Processed soy products may have less nutritional benefits than their more natural counterparts (e.g., soybeans, tofu, and soy milk).

The protein and caloric contributions from some soy products are shown in *Exhibit 5g*.

Exhibit 5g

Protein and Calories in Selected Soy Products

	Soybeans	½ c serving ~7g protein 190 calories
	Soy burger	1 each ~8g protein 100 calories
	Soy milk	1 c serving ~8g protein 110 calories
	Soy nuts	1 oz serving ~12g protein 150 calories
	Tempeh	½ c serving ~18g protein 200 calories
	Textured vegetable protein	¼ c serving ~14g protein ~50 calories
	Tofu	½ oz serving ~18–20g protein 50 calories

U.S. Department of Agriculture

Protein Changes during Cooking

Have you ever wondered why an egg becomes solid when heated? Or why the act of whipping cream produces the consistency it does? This happens because of the denaturation of the proteins in these food items. Denaturation occurs when the protein structure is changed from its naturally folded structure into an unfolded structure. Denaturation does not mean that the protein will not do its job in your body; because it still is composed of the same amino acids in the same sequence, it will. The protein has only uncoiled.

Causes of denaturation of a protein are:

- **Heat**—As in cooking an egg

- **Agitation or whipping**—As in mixing (or whipping) cream

- **Adding bases or acids to cause curdling**—As in adding lemon juice to milk

Excessive and Insufficient Protein in the Diet

The body needs a certain amount of protein on a regular basis, but it can metabolize an amount above the minimum amount of protein intake. However, when the minimum protein-intake amount is not met or the maximum protein-intake amount is passed, problems occur.

Excessive Protein Intake

Some scientific evidence points to harmful consequences when consuming protein in excess of seventy-two grams per kilogram of body weight. For example:

- Calcium losses from overconsumption of protein may lead to bone loss and osteoporosis.

- For those who have kidney stones made from calcium and oxalate, research has shown that the increased urinary losses of calcium increase the chances of forming these stones.

- High or excessive protein diets may also lead to dehydration, which causes the kidneys to work harder and might put extra stress on them.

- There is some evidence that reducing the amount of protein in the diet will prolong the function of the kidneys of a person who suffers from kidney disease.

Protein Deficiency

A lack of protein in the diet may lead to a **protein deficiency**—insufficient protein. Protein deficiency can result in loss of muscle mass, hormonal irregularities, fatigue, resistance to insulin, loss of hair or hair pigment, and loss of skin elasticity. Severe protein deficiency, which is seen only in instances of starvation, is fatal because it produces a shortage of amino acids used by the body to construct its own proteins.

Protein deficiency is not common in healthy individuals in the United States, where there are large amounts of protein food items available and intake of protein is usually more than adequate. However, for those restaurant or foodservice enterprises operating in the global market, the following protein deficiency diseases may be encountered.

Protein Energy Malnutrition

Protein energy malnutrition (PEM) can be related to the deficit of food or an underlying disease that causes a decrease in food consumption from a loss of appetite. PEM caused by a food deficit is usually seen in underdeveloped countries where food or protein sources are not plentiful. PEM also may occur in people and populations who do not consume nutritionally adequate diets although they have access to food. Both of these forms of PEM are most likely to happen in children from the ages of one to three years old, but they also can happen in adults who suffer from anorexia or some other illness or engage in excessive dieting.

The two major forms of PEM are marasmus and kwashiorkor. (See *Exhibit 5h*.)

- **Marasmus** is a form of PEM that includes muscle wasting and loss of stored fat. Those who have marasmus are also lacking other essential macronutrients besides protein over long periods of time.

- **Kwashiorkor**, another form of PEM, is a disease a weaned baby might get when the amino acids that had been supplied by the mother's milk are

Exhibit 5h

Differences between Kwashiorkor and Marasmus

Kwashiorkor	Marasmus
Protein-deficient, high-carbohydrate diet	Both protein- and calorie-deficient diet
Swollen belly from fatty liver	Does not have a fatty liver
Peeling skin	Muscle wastage and loss of fat stores
Happens fast	Develops slowly
Edema	No edema
Hair is thin and brittle, easily pulls out	Hair is thin and brittle, easily pulls out

not present in the subsequent diet. Kwashiorkor is caused mainly by a protein-deficient diet coupled with a high carbohydrate intake. Although people who suffer from kwashiorkor consume adequate carbohydrates, their intake of proteins is insufficient. People who have kwashiorkor also may have lesions on their bodies that look like a rash, peeling skin, edema (swelling of an organ or tissue due to accumulation of excess fluid in the cells), and a swollen belly.

In both cases of PEM, children also do not have a strong immune system because they lack antibodies to fight infections. Thus, it is common for them to suffer from infectious diarrhea or dysentery, which can even result in death. The symptoms of marasmus and kwashiorkor are similar, and the causes also are similar, as shown in *Exhibit 5h* on the previous page.

Exhibit 5i

Recommended Dietary Reference Intakes (DRI) for Protein for Persons of Average Body Weight

Age	Males (grams)	Females (grams)	Females Pregnant or Lactating (grams)
0–6 Months	9.1	9.1	NA
7–12 Months	11+	11+	NA
1–3 yrs	13	13	NA
4–8 yrs	19	19	NA
9–13 yrs	34	34	NA
14–18 yrs	52	46	71
19–30 yrs	56	46	71
31–50 yrs	56	46	71
51–70 yrs	56	46	NA
>70 yrs	56	46	NA

Reprinted with permission from *Dietary Reference Intakes for Energy, Carbohydrate, Fiber, Fat, Fatty Acids, Cholesterol, Protein, and Amino Acids (Macronutrients)*. ©2005 by the National Academy of Sciences, courtesy of the National Academies Press, Washington, DC.

Dietary Requirements for Protein

The Recommended Dietary Allowance (RDA) for protein for both men and women is 0.8 gram per kilogram (0.36 gram per pound) of healthy body weight; a healthy body weight means one that is not underweight or overweight. This translates into forty-six grams of protein daily for a 130-pound woman and fifty-six grams of protein daily for a 175-pound man. A table showing recommended intake levels by gender and age is seen in *Exhibit 5i*. The Acceptable Macronutrient Distribution Rate (AMDR) or percentage of total calories that should come from protein sources in the diet is 10 to 35 percent of total calories.

Exhibit 5j

Protein Content of Selected Food Items

Food	Protein (grams)
Apple, raw with skin	0.36
Asparagus, boiled and drained, four spears	1.4
Bagel, egg, four inches	9.4
Beans, baked vegetarian, one cup	12.0
Bologna, beef or pork, two slices	8.6
Bread, white, enriched, two slices	3.8
Cheese, cheddar, one slice	6.9
Half chicken breast, roasted	27.0
Chicken drumstick	13.0
Corn, sweet, yellow, cooked, half cup	2.5
Egg, large	6.3
Fish, white, uncooked, seven ounces	4.7
Hamburger, lean, three ounces	22.0
Hummus, four tablespoons	4.5
Milk, nonfat, one cup	8.2
Peanut butter, smooth, two tablespoons	8.0
Peanuts, whole with salt, one ounce	8.0
Potato, baked, flesh and skin	4.3
Spinach, cooked, one cup	5.0
Steak, top sirloin, lean, three ounces	23.0
Yogurt, plain, low-fat, one cup	12.0

U.S. Department of Agriculture

The RDA is higher for infants, children, and pregnant women because they are growing and require more protein. Athletes also may require more protein to help maintain their muscle mass; however, the amount of protein consumed daily in a typical American diet is well above the RDA, so an athlete may not necessarily need to increase protein intake.

There is no Tolerable Upper Intake Level (UL) established for protein, but this does not mean that it is safe to consume excessive amounts of protein on a regular basis. As you learned previously, there is evidence that high-protein diets may cause health problems.

Protein can be easily obtained through food. Besides meat, fish, and fowl, vegetables are also sources of protein, especially legumes. See *Exhibit 5j* for the protein content of some selected food items.

Activity

Determine Your Own Protein Needs

How much protein do you require each day according to the USDA's Recommended Dietary Allowance (RDA)? Are you getting what you need, more, or less? You can calculate it yourself.

Part One: Your Daily Protein Needs

Use your weight (or a healthy weight from *Exhibit 2b* on page 21 if you are over or underweight) to determine your protein needs using the following table.

Calculation Steps	Numbers
1 Enter your healthy weight in pounds.	
2 Divide #1 by 2.2 (= your weight in kilograms).	
3 Multiply #2 by 0.8 (= your daily protein requirement in grams).	

Example Calculation	Numbers
1 Enter your healthy weight in pounds.	125
2 Divide #1 by 2.2 (= your weight in kilograms).	57
3 Multiply #2 by 0.8 (= your daily protein requirement in grams).	46

Part Two: Your Actual Protein Intake

In the table on the next page, keep a log of the food you eat. Look up the protein content of each food on the USDA Web site at *www.nal.usda.gov/fnic/foodcomp/search*. Then calculate the protein you ingested during the week using the remaining columns in the table. Finally, calculate your average protein intake per day.

Compare the amount of protein you need to what you are consuming. Do you think you are consuming too little, enough, or too much?

Activity

Protein Intake Log Table				
Day	Meal	Protein Item (name)	Protein Item (ounces)	Number of grams of protein for this amount (from USDA)
Sunday	Breakfast			
	Lunch			
	Dinner			
	Other			
Monday	Breakfast			
	Lunch			
	Dinner			
	Other			
Tuesday	Breakfast			
	Lunch			
	Dinner			
	Other			
Wednesday	Breakfast			
	Lunch			
	Dinner			
	Other			
Thursday	Breakfast			
	Lunch			
	Dinner			
	Other			
Friday	Breakfast			
	Lunch			
	Dinner			
	Other			
Saturday	Breakfast			
	Lunch			
	Dinner			
	Other			
Total protein for the week (grams)				
Divide by 7 to get average protein per day				

Summary

Protein is made up of amino acids and has four kilocalories per gram. Protein is found in food like beef and chicken as well as in grains and vegetables; however, fruit is relatively low in protein. Vegetarians can obtain adequate amounts of protein from vegetable and grain sources, as long as all of the essential amino acids are consumed. Typically, vegetarians must consume complementary protein food items to do this.

Protein is an important macronutrient in people's diets that carries out numerous essential functions. However, consuming more protein than required by the body does not increase muscle mass or necessarily make you healthier.

The information in this chapter should serve as a foundation of knowledge regarding protein that will inform both your daily activities in the culinary world and your own dietary standards.

Review Your Learning

1 Protein is composed of

   A. meat, fish, or beans.

   B. carbon and water.

   C. vitamins and minerals.

   D. chains of amino acids.

2 A complete or high-quality protein contains

   A. all the amino acids.

   B. the amino acid alanine.

   C. all nine essential amino acids.

   D. at least four amino acids plus water.

3 All of the following are effects of a low-protein diet *except*

   A. a swollen belly.

   B. peeling skin.

   C. blood in the urine.

   D. hair that is thin and brittle.

4 All of the these food products are good sources of protein *except*

   A. soy.

   B. apples.

   C. hamburgers.

   D. chicken.

5 Which is *not* a function of protein in the body?

   A. Act as hormones

   B. Act as enzymes

   C. Promote growth and maintenance of body cells and tissues

   D. Serve as the primary source of energy

6 An essential amino acid is one that

   A. must be obtained from the diet.

   B. is made easily by the body.

   C. contains all the necessary nutrients.

   D. None of the above

7 The result of ingesting significantly more protein than needed is

   A. increased strength.

   B. decreased vulnerability to disease.

   C. increased fat.

   D. decreased stamina.

8 The daily recommended protein intake for most adults for each pound of healthy body weight is about

   A. 0.25 gram.

   B. 0.36 gram.

   C. 0.50 gram.

   D. 0.75 gram.

9 An example of complementary proteins is

   A. beans and rice.

   B. potatoes and butter.

   C. corn and margarine.

   D. rice with lemon.

10 All of the following are examples of protein denaturation *except*

   A. cream partially solidifying when whipped.

   B. freezer burn on chicken or steak.

   C. an egg becoming solid when cooked.

   D. clotting of milk when vinegar is added.

Notes

Fats and Other Lipids

6

Inside This Chapter

- Lipids: Structure and Type
- The Role of Lipids in the Body
- Cooking with Fats and Oils
- Dietary Intakes of Lipids
- Lipid Digestion and Absorption
- Lipids and Health

After completing this chapter, you should be able to:

- Describe the types of lipids found in food and their characteristics.
- Define these terms: fatty acids, cholesterol, and triglyceride.
- Explain the difference between saturated, monounsaturated, and polyunsaturated fatty acids.
- Describe how trans fatty acids are produced and their effect on health.
- List the essential fatty acids and their food sources.
- State the daily requirement for fats.
- Describe the digestion and absorption of fats.
- Explain the role of fats, oils, and cholesterol in health and disease.
- Describe the omega-3 and omega-6 fatty acids and their effects on health.

Test Your Knowledge

1. **True or False:** The fatty acids in butter and lard are mostly monounsaturated. *(See p. 113.)*

2. **True or False:** Most trans fats in the diet are a product of the hydrogenation of oils. *(See p. 108.)*

3. **True or False:** Cholesterol is found in each cell membrane. *(See p. 105.)*

4. **True or False:** Omega-6 fatty acids are known to decrease inflammatory processes in the body. *(See p. 116.)*

5. **True or False:** Lipids must be attached to proteins to be transported in the blood. *(See p. 114.)*

Key Terms

Acrolein

Alpha-linolenic acid

Cholesterol

Chylomicron

Diglyceride

Docosahexenoic acid (DHA)

Eicosapentaenoic acid (EPA)

Emulsification

Essential fatty acid

Fatty acid

Flavor reversion

Glycerol

High-density lipoprotein (HDL)

Hydrogenated

Hydrolytic rancidity

Intermediate-density lipoprotein (IDL)

Lecithin

Linoleic acid

Low-density lipoprotein (LDL)

Monoglyceride

Monounsaturated

Omega-3 fatty acid

Omega-6 fatty acid

Oxidative rancidity

Partially saturated

Phospholipid

Plaque

Polyunsaturated

Rancidity

Saturated fatty acid

Shortening effect

Sterol

Trans fat

Triglyceride

Unsaturated fatty acid

Very low-density lipoprotein (VLDL)

Introduction

Most chefs will agree that fats contribute to the texture, mouth feel, shortening effect, viscosity, and taste of food. While there are many cooking techniques that can be used to make food healthier with lower amounts of fat, people still cook with more fat and more saturated fat than recommended for good health.

Exhibit 6a

Fat used for deep-frying can be more or less healthful.

Think About It...

What factors might restaurants be considering when selecting recipes and ingredients high in fat for their menus?

The quantity and type of fats consumed by your customers can have positive or negative effects on their health. For example, the fat used for deep-frying food, like those shown in *Exhibit 6a,* can be saturated or polyunsaturated. The meanings of these terms are explained later in this chapter. It is now known that even small increases in dietary saturated fats increase the risk of heart disease; therefore, these fats should be consumed in moderation. On the other hand, certain oils are recommended for their positive effects on cardiovascular health. Understanding the types of fats used in your establishment, cooking methods, and dishes and their nutritional impact will help you to provide more nutritious menu offerings.

Although your customers' eating habits are their responsibility, providing a variety of nutritional menu items is the responsibility of chefs, menu planners, foodservice managers, and restaurant owners. Many customers desire food that enables them to follow nutritional guidelines for the amount and types of fat in their diet. Ensuring that the proper quantity and type of fat is used when preparing food will not only provide a tasty alternative for your customers, but also serve as a good business decision. When customers recognize your operation for providing great taste in healthy cuisine, they are likely to visit again.

Lipids: Structure and Type

The proper term for fats is "lipids." Lipids are a class of nutrient; fats actually are a subclass of this larger class of organic molecules. This chapter examines fats and other lipids of dietary interest, including triglycerides, cholesterol, and phospholipids.

All lipids are soluble in the major organic solvents of alcohol, acetone, ether, and chloroform, but they differ in their solubility in water. Triglycerides and cholesterol are insoluble in water, but phospholipids have both a fat-soluble side and a water-soluble side, enabling them to dissolve in both water and organic solvents. About 95 percent of all lipids in the diet are triglycerides, while phospholipids and sterols make up the other 5 percent of dietary intake.

Cholesterol

Cholesterol is one of the sterols—hydrocarbons consisting of a steroid and an alcohol and having carbon bonded to carbon in a closed ring. The sterols are an important part of the cellular membrane. Cholesterol is a waxy substance, found only in animal food such as meat, fish, poultry, and cheese. It has multiple hydrocarbon rings and does not

Exhibit 6b

Cholesterol Content of Selected Food Items

Food Item	Cholesterol (Milligrams)
Beef liver, three ounces	356
Large egg	213
Leg of roasted lamb, three ounces	82
Roasted chicken breast, three ounces	76
Lean roasted beef, three ounces	74
Baked salmon, three ounces	60
Cream cheese, two tablespoons	32
Butter, one tablespoon	31
Cheddar cheese, one ounce	30
Milk (3.5 percent), one cup	24
Ice cream, half cup	22
Tofu, quarter cup	0

U.S. Department of Agriculture

contain fatty acids. While greater proportions are found in eggs, the amount of cholesterol varies from food to food. In the body, cholesterol is also the precursor for many substances such as bile acids, vitamin D, and hormones. Cholesterol is a natural component of the body, and the body can synthesize it when needed; therefore it is not required in the diet. *Exhibit 6b* lists the cholesterol content of some popular food items.

The greatest concern with cholesterol is having extra amounts in the diet that are not needed in the body. Due to multiple factors, including genetics and excessive weight, cholesterol builds up in the body and may begin to negatively affect health. It may settle in the artery walls, creating **plaque** deposits— fatty deposits on the wall of a blood vessel—possibly causing cardiovascular disease.

Although too much cholesterol in the diet is undesirable, saturated fat is even more serious, since more dietary cholesterol is absorbed in the presence of saturated fatty acids.

Triglycerides

Triglycerides are the form in which fats are stored in the body. **Triglycerides** are molecules formed by one glycerol molecule and three fatty acids. **Glycerol** is a three-carbon alcohol that bonds with three fatty acids to produce a single structure. A **fatty acid** is an organic molecule, found in animal and vegetable fats, consisting of a carbon-hydrogen chain with an organic-acid group (COOH) at one end, as shown at the right end of the molecule in *Exhibit 6c*. In food, triglycerides are mixed, meaning that different types of fatty acids can be found on the same triglyceride. All three fatty acids can be different, or two can be one type with one fatty acid as another type.

Triglycerides contain fatty acids ranging from four to twenty-four carbons in length. Three types of fatty acids commonly found in food are saturated, monounsaturated, and polyunsaturated. **Saturated fatty acids** have no double bond present between the carbon atoms in their carbon chain; an example is shown in the left image of *Exhibit 6c*. Saturated fatty acids cannot accept or bond with any more hydrogen atoms, because these fatty acids are already saturated with hydrogen. **Unsaturated fatty acids** contain one or more double bonds in the carbon chain; an example is shown in the right image of *Exhibit 6c*. A fatty-acid molecule is **monounsaturated** if it contains one double bond or **polyunsaturated** or **partially saturated** if it contains more than one double bond.

Exhibit 6c

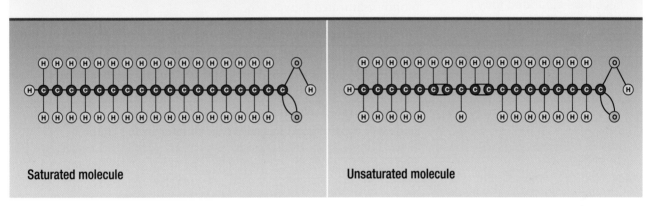

Saturated versus Unsaturated

Saturated molecule

Unsaturated molecule

The saturated molecule on the left has all single bonds and all possible hydrogen atoms in the molecule. The unsaturated molecule on the right has two double bonds near the middle, and as a result, has four fewer hydrogen atoms than the saturated molecule.

Triglycerides in the diet are divided into fats and oils. Fats are triglycerides that are solid at room temperature and come from animal sources; oils are liquid at room temperature and originate from plant sources. Both fats and oils are found in food items and in food preparation. Some of the more common fats are butter, sour cream, lard, cream cheese, and animal fat. Oils that are commonly used in cooking are soybean, corn, safflower, sunflower, canola, olive, sesame, and vegetable-oil blends.

The majority of saturated fatty acids are found in animal products such as meat and meat products like bacon, sausage, tallow, and lard made from meat. They are also found in milk and milk products such as butter, cheese, and cream cheese. Plant sources and tropical oils such as palm, palm kernel, and coconut are other concentrated sources of saturated fatty acids.

Exhibit 6d

Vegetable oils generally have less saturated fatty acid content than animal fats.

Since fatty acids are mixed in nature, it is misleading to refer to them as saturated, polyunsaturated, and monounsaturated. Fatty acids are better identified by their properties. This includes the length of the carbon chain and the number of double bonds located within the carbon chain. They are considered saturated when they contain a higher percentage of saturated fatty acids than any other in their fatty-acid profile. Generally, fats and oils are referred to by the name of the fatty acid that has the greatest concentration in that food. Therefore, it is common practice to call corn oil polyunsaturated, olive oil monounsaturated, and butter a saturated fat.

In studies involving cardiovascular health, monounsaturated fats have been shown to be beneficial for the heart. The monounsaturated fatty acids, by having only one double bond in the carbon chain, allow less hydrogen to be bonded. Olive oil, like the example in *Exhibit 6d,* and canola oil, for example, contain large amounts of monounsaturated fatty acids.

Polyunsaturated fatty acids, by having two or more double bonds in the carbon chain, allow more hydrogen molecules to bond. Oils such as safflower, sunflower, soybean, and corn oil all have large quantities of polyunsaturated fatty acids. Two essential fatty acids found in polyunsaturated oils are linoleic and alpha-linolenic acid. These acids will be discussed in greater detail later in the chapter.

Trans Fats

Oils can be **hydrogenated** (chemically reacted with hydrogen) to make them more solid and to increase their shelf life. By hydrogenating oil, it becomes more saturated and has properties similar to saturated fat. The oil can be totally hydrogenated all the way to being a saturated fat, or the oil can be partially hydrogenated, resulting in less unsaturated fat than it started with.

Trans fats are formed when oils have been partially hydrogenated, allowing some of the double bonds to be broken and rebounded with hydrogen atoms. During this process, some of the hydrogen molecules are bonded differently, forming a slightly different version of the molecule called an isomer. On this isomer, hydrogen is bonded across ("trans" means "across") from the normal position in which it appears in nature. *Exhibit 6e* shows the difference between the normal hydrogen position and the trans hydrogen position. The isomer behaves differently in the body.

Trans fat formed by hydrogenation has been the focus of much attention because it affects people's cholesterol levels. It acts similarly in the body to saturated fat, raising low-density lipoprotein cholesterol (LDL-C) levels and decreasing high-density lipoprotein cholesterol (HDL-C) levels, both undesirable to heart health.

Exhibit 6e

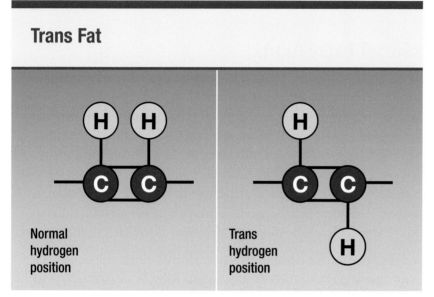

Trans Fat

Normal hydrogen position

Trans hydrogen position

The normal hydrogen position in the molecule is shown on the left; the trans position is shown on the right. This slight variation affects how the molecule reacts.

Dairy products have another form of trans fatty acid called conjugated linoleic acid. This is currently being studied because it may have some benefits to health.

Phospholipids

Phospholipids have a structure similar to triglycerides; however, in place of one of the fatty acids, there is a phosphate and nitrogen attached to the glycerol. Like cholesterol, phospholipids are part of the cell membrane. Phospholipids have a very important role due to their ability to link with both water and fat, forming an emulsion. The fat part of the phospholipid is attracted to other fats, while the phosphorus and nitrogen portion is attracted to acidic molecules like vinegar or lemon juice. Mayonnaise is a familiar emulsion. Lecithin is the most common phospholipid in food; found in egg yolks, it holds oil and lemon juice or vinegar in an emulsion.

The Role of Lipids in the Body

Lipids provide nine kilocalories of energy per gram of food. Adipose tissue is the largest storage area for energy, in the form of fat, in the body and is the body's preferred storage compartment. Although the body stores carbohydrates as glycogen, these are relatively small stores in comparison to the almost infinite supply of adipose fat that can be stored by the body. Excess dietary intake from all nutrient sources, carbohydrates, protein, and lipids, can be stored as adipose tissue. This includes carbohydrates that cannot be stored as glycogen because the liver and muscle stores are full, as well as excess protein, fat, and non-nutrient alcohol.

The body's lipids are stored in many different places, varying from person to person based on gender, genetics, and total weight. There are adipose-tissue stores that surround the organs for cushion and protection, adipose-tissue stores under the skin for insulation, and adipose tissue in muscles. Apart from these functions, lipids in the body are needed to absorb fat-soluble vitamins, spare body protein from being used for energy, act structurally as a part of every cell membrane, form the base for many hormones, and act as lipoproteins.

Essential Fatty Acids

As much as people fret about fats, people cannot live without lipids because they are essential nutrients. As previously mentioned, linoleic acid and alpha-linolenic acid are two essential fatty acids necessary for normal growth and development; they are essential fatty acids because they cannot be manufactured by the body and must be obtained from food. Linoleic acid is found in corn, safflower, soybean, cottonseed, and canola oil. Alpha-linolenic acid is found in canola, soybean, walnut, peanuts, pecans, almonds, wheat germ, and flaxseed oils. These acids will be discussed in greater detail later in the chapter.

A deficiency in these essential fatty acids may cause dermatitis, a condition where skin becomes itchy and flaky. Increased fatty acid deficiency can lead to diarrhea, infections, and a halt in growth and wound healing. People need very little oil to provide enough of the essential fatty acids, as you can see from the small Adequate Intakes listed in *Exhibit 6f*. Since there are usually ample oils used in cooking food, it is unusual to see fatty-acid deficiencies in the population.

Exhibit 6f

Adequate Intakes for Linoleic and Linolenic Acids (grams per day)

Age (yrs)	Males		Females		Pregnant and Lactating Females			
	Linoleic Acid	Linolenic Acid	Linoleic Acid	Linolenic Acid	During	When	Linoleic Acid	Linolenic Acid
1–3	7	0.7	7	0.7	**Pregnancy**	First trimester	13	1.4
4–8	10	0.9	10	0.9		Second trimester	13	1.4
9–13	12	1.2	10	1.1		Third trimester	13	1.4
14–18	16	1.6	11	1.1				
19–30	17	1.6	12	1.1	**Lactation**	First 6 months	13	1.4
31–50	17	1.6	12	1.1		Second 6 months	13	1.4
>50	14	1.6	11	1.1				

Exhibit 6g

Pan-frying is a low-heat method that does not cause oil to deteriorate.

Cooking with Fats and Oils

Since fried food is popular, the restaurant and foodservice industry is not going to eliminate frying. Chefs, recipe developers, and restaurant managers should choose healthy cooking oils that have little or no trans fatty acids. Healthier oils like canola and special oil blends will provide customers with less of these harmful fatty acids.

By using healthy oils, you are not changing the amount of fat used, but you are changing the type of fat used. For example, pan-frying, as shown in *Exhibit 6g,* is not a low-fat cooking method, but using healthy oils such as canola, olive, or peanut provides a healthier ingredient than frying in butter or lard. It also enhances flavor.

One of the challenges in following current guidelines when preparing food is that it is very difficult to replace saturated fat in some items because of the unique properties of saturated fat. Butter and other fats with high levels of saturated fats are ideal for baking because of their shortening effect—an interference with the formation of long gluten strands in wheat-based dough, causing it to have a crumbly texture.

Some margarine brands are now devoid of trans fatty acids but may have a small amount of palm oil or other saturated fat to allow using them as spreads and for baking and cooking. If substituted for shortenings or butter, these products may reduce the amount of saturated fatty acids while still allowing customers to enjoy pastries and cookies. Low trans-fat shortenings are currently being produced and have the qualities of a trans-fat shortening without the harm of trans fats. Unfortunately, when trans fats are reduced in oils, some saturated fatty acids are usually the replacement. When purchasing fats and oils for your restaurant or foodservice operation, try to use only unsaturated ones with little or no trans fats.

Oils deteriorate and need to be changed frequently. Oil used for deep-frying must be filtered regularly. In addition, when oil is overheated to its smoking point, it produces acrolein, which irritates the throat and eyes. The moisture in the food being fried may lower the smoking point, which also contributes to this effect.

Rancidity

As previously described, poor methods of cooking with oils may threaten the food's flavor quality if the oils deteriorate. When fats and oils deteriorate and develop an off flavor and bad taste, it is called rancidity. Any fat can become rancid; however, it is much more common in unsaturated fats due to their double bonds. Hydrogenated fats and saturated fats are more resistant to rancidity because they have fewer double bonds.

There are two general types of rancidity: hydrolytic rancidity and oxidative rancidity.

■ **Hydrolytic rancidity** is caused by the hydrolysis or separation of glycerol from the fatty acids in a triglyceride, yielding water. This occurs with some short-chain fatty acids. Butter contains butyric acid, a short-chain fatty acid; thus hydrolytic rancidity affects butter.

■ **Oxidative rancidity** occurs when oils are exposed to air and heat; they become rancid due to oxidation of their double bonds.

Flavor reversion is a problem with some types of fats. **Flavor reversion** is a slight oxidation of a fat before rancidity is apparent. Soy oil is highly susceptible to flavor reversion because it may contain iron and copper, which may help the breakdown and oxidation of the fat.

The method for keeping most oils from going rancid is to store them in dark-colored, tightly sealed containers in a cool, dry place out of the light; this will retard their oxidation. Many oils have an antioxidant like vitamin C, beta-carotene, or vitamin E added to prevent oxidation and rancidity.

Think About It...

Which fat do you prefer with your bread: butter, margarine, or oil?

Dietary Intakes of Lipids

Recent research supports a moderate intake of fat. Most information suggests that people do not like low-fat diets and that a moderate approach is best, with emphasis put on a dietary intake of fat from healthy oils. The Food and Nutrition Board has set the Acceptable Macronutrient Distribution Range (AMDR) for total lipids at 20 to 35 percent of calories from lipids per day. The type of fat matters more than the quantity of fat in a diet within the range of dietary intake. The Food and Nutrition Board has indicated that even small quantities of saturated fats increase the risk of heart disease. The *Dietary Guidelines for Americans 2005* and MyPyramid encourage the use of oils over solid fats. The same holds true for trans fatty acids, and recommendations are to eat as little as possible. To do this, restaurant and foodservice professionals as well as consumers should read labels to identify and avoid products that contain trans fatty acids.

The 2006 fat-consumption recommendations of the American Heart Association state that people should follow a diet with less than 7 percent of calories from saturated fat and less than 1 percent from trans fat, and to limit cholesterol intake of 300 milligrams per day. (For the entire statement, see "Diet and Lifestyle Recommendations Revision 2006," a scientific statement by the American Heart

Association published online at *www.americanheart.org* on June 21, 2006, in the *Circulation* newsletter.)

Exhibit 6h

Soft margarine contains less saturated fat than butter.

Margarine or Butter: Which Is Better?

When research indicated that trans fatty acids were harmful, people turned from eating margarine to eating butter, thinking it was better for them. The public's perception was that butter was better for them because most margarines have partially hydrogenated fats, although in small amounts. However, what many people did not understand is that butter is a very concentrated form of saturated fatty acids, which are connected with a higher risk of heart disease.

To create the characteristics of a spread, manufacturers add small amounts of either saturated fat or partially hydrogenated fats to margarine. If the ingredients indicate there are partially hydrogenated fats in the product, it will contain trans fatty acids. Otherwise, they use a small amount of saturated fat, like palm oil, to replace hydrogenated fats.

Soft margarine, as shown in *Exhibit 6h,* with a small amount of added saturated fatty acids will still be healthier than butter, based on current recommendations. In response, many people choose to avoid partially hydrogenated fats altogether, instead using spreads that contain monounsaturated or polyunsaturated fats.

Lipid Digestion and Absorption

No matter what type of lipid is consumed, it must be incorporated into the body through the process of digestion. This process breaks down the lipid into the form that can pass across the intestinal wall and enter the bloodstream, which carries it to its final destination.

The digestive system (see *Exhibit 6i* on the next page) handles lipids somewhat differently than it does carbohydrates and proteins. With lipids, digestion begins in the mouth by the action of lingual lipase, an enzyme that is secreted by the salivary glands. Lingual lipase continues to work as the food travels from the mouth to the stomach. In the stomach, it is joined with gastric lipase, an enzyme that helps to further break down the lipid. The stomach continues mixing the food until the original bolus of food that arrived in the stomach is now a watery fluid called chyme, which travels to the small intestine. In the small intestine, bile is secreted at just the right time, along with pancreatic juices containing a pancreatic lipase, to complete the digestive process. The emulsification of lipids is a complicated process, with fat forming into tiny globules called micelles. These tiny globules of fat are formed to allow for the complete breakdown of lipid to monoglycerides and free

Exhibit 6i

The Digestive System

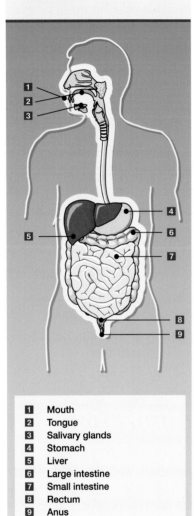

1. Mouth
2. Tongue
3. Salivary glands
4. Stomach
5. Liver
6. Large intestine
7. Small intestine
8. Rectum
9. Anus

Lipid digestion begins in the mouth, continues to the stomach, and is completed in the small intestine.

fatty acids that can then cross through the villi of the small intestine and be absorbed. Most of the lipid is absorbed in the duodenum and jejunum of the small intestine.

As these **monoglycerides** (molecules formed by one glycerol molecule and one fatty acid) and **diglycerides** (molecules formed by one glycerol molecule and two fatty acids) make their way through the digestive and absorptive processes in the intestinal wall, they are reformed into triglycerides. At this point, the lipid joins a protein to form lipoproteins. These digestive lipoproteins are called **chylomicrons.** These chylomicrons then journey to the central lacteal (intestinal lymph-carrying vessels) of the villi and enter the lymphatic system. Small-chain fatty acids that are water soluble can enter the villi and go directly to the portal vein. Phospholipids are digested very similarly to triglycerides. Only about 50 percent of the cholesterol eaten in the diet will be absorbed. The body can add a fatty acid to the cholesterol, and it can be absorbed or be bound in the soluble dietary fibers in the colon and pass out of the body.

Lipids and Health

Lipoproteins, introduced in Chapter 2, are the transport mechanism for fat in the body. Proteins are linked to lipids, including triglyceride, cholesterol, and phospholipids, to keep them in solution in the water environment of the body. These lipoproteins are important markers of health. They travel throughout the body, passing their contents of cholesterol, triglyceride, and phospholipids to cells. They also transport the fat-soluble vitamins. Lipoproteins are considered dense if they have a significant amount of protein in relation to the lipid they carry.

The most basic lipoproteins are chylomicrons. These start out rich in triglyceride from digestion. They are absorbed into the lymphatic system and released at the thoracic duct. On their surface, cells have the enzyme lipoprotein lipase, which breaks up the triglyceride for cell use. Lipoprotein lipase breaks the bond, releasing fatty acids and glycerol from triglyceride. Moving through the body, chylomicrons give up their triglyceride to the cells and become "remnants" now that they lack their lipid load. The liver captures these remnants and uses their cholesterol to construct low-density lipoproteins.

Very low-density lipoprotein (VLDL) is made in the liver and the intestines. It is the second lipoprotein that carries triglyceride to the cells, picking up some cholesterol, phospholipid, and protein along the way, becoming more dense, or protein-laden, as it circulates. VLDL develops into an **intermediate-density lipoprotein** (IDL). It returns to the liver, where it acquires more cholesterol and becomes a **low-density lipoprotein** (LDL).

Exhibit 6j

Recommended LDL and HDL Levels (mg per deciliter)

Cholesterol Type	Recommended Level
LDL "bad" cholesterol **(There are different goals for each level of risk for heart disease.)**	■ People who are at low risk for heart disease: Less than **160 mg/dL** ■ People at intermediate risk for heart disease: Less than **130 mg/dL** ■ People at high risk for heart disease, including those who have heart disease or diabetes: Less than **100 mg/dL** ■ People at very high risk for heart disease: Less than **70 mg/dL**
HDL "good" cholesterol	■ Women: **50 mg/dL** or higher ■ Men: **40 mg/dL** or higher
Total cholesterol	**Less than 200 mg/dL**

From "Numbers That Count for a Healthy Heart." Reproduced with permission: www.americanheart.org.
©2006, American Heart Association.

Low-density lipoproteins have considerable amounts of cholesterol that they deliver to the cells. This cholesterol is taken up by the cells, incorporated into cell membranes, and made into hormones and other important, complex substances. In the liver, receptor cells regulate cholesterol levels in the blood by binding with LDL. These receptors are blocked from working correctly by saturated fatty acids, allowing cholesterol levels of the body to rise. This is part of the reason for the advice to eat saturated fat in moderation. High saturated-fat intake can raise LDL cholesterol levels. LDL has been called the "bad" cholesterol, since it can increase risk of cardiovascular disease. The cholesterol levels recommended for Americans by the American Heart Association are shown in *Exhibit 6j*.

High-density lipoproteins (HDL) are made in the liver and intestines and are believed to be heart healthy. HDL has been called the "good cholesterol," since it removes or lowers blood cholesterol levels. HDL has more protein and is denser than other lipoproteins. HDL (good cholesterol) is able to remove LDL (bad cholesterol) from the blood and plaque in the artery walls. This reduction in LDL not only brings down LDL cholesterol levels in the blood, but also brings down total cholesterol. The cholesterol collected by HDL is returned by IDL to the liver for recycling. The body is very efficient at handling all types of cholesterol because it is needed for so many complex substances. If the control mechanisms set by the body do not respond properly, cholesterol can build up in vessel walls, causing strokes and heart attacks.

Are There Heart-Healthy Fats?

As mentioned earlier in this chapter, there are two essential fatty acids: linoleic and alpha-linolenic. These fatty acids are required by the body and need to be included in the diet each day. If a fatty acid has a double bond, it is named by the position of the first double bond from the methyl group. The methyl group is a carbon bonded by three hydrogen atoms on the end of the molecule of fatty acid. Nutritionists count from this end when naming fatty acids. It is called the omega end of the molecule.

Omega-6 Fatty Acid

Linoleic acid is an **omega-6 fatty acid**, as is arachidonic acid. Both are essential and must be obtained from food. They are necessary for stimulating skin and hair growth, aiding with bone health, controlling metabolism, and aiding reproductive capacity. These are important reactions for the body, so omega-6 fats are so-called good fats. On the other hand, some research has suggested that excessive levels of omega-6 fatty acids may increase the probability of a number of diseases. *Exhibit 6j* shows common food sources of omega-6 fatty acid.

Omega-3 Fatty Acid

Omega-3 fatty acids are considered essential because they cannot be made by the body. When you have appendicitis, you want inflammation to warn you there is a problem; but in chronic diseases like arthritis, it is helpful to have the action produced by omega-3 fatty acids, which follow a different pathway and help to reduce inflammation, thin the blood, and prevent stroke. Alpha-linoleic is an **omega-3 fatty acid**, another so-called good fat. Some good sources of omega-3 fatty acids are listed in *Exhibit 6k*.

Ratio of Omega-6 to Omega-3 Fatty Acids

It is now known that the omega-6 arachidonic acid is converted by the body into chemicals that promote inflammation. The omega-3 fatty acids also are converted but at a slower rate. Of the two, omega-6 fatty acids are much more inflammatory. However, if both omega-3 and omega-6 are present, they will "compete" to be transformed. If there is sufficient omega-3 present, it will slow the overall production of inflammatory agents. Thus, the current recommendation is that three to five times as much omega-6 be consumed as omega-3. Studies suggest that the evolutionary human diet, rich in seafood, nuts, and other sources of omega-3, may have provided such a ratio. The typical Western diet, however, provides ratios of between 10:1 and 30:1, radically overemphasizing omega-6.

The other two fatty acids of particular interest are **eicosapentaenoic acid** (EPA), an omega-3 fatty acid, and **docosahexaenoic acid** (DHA). Both are polyunsaturated fatty acids that are so-called good fats. EPA and DHA are found in cold-water fish such as salmon, trout, bluefish, sablefish, mackerel, mullet, sardine, and tuna. EPA is found in quite a few places in the body, including brain tissue, the cornea, and the skin. DHA is found in breast milk and is believed to participate in the development of normal vision in the newborn. The current recommendation to eat two servings of fatty fish a week is aimed at increasing the EPA and DHA content of the diet. Some people have decided to take fish-oil supplements to get fatty acids. At this time, there is no way to ensure that fish oils are low in mercury. It seems that getting these fatty acids from fish is still the best answer with a caution that some of the most popular fish, like tuna and salmon, do contain mercury in varying amounts. Pregnant women are advised to only eat fish known to have lower mercury levels, since it has negative effects on the fetus.

Exhibit 6k

Dietary Sources of Omega Fatty Acids

Omega-3 Fatty Acids

Cold-water oily fish | Flax | Canola oil | Green leafy vegetables | Walnuts

Omega-6 Fatty Acids

Cereals | Whole-grain breads | Most vegetable oils | Sesame seeds or oil | Soybeans

Activity

Your Fat Intake

In the following table, keep a log of the food you eat. Then look up the fat content of each food on the USDA Web site at *www.nal.usda.gov/fnic/foodcomp/search*. Finally, calculate the fat you ingested during the week and your average daily fat intake using the remaining columns in the table.

Day	Meal	Name of Food Item	Ounces of Food Item	Saturated Fat Grams of Item (from USDA)	Total Fat Grams of Item (from USDA)
Sunday	Breakfast				
	Lunch				
	Dinner				
	Other				
Monday	Breakfast				
	Lunch				
	Dinner				
	Other				
Tuesday	Breakfast				
	Lunch				
	Dinner				
	Other				
Wednesday	Breakfast				
	Lunch				
	Dinner				
	Other				
Thursday	Breakfast				
	Lunch				
	Dinner				
	Other				
Friday	Breakfast				
	Lunch				
	Dinner				
	Other				
Saturday	Breakfast				
	Lunch				
	Dinner				
	Other				
Total fat for the week (grams)					
Divide by 7 = Average fat per day (grams)					

Summary

Fat is an essential nutrient to the human body. Tissue development, energy, and the body's ability to heal all depend on fatty acids found in food. When determining what food is best for the diet, people must pay more attention to the type of fat rather than the amount of fat found in the nutritional makeup of food items.

Lipids include triglycerides, cholesterol, and phospholipids. Whether found in plants, animals, or eggs, each of these types of fats must be stored, prepared, and consumed in ways that will not cause harm to the body. Linoleic and alpha-linolenic acid are two essential fatty acids found in polyunsaturated oils. These acids are necessary for normal growth and development. A deficiency in these may cause dermatitis, diarrhea, infections, and stunted growth and wound healing.

Rancidity is most common in unsaturated fats. Two general types of rancidity are hydrolytic and oxidative, which either yield water or react to air. Proper storage will prevent most fats from going rancid and losing flavor.

Lipoproteins are the combination of lipids and protein as they link together before passing cholesterol, triglycerides, and phospholipids to cells throughout the body. The density of these lipoproteins is based upon the amount of protein contained in the molecule. A lipoprotein molecule is created in the liver and intestines and travels through the body as a very low-density lipoprotein (VLDL), picking up cholesterol, phospholipids, and protein until it develops into a low-density lipoprotein (LDL). LDL is often blocked by saturated fats that cause cholesterol levels to rise, whereas HDL can lower cholesterol levels.

The body is equipped to handle all types of fat and fat-like substances, but it is very easy to harm the body by following poor dietary practices. The Food and Nutrition Board does not recommend frequent consumption of products with saturated fats or trans fatty acids. The American Heart Association recommends that people follow a diet regulating the quantities of calories from fat. They also have indicated a limit on cholesterol intake of less than 300 milligrams per day. By following these and other recommended dietary practices, the body can remain healthy by consuming the right food more often.

Review Your Learning

1 Lipids are a class of nutrients that contain all of the following *except*

  A. triglycerides.
  B. cholesterol.
  C. trans fat.
  D. phospholipids.

2 The following items contain mostly saturated fats *except*

  A. coconut oil.
  B. butter.
  C. cream cheese.
  D. corn oil.

3 Fats are digested and absorbed almost entirely in the

  A. stomach.
  B. large intestine.
  C. gall bladder.
  D. small intestine.

4 Low-density lipoprotein (LDL) is the most important of the lipoproteins to monitor because

  A. high LDL levels in the blood show increased risk of heart problems.
  B. when LDL is high, a person is in a heart-healthy state.
  C. a person with high LDL levels is definitely eating too much cholesterol.
  D. high LDL is proof that a person is obese.

5 Trans fats are not heart healthy because

  A. they have been found to raise HDL.
  B. they act like saturated fatty acids and lower LDL.
  C. they act like saturated fats and raise LDL.
  D. they raise LDL and decrease HDL.

6 The essential fatty acids are

  A. linoleic acid and alpha-linolenic acid.
  B. saturated and unsaturated fatty acids.
  C. acetic acid and oleic acid.
  D. omega-3 and omega-6 fatty acids.

7 Which is found in animal meat and eggs?

  A. Fat
  B. Polyunsaturated fatty acids
  C. Cholesterol
  D. Oil

8 Rancidity of oil is caused by

  A. cool temperatures.
  B. placing oil in dark containers.
  C. oxidation of its carbon-carbon double bonds.
  D. dimly lit storerooms.

9 The amount of cholesterol recommended as a limit for daily cholesterol is

  A. 100 milligrams.
  B. 200 milligrams.
  C. 300 milligrams.
  D. 400 milligrams.

10 Which fish is *not* listed as a source of EPA and DHA?

  A. Tilapia
  B. Blue fish
  C. Trout
  D. Salmon

Vitamins, Minerals, and Water

7

Inside This Chapter

- What Are Vitamins and Minerals?
- Vitamins in the Diet
- Minerals in the Diet
- Retaining Vitamins and Minerals When Cooking
- Supplementation of Vitamins and Minerals
- Water in the Diet

After completing this chapter, you should be able to:

- List the functions of vitamins, minerals, and water in the body.
- Distinguish between fat-soluble and water-soluble vitamins.
- State good food sources for specific vitamins and minerals.
- List vitamin- and mineral-deficiency diseases.
- List ways to retain the vitamin and mineral content of food while cooking.
- State when it is appropriate to supplement vitamins and minerals.

Test Your Knowledge

1. **True or False:** Vitamins contain calories for energy. *(See p. 123.)*

2. **True or False:** There are three categories of vitamins. *(See p. 124.)*

3. **True or False:** Peppers are a good source of vitamin C. *(See p. 127.)*

4. **True or False:** Rickets is a vitamin D deficiency in children. *(See p. 126.)*

5. **True or False:** Most people should take supplemental vitamins every day. *(See p. 136.)*

Key Terms

Antioxidant	Hard water	Micronutrient
Beta carotene	Heme iron	Nonheme iron
Coenzyme	Hemoglobin	Retinol
Cruciferous vegetable	Hydrated	Soft water
DASH	Intrinsic factor	Trace mineral
Dehydrating	Iron-deficiency anemia	Water-soluble vitamin
Fat-soluble vitamin	Major mineral	

Think About It...

Vitamins and minerals are measured in thousandths of a gram and millionths of a gram. Imagine how small one millionth of a gram is: a quarter teaspoon of sugar weighs about one gram and does not even come close to having a million granules.

Introduction

Vitamins and minerals are important in the human diet because they promote growth and optimum health. Both vitamins and minerals are essential for body functioning. Some food items have more vitamins and minerals than others. Consuming a variety of food items from each food group helps meet the body's need for specific vitamins and minerals.

Water also is important to the human body because almost all the chemical reactions that make the body work involve water in one way or the other. The body needs a certain amount of water every day, and food and drink are the primary sources of this water.

In this chapter you will learn specific functions and food sources of vitamins, minerals, and water. You will also learn the consequences of insufficient amounts of these important nutrients.

Vitamins

Vitamin A (retinol)

B Vitamins

- B_1 (thiamin)
- B_2 (riboflavin)
- B_3 (niacin)
- B_5 (pantothenic acid)
- B_6 (pyridoxine, pyridoxal, and pyridoxamine)
- B_7 (biotin)
- B_9 (folic acid or folate)
- B_{12} (cyanocobalamin)

Vitamin C (ascorbic acid)

D Vitamins

- D_1 (lamisterol)
- D_2 (gocalciferol)
- D_3 (cholecalciferol)*
- D_4 (dihydrotachysterol)
- D_5 (sitocalciferol)
- D_7 (dehydrositosterol)

Vitamin E (tocopherol)

Vitamin K (naphthoquinone)

*Cholecalciferol is the natural human form of vitamin D.

Think About It...

An old nickname for a sailor is "limey." Do you know why?

What Are Vitamins and Minerals?

As you learned in Chapter 1, scientists began discovering vitamins in the early twentieth century. They assigned letters and numbers to unknown properties in food and later named them vitamins. The Polish scientist Casimir Funk originally named these "vitamines" for the Latin word "vita" meaning life and "amine" for the type of organic chemical that scientists originally thought they were. Vitamins are organic compounds, meaning they contain carbon and are made from plants or animals.

Once vitamins were identified, scientists conducted experiments to learn more about them, which eventually lead to the discovery of the vitamins A and D and the B complex of several vitamins. Now scientists know that there are thirteen vitamins. Each vitamin has a letter resulting from its original discovery, and each has a chemical name; *Exhibit 7a* lists both. You will note that some of the letters in the vitamin names have been skipped. Originally, the missing letters were assigned as the vitamin was discovered. Later, these vitamins were found to be one of the vitamins in a group of vitamins called the B-vitamin complex, so the names were changed to B_1, B_2, and so on. A similar thing happened with the D vitamins.

Vitamins are called **micronutrients** because the amount of each vitamin needed in the body is very small; carbohydrates, fats, and proteins are called macronutrients because the body needs large amounts of them. To get a mental picture, think of the size of a meal that provides enough macronutrients versus the size of a vitamin tablet with 100 percent of the Recommended Dietary Allowance (RDA) for most of the vitamins; this is shown in *Exhibit 7b* on the next page.

Vitamins are essential for life and must be obtained from food because the human body makes insufficient amounts or none at all. Unlike carbohydrates, fats, and proteins, vitamins and minerals do not contain energy or kilocalories. Instead, vitamins facilitate the operation of other nutrients. Some vitamins act as **coenzymes** because they are activators of other enzymes—body chemicals that catalyze, or speed up, a specific chemical reaction important to the body. Think of a coenzyme as a puzzle piece that completes the puzzle; they are specific to and combine with the target enzyme to enable certain reactions to take place in the body.

Exhibit 7b

Vitamins are miniscule compared to food.

Exhibit 7c

Vitamins by Category

Fat-Soluble Vitamins	Water-Soluble Vitamins
■ Vitamin A	■ Vitamin C
■ D Vitamins	■ B Vitamins
■ Vitamin E	
■ Vitamin K	

Vitamins are classified as either water soluble or fat soluble. **Water-soluble vitamins** are soluble in water but not in fat, and they are not generally stored in the body. **Fat-soluble vitamins** are soluble in fat but not in water, and they can be stored in the body's adipose (fat) tissue. *Exhibit 7c* shows which vitamins are water soluble and which are fat soluble.

Minerals, on the other hand, are inorganic elements and do not contain carbon. Technically, the word "mineral" refers to mixtures and compounds of chemical elements found in the earth. However, in nutrition, the chemical elements found in the soil or ground water are simply called minerals. Like vitamins, minerals are needed by the body to stay healthy. For example, calcium is needed to build bones, maintain bone health, and operate molecular passages into each cell of the body called calcium channels. This chapter explains which minerals are needed by the human body and the amounts needed. It also explains the effect on the body of a deficiency in these minerals.

Vitamins in the Diet

Vitamins have specific functions in the body, which are listed in *Exhibit 7d* along with the primary diseases caused by a deficiency in each vitamin. Some noteworthy characteristics and sources of vitamins are discussed on pages 126–127.

Exhibit 7d

Vitamins: Primary Functions and Deficiency Diseases

Vitamin	Primary Function	Deficiency Diseases
Vitamin A (retinol)	Normal vision and normal cell development in the body	Night blindness, dry eyes, softening of the cornea
Vitamin B_1 (thiamin)	A coenzyme for energy metabolism, nervous-system function	Beriberi
Vitamin B_2 (riboflavin)	A coenzyme in energy metabolism, normal vision	Ariboflavinosis
Vitamin B_3 (niacin)	A coenzyme in energy metabolism	Pellagra
Vitamin B_5 (pantothenic acid)	Part of a coenzyme used in energy metabolism	Convulsions or anemia
Vitamin B_6 (pyridoxine, pyridoxal, and pyridoxamine)	Part of a coenzyme used in amino-acid metabolism, helps make red blood cells, and assists in the conversion of the amino acid tryptophan to the vitamin niacin	Anemia, nerve damage, seizures, skin problems, sores in the mouth
Vitamin B_7 (biotin)	Part of a coenzyme used in energy metabolism, used in cell growth, helps maintain a steady blood-sugar level, strengthens hair and nails	Changes in mental state, dry skin, fine and brittle hair, fungal infections, hair loss or total alopecia, muscular pain, skin rash, seborrheic dermatitis
Vitamin B_9 (folic acid or folate)	Part of a coenzyme used in the synthesis of new cells	Behavioral disorders, diarrhea, loss of appetite, sore tongue, headaches, heart palpitations, infant neural tube defects, irritability, low birth weight babies, megaloblastic anemia, premature babies, weakness, weight loss
Vitamin B_{12} (cyanocobalamin)	Part of a coenzyme used in the synthesis of new cells	Megaloblastic anemia, nerve-cell death, numbness or tingling of the extremities, pernicious anemia
Vitamin C (ascorbic acid)	Antioxidant, collagen formation in the skin, helps immunity	Scurvy
Vitamin D (five forms)	Maintains the normal levels of calcium and phosphorus in the blood	Osteomalacia, osteoporosis, rickets
Vitamin E (tocopherol)	Antioxidant	Neurological disorders leading to poor transmission of nerve impulses, muscle weakness, and degeneration of the retina
Vitamin K (napthoquinone)	Blood clotting	Bleeding diathesis (causing problems with blood coagulation)

- **Vitamin A:** It is commonly known that carrots are good for eyesight. This is because the main function of vitamin A is to promote good vision through the health of the retina—the light sensitive portion of the eye—and the cornea—the clear layer covering of the eye. That is why vitamin A is called **retinol.** Some other functions of vitamin A include the development of new cells and bones and maintenance of a healthy immune system. Retinol is the active form of vitamin A; it is obtained from animal products in a person's diet. **Beta carotene**—the most common precursor or inactive form of vitamin A that becomes active in the body—is obtained from a variety of plant sources. Beta-carotene is an **antioxidant**—a chemical that fights the excessive oxidation of molecules in the human body. Beta-carotene is orange in color; it is what gives carrots and sweet potatoes their color. A deficiency of vitamin A may lead to several deficiency diseases: night blindness (the inability to see clearly at night) or xerophthalmia (dry eyes), which could lead to permanent blindness, and keratomalacia (softening of the cornea). Excessive vitamin A, however, is highly toxic.

- **Vitamin D:** Rickets is a disease that occurs in children with a vitamin D deficiency. Rickets causes bowing of the legs or knocked knees. The main function of vitamin D in the body is to regulate the blood calcium levels to maintain bone health. Vitamin D is activated in the skin by sunlight. Additionally, milk is fortified with vitamin D, as are other food sources discussed later in this chapter. A vitamin D deficiency in adults called osteomalacia involves softening of the bones and can lead to bone deformities. As people age, osteoporosis (a bone-thinning disorder) is another disease caused by a vitamin D deficiency. Having a vitamin D deficiency is a concern in climates that do not have a lot of sun exposure; moreover, people who use sunscreen extensively are also at risk because they are blocking the activation of vitamin D by the sun.

- **Vitamin K:** The primary function of vitamin K is to enable blood to clot, but it also plays a role in the health of bones. The body can make vitamin K in the intestines. However, the body does not make enough, so it must be obtained from food sources as well, such as green, leafy vegetables.

- **Vitamin C:** Sailors are sometimes referred to as "limeys" because they used to suck on lemons or limes to avoid the illness later named scurvy. The lack of fresh fruit and certain vegetables in the diet of sailors hundreds of years ago caused this vitamin C deficiency. Scurvy causes swollen gums, loose teeth, a rash that looks like red spots, and hair loss. Other functions of vitamin C

Exhibit 7e

A varied diet will help people obtain all of the vitamins needed for optimal health.

are to act as an antioxidant and to assist the body in the absorption of **nonheme iron,** the mineral iron from plant sources, as distinct from the form carried in blood (blood is also called heme).

■ **Vitamins B_1, B_2, and B_3:** The major function of thiamin (vitamin B_1), riboflavin (vitamin B_2), and niacin (vitamin B_3) is to act as a coenzyme in energy metabolism. In the process of refining grain, the B vitamins are removed; therefore, they are added to grain products. This makes the products enriched.

■ **Vitamin B_9:** Folic acid, also known as folate, is important in the early stages of pregnancy to avoid neural-tube defects—a disorder of the brain or spinal column in the early stages of pregnancy. Folate is put into fortified food products for this reason. Folate is also important in the development of red and white blood cells. Megaloblastic anemia is caused by a folate deficiency; it is a disease that causes abnormally large red blood cells.

■ **Vitamin B_6:** Pyridoxine has the ability to be stored in your muscles. Its primary function is to act as a coenzyme in amino-acid and protein metabolism.

Food Sources of Vitamins

Consuming a varied diet of vegetables, fruit, dairy, grains, and animal products (like those shown in *Exhibit 7e*) will help people obtain all the vitamins needed for optimal health. Although oranges are known as a good source of the vitamin C, there are other good sources such as peppers. Adding peppers to an omelet incorporates vitamin C into this food item without adding many calories. On the other hand, orange juice, although an excellent source of vitamin C, includes calories from the sugar in the oranges. Those who are calorie conscious or diabetic may choose peppers instead of orange juice as their source of vitamin C.

Exhibit 7f on the next page identifies good sources of each of the vitamins from vegetarian and animal sources. The different colors of fruit and vegetables often indicate the presence of different vitamins. For example, dark orange vegetables like carrots contain beta-carotene, and dark green vegetables often contain vitamin K. Notice that people have the ability to make vitamin K in the intestines with the help of "friendly" bacteria that live in the intestines; but not enough is synthesized by the body, so vitamin K is still considered an essential vitamin. Biotin is also made in the intestine by these bacteria in insufficient amounts, and it may not be absorbed well by humans when produced in the intestines. Vitamin B_{12} is available only from animal sources and should be supplemented in the diets of vegans since they do not consume any animal products.

Exhibit 7f

Food Sources of Vitamins

Vitamin	Vegetarian Sources	Animal Sources
Vitamin A	Dark orange and green vegetables, sweet potatoes, mangos	Fortified milk or dairy products, liver, eggs
Vitamin B$_1$	Whole grains, enriched products, fortified products, nuts, legumes	Pork
Vitamin B$_2$	Whole grains or enriched grains	Milk and milk products
Vitamin B$_3$	Whole grains, enriched products, nuts	Milk, eggs, meat, poultry and fish
Vitamin B$_5$	Most	Most
Vitamin B$_6$	Green vegetables, green leafy vegetables, fruit, whole grains	Meat, fish, poultry
Vitamin B$_7$	Most; people make small amounts in the intestines	Most
Vitamin B$_9$	Green leafy vegetables, legumes, seeds, enriched products	Liver
Vitamin B$_{12}$	None naturally; may be fortified in cereals	All
Vitamin C	Citrus fruit, peppers, strawberries, tomatoes, potatoes	None
Vitamin D	None, but made with the help of sunlight	Fortified milk, fatty fish, some fish-liver oils, eggs
Vitamin E	Green leafy vegetables, mayonnaise made with vegetable oil, nuts, peanut butter, sunflower seeds, sea buckthorn berries, seeds, vegetable oils (palm, sunflower, canola, corn, soybean, and olive), wheat germ, whole grains	Fish, only small amounts in some, not a good source
Vitamin K	Green, leafy cabbage-type vegetables, collards, spinach, also made by bacteria in the intestine	Minimal amounts in liver and eggs

Dietary Reference Intakes for Vitamins

The National Academy of Sciences has established recommended amounts of vitamins that people should obtain each day. The key data about these recommended intakes is listed in *Exhibit 7g*. Notice that some vitamins have maximum amounts that should not be exceeded; these are called the Tolerable Upper Intake Level; they were developed in response to increasing incidents of toxicity due to oversupplementation.

Exhibit 7g

Dietary Reference Intakes for Vitamins

Vitamin	Male, age 14–70 years		Female, age 14–70 years	
	Recommended Dietary Allowance, (mg)	Tolerable Upper Intake Level, (mg)	Recommended Dietary Allowance, (mg)	Tolerable Upper Intake Level, (mg)
Vitamin A	0.9	2.8 (3.0 after age 19)	0.7	2.8 (3.0 after age 19)
Vitamin B_1	1.2	not determined	1.0 (1.1 after age 19)	not determined
Vitamin B_2	1.3	not determined	1.0 (1.1 after age 19)	not determined
Vitamin B_3	16.0	30.0 (35.0 after age 19)	14.0	30.0 (35.0 after age 19)
Vitamin B_5	5.0	not determined	5.0	not determined
Vitamin B_6	1.3 (1.7 after age 50)	80.0 (100.0 after age 19)	1.2 (1.3 after age 19) (1.5 after age 50)	80.0 (100.0 after age 19)
Vitamin B_7	0.025 (0.03 after age 19)	not determined	0.025 (0.03 after age 19)	not determined
Vitamin B_9	0.4	0.8 (1.0 after age 19)	0.4	0.8 (1.0 after age 19)
Vitamin B_{12}	0.0024	not determined	0.0024	not determined
Vitamin C	75.0 (90.0 after age 19)	1,800.0 (2,000.0 after age 19)	65.0 (75.0 after age 19)	1,800.0 (2,000.0 after age 19)
Vitamin D	0.005 (0.01 after age 50)	0.05	0.005 (0.01 after age 50)	0.05
Vitamin E	15.0	800.0 (1,000.0 after age 19)	15.0	800.0 (1,000.0 after age 19)
Vitamin K	0.075 (0.12 after age 19)	not determined	0.075 (0.09 after age 19)	not determined

The amounts of vitamins needed by the body are very small when compared to its need for carbohydrates, proteins, and fats. That is why vitamins are considered to be micronutrients and the others are considered macronutrients. Ensuring that the needed amounts of vitamins are present in restaurant and foodservice food is an easy thing to do. As described in the previous three chapters, preparing food using fresh fruit and vegetables, whole grains, and either complete-or complementary-protein food items will supply the needed micronutrients along with macronutrients. In addition, the dishes your operation prepares will taste better and be more appealing to the customer.

Exhibit 7h

Primary Functions of Important Minerals

Mineral	Function
Calcium	Bone health, helps maintain normal blood pressure, muscle contraction
Chloride	Maintains fluid and electrolyte balance in the body
Chromium	Required for carbohydrate metabolism
Copper	Part of various enzymes; used for electron transport
Fluorine	Bone and tooth health
Iron	Part of hemoglobin
Magnesium	Part of bones and teeth, making protein, muscle activity, activator of metabolism of carbohydrates, fats, and proteins
Manganese	Part of many enzymes
Molybdenum	Necessary for purine degradation and formation of uric acid and used in many enzyme reactions
Phosphorus	Part of the bones and teeth
Potassium	Maintains fluid and electrolyte balance in the body
Selenium	Antioxidant
Sodium	Maintains the fluid and electrolyte balance in the body
Zinc	Taste perception, coenzyme

Minerals in the Diet

The minerals (really, chemical elements) of dietary concern are calcium, chlorine, chromium, copper, fluorine, iron, magnesium, manganese, molybdenum, phosphorus, potassium, selenium, sodium, and zinc. These minerals have many important functions in the body; for example:

- Sodium and potassium work together to regulate the heartbeat.

- Calcium, along with phosphorus and magnesium, assists in keeping bones healthy.

The primary functions of these minerals are listed in *Exhibit 7h.*

Amounts of Minerals Needed

For nutritional purposes, minerals are classified as either trace minerals or major minerals. These classifications are only descriptive of the quantities needed by the body, not the importance of the different minerals. **Major minerals** are needed in larger amounts in the body; **trace minerals** are needed in smaller amounts. One example of a major mineral is calcium; it is needed in larger quantities from the diet than other minerals. Iron is an example of a trace mineral; it is needed in small amounts but is equally important.

The human body's need for minerals varies somewhat with age and gender. The Food and Nutrition Board publishes the intake needed as either Adequate Intake (AI) or Recommended Dietary Allowance (RDA), depending on the mineral involved; both are used for dietary intake levels. Also, they publish the Tolerable Upper Intake Level (UL) that is considered safe. The dietary intakes for the minerals are shown in *Exhibit 7i* on the next page.

Food Sources of Minerals

The best way for people to obtain the minerals their bodies need is through food. (The use of supplements is discussed later in this chapter.) Obtaining them through the diet is not difficult, and restaurant and foodservice professionals should know what food to include in the diet in order to do this. *Exhibit 7j* on page 133 shows common food sources that are rich in the various minerals. By including all of these food items in their diet in reasonable quantities, people will obtain their recommended daily amounts of minerals.

Obtaining sufficient minerals through food is as easy to do as with vitamins. Simply include all the sources of minerals listed in *Exhibit 7j* in the diet. The more of these food items that your restaurant or foodservice operation can supply as part of its marketing plan, the easier it is for customers to obtain the needed minerals at your operation.

Minerals and Health

From the functions of the different minerals previously described, you can see that they are all important for health. However, several health issues related to minerals merit further discussion.

Minerals and Blood-Pressure Regulation

Minerals play an important role in blood-pressure regulation. It appears that deficiencies of the minerals potassium, calcium, and magnesium may contribute to the incidence of high blood pressure. Also, for those who have a genetic tendency towards high blood pressure, excessive sodium intake may increase the likelihood of developing it. The National Institutes of Health publishes the

Exhibit 7i

Dietary Intakes for Minerals

Mineral (Element)	Male, age 14–70 years		Female, age 14–70 years	
	Adequate Intake (mg)	Tolerable Upper Intake (mg)	Adequate Intake (mg)	Tolerable Upper Intake (mg)
Major Minerals				
Calcium	Age 14–18: 1,300 Age 19–50: 1,000 Over age 50: 1,200	2,500	Age 14–18: 1,300 Age 19–50: 1,000 Over age 50: 1,200	2,500
Chloride	Age 14–50: 2,300 Age 51–70: 2,000 Over age 70: 1,800	3,600	Age 14–50: 2,300 Age 51–70: 2,000 Over age 70: 1,800	3,600
Magnesium	Age 14–30: 410 Age 19–30: 400 Over age 30: 420	350	Age 14–30: 360 Age 19–30: 310 Over age 30: 320	350
Phosphorus	Age 14–18: 1,250 Over age 18: 700	Age 14–70: 4,000 Over age 70: 3,000	Age 14–18: 1,250 Over age 18: 700	Age 14–70: 4,000 Over age 70: 3,000
Sodium	Age 14–50: 1,500 Age 51–70: 1,300 Over age 70: 1,200	2,300	Age 14–50: 1,500 Age 51–70: 1,300 Over age 70: 1,200	2,300
Trace Minerals				
Chromium	Age 14–50: 0.035 Over age 50: 0.030	not determined	Age 14–18: 0.024 Age 19–50: 0.025 Over age 50: 0.020	not determined
Copper	Age 14–18: 0.89 Over age 18: 0.90	Age 14–18: 8 Over age 18: 10	Age 14–18: 0.89 Over age 18: 0.90	Age 14–18: 8 Over age 18: 10
Fluorine	Age 14–18: 3 Over age 18: 4	10	3	10
Iron	Age 14–18: 11 Over age 18: 8	45	Age 14–18: 15 Age 19–50: 18 Over age 50: 8	45
Manganese	Age 14–18: 2.2 Over age 18: 2.3	Age 14–18: 9 Over age 18: 11	Age 14–18: 1.6 Over age 18: 1.8	Age 14–18: 9 Over age 18: 11
Molybdenum	Age 14–18: 0.043 Over age 18: 0.045	Age 14–18: 1.7 Over age 18: 2.0	Age 14–18: 0.043 Over age 18: 0.045	Age 14–18: 1.7 Over age 18: 2.0
Potassium	4,700	not determined	4,700	not determined
Selenium	0.055	0.4	0.055	0.4
Zinc	11	Age 14–18: 34 Over age 18: 40	Age 14–18: 9 Over age 18: 8	Age 14–18: 34 Over age 18: 40

Exhibit 7j

Food Sources of Minerals

Mineral	Food Sources
Calcium	Broccoli, Chinese cabbage, corn tortillas, dairy products, fortified fruit juice, greens, kale, legumes, milk, salmon, sardines, soy milk
Chloride	Baking soda, baking powder, bread, cheese, eggs, meat, milk, processed food, seafood, table salt, vegetables
Chromium	Brewer's yeast, cheeses, fish, liver, meat, nuts, poultry, whole grains
Copper	Cocoa, legumes, organ meat, nuts, seafood, seeds, wheat bran, whole-grain products
Fluorine	Fluoridated water, legumes, marine fish, organ meat, nuts, seeds, whole grains
Iodine	Iodized salt, seafood, vegetables, small amounts in milk
Iron	Cereals/breads, egg yolks, fish, fruit, greens, legumes, liver, meat, nuts, poultry, enriched or whole grains
Magnesium	Alfalfa, almonds, apples, brown rice, cocoa, figs, greens, lemons, legumes, meat, peaches, nuts, seafood, sesame seeds, soybeans, sunflower seeds, vegetables, whole grains
Manganese	Fruit, nuts, whole grains
Molybdenum	Bread, cereal, grains, nuts
Phosphorus	Cereals, eggs, fish, meat, milk, peas, poultry, whole grains
Potassium	Bananas, citrus fruit, legumes, meat, melons, milk, potatoes, tomatoes, vegetables, whole grains
Selenium	Dairy products, fish, organ meat, poultry, seafood, vegetable, whole grains
Sodium	Table salt, milk, processed food, spinach
Zinc	Enriched cereals, red meat, seafood, whole grains

DASH Eating Plan as a heart-healthy plan. **DASH** stands for Dietary Approaches to Stop Hypertension. The DASH plan is a diet that is low in sodium but high in the other minerals to help normalize blood pressure. The DASH plan is available at *www.nhlbi.nih.gov/ health/public/heart/hbp/dash*. For restaurant and foodservice professionals, effort should be made to utilize as much variety as possible in menu items using food items like those shown in *Exhibit 7k* on the next page, and to keep salt to a minimum in recipes.

Exhibit 7k

Heart-Healthy Food Items

Food low in sodium but rich in other nutrients is important for controlling blood pressure.

Minerals and Bone Health

Minerals work to maintain bone health since bone is constantly being built up and broken down. Calcium is well recognized for its role in healthy bones and teeth; it is also the most common mineral in the body. Phosphorus and magnesium are also present in the bones. Osteoporosis is a disease causing the bones to become porous so they easily fracture. Osteoporosis affects millions of Americans. When an elderly person seems to be losing height, osteoporosis is a possible cause.

Osteoporosis has several risk factors:

- **Gender**—Females are more likely to have osteoporosis than men; however, men do develop it.

- **Age**—The risk of osteoporosis increases with age.

- **Race**—Caucasian and Asian women are at a higher risk.

- **Family history**—A family history of osteoporosis increases risk.

- **Frame size**—Those who have a smaller frame have a higher risk.

- **Medications**—Some medications can increase the development of osteoporosis.

Osteoporosis can be prevented by taking some simple steps:

- **Doing weight-bearing exercise**—Participation in weight-bearing exercise, like jogging or walking, helps build bones.

- **Smoking and drinking less or not at all**—Stopping smoking or drinking alcohol may decrease the risk.

- **Obtaining enough vitamins and minerals**—Consuming the recommended amounts of calcium and vitamin D. If calcium supplements are taken, they should contain vitamin D because it enables calcium to pass through the intestinal wall and into the bloodstream.

Minerals in the Blood

Iron, zinc, and copper are important minerals that form hemoglobin. **Hemoglobin** is the active molecule in red blood cells; it is a protein in the body that carries oxygen through the blood. **Iron-deficiency anemia** occurs when there is a lack of iron in the diet or a problem with absorption of iron in the body resulting in low levels of hemoglobin in the blood. Iron-deficiency anemia causes weakness, irritability, headaches, pale skin, and sensitivity to cold temperature. Iron deficiency is more common in women and children than in men. Iron-deficiency anemia is the most common nutritional deficiency in the world.

Iron comes in two forms in the diet: heme and nonheme. **Heme iron** is iron from animal sources, whereas **nonheme iron** is from vegetarian sources. Heme iron is better absorbed by the body than nonheme iron.

Exhibit 7I

Steaming vegetables preserves vitamins and minerals.

Retaining Vitamins and Minerals When Cooking

If the color of water after boiling a green vegetable is green, there is a good chance that some vitamins were lost. Minimal cooking time helps preserve vitamins and minerals, especially water-soluble vitamins. Steaming, shown in *Exhibit 7I*, is the best process for preserving the vitamin content of vegetables; microwaving and stir-frying are other good methods. It is best not to overcook vegetables so their vitamin and mineral content is preserved. Even rinsing or soaking produce can result in lost vitamins, because the water-soluble vitamins are leached out.

Minerals and fat-soluble vitamins are not as fragile as water-soluble vitamins. However, avoid soaking produce because it will leach out minerals like potassium. Cooking or boiling food for extended periods of time on high heat may destroy vitamins and minerals, so you should keep cooking times to a minimum to maintain the nutritional content. Also, storing food for extended periods of time and simple exposure to air or light can destroy vitamins in food. For example, exposure to light destroys riboflavin. Riboflavin is found in milk products. The amount of light that passes through cardboard cartons, glass, and plastic may result in lost riboflavin.

Supplementation of Vitamins and Minerals

Although it is possible to obtain the needed vitamins and minerals from food in a healthy diet, millions of Americans spend many billions of dollars each year on vitamin and mineral supplements. There are some instances in which vitamin and/or mineral supplements may be needed; however, in healthy adults who are free of chronic diseases and consume varied diets, nothing more than a multivitamin is usually warranted.

Missing Out on Phytochemicals

It is best to obtain essential vitamins and minerals from food because food usually contains fiber and other qualities like phytochemicals. Phytochemicals are compounds found in plant-food items that protect the plant, but they are considered non-nutrients for humans. Although humans technically do not need phytochemicals in their diets and they are not considered essential for life, they may enhance the quality of life. For example, the isoflavones in soy (discussed in Chapter 5) are phytochemicals. Phytochemicals have a strong antioxidant effect, which means they help protect the body from cancer and heart disease. These phytochemicals are not in vitamin and mineral supplements. **Cruciferous vegetables** (broccoli, cauliflower, and cabbage) are potent in phytochemicals. *Exhibit 7m* gives some examples of food items that are known sources of phytochemicals. Actually, most fruit and vegetables contain at least one phytochemical even if they are not listed here. This list is for examples only; it is not complete.

Taking Vitamin and Mineral Supplements

Sometimes, healthy people choose to take a multivitamin as "insurance," to make sure they obtain all the vitamins and minerals they need each day. Supplementing the diet with vitamins and minerals means taking a tablet that usually contains synthetic forms of a single or mixed variety of vitamins and minerals. Vitamin tablets should be taken with a meal or snack to increase absorption; otherwise it is more likely that the vitamin will be excreted into the urine. In other words, it will be wasted and not absorbed.

Exhibit 7m

Some Food Items with Known Phytochemicals

Yellow and orange vegetables

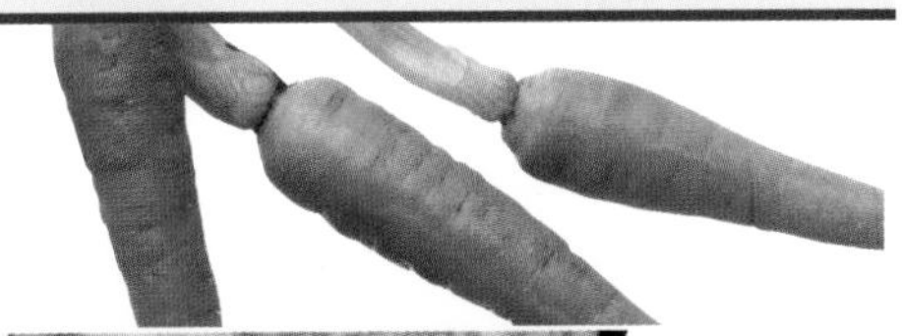

Cruciferous vegetables (broccoli, cauliflower, and cabbage)

Citrus fruit

Onions

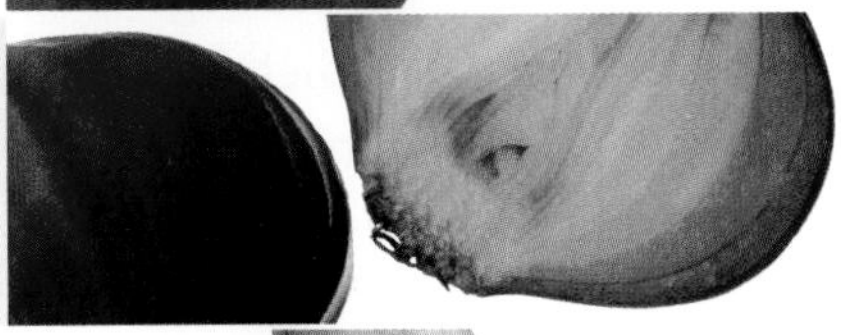

Garlic

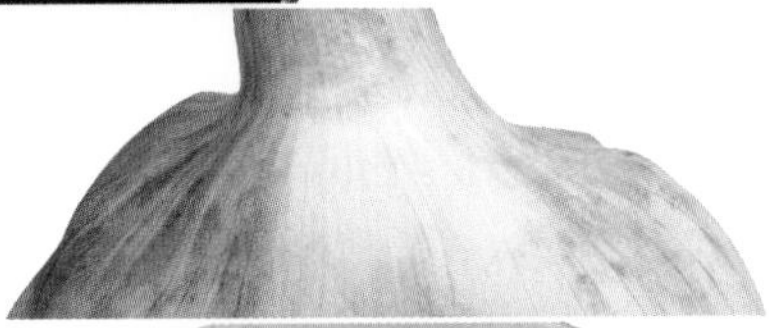

Green tea

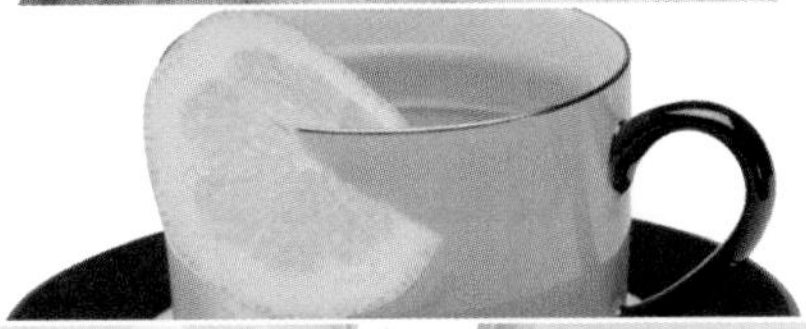

Wine

Soybeans

Leeks

Chives

There are times when the supplementation of vitamins and minerals is necessary. Listed below are the major health conditions that call for vitamin and/or mineral supplementation. Although this is not a complete list, you can see the types of medical conditions that make supplementation necessary.

- **Pregnancy and breast-feeding**—One exception to the general absence of need for supplemental vitamins and minerals is pregnancy and breast-feeding. During these conditions some vitamins and minerals are needed in larger amounts. For example, the B vitamin folic acid (or folate) is important for the prevention of neural tube defects mentioned earlier in this chapter. Spina bifida and cleft palate are examples of birth defects that result from inadequate folate intake during pregnancy. Folic acid is added to prenatal vitamins for women whose intake is suboptimal and, therefore, puts the fetus at risk. The mineral iron is usually supplemented during pregnancy and breast-feeding as well.

- **Iron-deficiency anemia**—Another exception that results in a need for mineral supplementation is iron-deficiency anemia.

Those with iron-deficiency anemia lack sufficient iron in the blood. When a person is diagnosed with this disease, the physician may prescribe a daily iron tablet. Iron supplements should be taken only if prescribed by a physician; excess iron can be harmful.

■ **Low-calorie diets and chronic dieting**—People who diet frequently or otherwise restrict their food consumption may also be restricting their vitamin and mineral intake. These people will benefit from a multivitamin to supply the necessary vitamins and minerals from the food items they are not eating. Those who follow diets that eliminate an entire food group should consider a multivitamin as well.

■ **Osteoporosis**—Calcium and vitamin D supplements are prescribed to people who have osteoporosis or a family history of osteoporosis to help prevent the disease.

■ **Vegan diet**—Vegans are vegetarians who eliminate all animal products from their diet. They should supplement B_{12} because it is only available from animal products. Vitamin D, iron, and zinc also may need to be supplemented by vegans. See Chapter 5 for more information about vegan and other vegetarian diets.

■ **Lacking intrinsic factor**—Intrinsic factor is a chemical made in the intestines that facilitates the absorption of vitamin B_{12}. There is a rare genetic disorder in which people lack intrinsic factor, but a more common instance of lacking intrinsic factor happens during the aging process, at which time an elderly person may lose the ability to produce intrinsic factor and become deficient in vitamin B_{12}. Some types of abdominal surgery may also impact the ability to process B_{12}. These instances would involve obtaining a B_{12} injection from a doctor for direct absorption into the blood stream, not a vitamin pill.

Potential for Toxicity

If a person consumes more calories than needed, the calories are stored as fat. In a similar way, consuming more vitamins or minerals does not mean better health and may actually be detrimental to health. For example, vitamin A toxicity can cause a skin rash as well as hair loss, bone problems, birth defects, and even death.

It is difficult to obtain toxic levels of vitamins and minerals from food sources. Usually, attaining a toxic level of a vitamin or mineral is the result of unnecessary or excessive supplementation resulting in more than 100 percent of the RDA for that nutrient. This could be because the supplement contains more than 100 percent or because the supplement was taken more than once each day.

The Tolerable Upper Limit (UL) is the amount of a vitamin or mineral that the body can tolerate. Some vitamins and minerals are beneficial up to a certain dosage, and at a higher level they are toxic to the body and have the potential to cause harm. The UL is set for some vitamins and minerals; they are listed in *Exhibit 7g* on page 129 and *Exhibit 7i* on page 132.

Because the fat-soluble vitamins are stored in adipose tissue, they are more likely to be toxic at excessive levels. Two water-soluble vitamins, B_6 and B_{12}, also have potential for storage and, therefore, are more likely to become toxic than the other water-soluble vitamins.

Water in the Diet

Water is the most abundant and important macronutrient in the body. It makes up about 50 to 70 percent of body weight and is essential for life. Water has many important roles in the body— it not only keeps you hydrated but helps regulate body temperature, transport nutrients, is part of all cells, hydrates the skin, lubricates joints, and facilitates digestion, absorption, and excretion.

A thirsty feeling is the body's way of telling a person that it does not have enough water. The body must be **hydrated** (contain enough water) for proper operation. This section examines the nutritional role of water in the body.

A lack of water in the body causes dehydration (too little water in the body's cells and fluids), and too much water can cause water intoxication, a rare condition in which there is too much water in the body causing a shift in the amount of water in body cells. Both dehydration and water intoxication can be life threatening. A rapid weight loss might be a sign of dehydration whereas a rapid weight gain could be water intoxication. Consuming too much water at a time is dangerous and may prove fatal.

Water Requirements

Your body requires somewhere between 1.0 milliliters to 1.5 milliliters of water per calorie consumed. For a person on a 2,000-calorie diet, this equals the equivalent of about eight glasses (like the one shown in *Exhibit 7n* on the next page) at eight ounces each (for a total of sixty-four ounces) every day. This is the requirement for total daily water from all sources: food, beverages, and drinking water. Of course, there are times when more water may be necessary, such as during athletics or when sweating. Most people get enough water by letting thirst be their guide.

Exhibit 7n

Consuming sufficient water is essential for life and well being.

The amount of water to be obtained through drinking depends on the amount of fluid that comes from food items consumed because fluid from other liquids and food items counts toward this goal for water consumption. For example, if a person consumes several servings of fruit and vegetables daily, he or she can drink less because these food items contain a significant amount of water. In the opposite case, a person who consumes cheese and meat frequently must drink more water because these food items contain less water. When planning a menu, liquids should be available at each meal. Drinking water can be included at the table with each individual place setting, and watery drinks like soda and milk are significant sources of water in the diet. However, although soda contains water, consuming sixty-four ounces of soda would not be healthy because of the amount of sugar and caffeine it may contain. Beverages that contain alcohol or caffeine may actually increase a person's daily need for fluids because these chemicals are **dehydrating** (reducing the available water by chemically tying it up). Additionally, alcohol contains calories but no other nutrients.

Hard and Soft Water

Hard water contains large amounts of minerals like calcium, magnesium, and sulfur; **soft water** contains minerals but in a smaller amount. The distinction is mostly related to the interaction of soap with these minerals. In hard water, the soap reacts with the hard water's minerals instead of being used for cleaning. Softened water is hard water that has had these minerals removed through a chemical process in a purification facility or water softener; it usually contains extra sodium or other minerals instead of the ones that make the water hard. Additionally, soft or softened water can dissolve lead from pipes. Hard water has more minerals but has the possibility of containing lead, especially in older pipes. Running cold water minimizes the amount of total lead in the hard water from the tap. Consequently, restaurant and foodservice operations should run the cold water for a few minutes at the start of each day to remove the possibility that lead collected in the water while it was standing in the pipes.

Summary

Vitamins, minerals, and water are essential to the human diet. Each vitamin has one or more specific functions and can be obtained from specific food sources. Vitamins are classified as either water-soluble or fat-soluble vitamins. The fat-soluble vitamins are important for human health for many reasons: vitamin A facilitates vision, vitamin D is necessary for bone health, vitamin E acts as an antioxidant, and vitamin K helps prevent blood clotting. Among the water-soluble vitamins, the B vitamins act primarily as coenzymes for energy metabolism, and vitamin C acts as an antioxidant in the body. Deficiencies and toxicities of vitamins are possible, and some are serious.

The word "mineral" refers to chemical elements in the diet. Several elements are necessary for a variety of functions, and a deficiency in a needed mineral results in a deficiency disease. Deficiencies of the minerals potassium, calcium, and magnesium may contribute to the incidence of high blood pressure. Calcium is well recognized for its role in healthy bones and teeth. Iron, zinc, and copper are important minerals that form hemoglobin.

There are established intake levels for vitamins and minerals, and obtaining too much can be a problem. Supplementation of vitamins and minerals may be warranted for specific people to avoid deficiencies, and some people choose to take a multivitamin each day to ensure receiving all of the needed vitamins and minerals. However, it is best to obtain vitamins and minerals from food sources because of the added benefits from fiber and phytochemicals in food. There are ways to minimize vitamin and mineral losses when cooking.

Water, the most important nutrient in the body, has several important functions that are necessary for health. The average-sized adult should have sixty-four ounces of water each day from food and liquids combined. Consuming a variety of food items from all of the food groups helps attain the recommended dietary allowance for vitamins, minerals, and water in your diet.

Activity

Your Vitamins and Minerals

How are you doing at achieving the Recommended Dietary Allowance for vitamins and minerals? Keep a log of what you actually eat, then analyze your diet on the MyPyramid Web site.

1. Keep an exact log of what you eat for several days or a week. Include everything at every meal and all snacks.

2. Go to *www.MyPyramidTracker.gov* and then click on the Assess Your Food Intake link.

3. Either log in or create a new login.

4. If you haven't already done so, fill out your personal profile. Be honest; no one will see it. Set the Entry Date field to the first day of your diet log.

5. Save your profile, and then click on Proceed to Food Intake.

6. In the Enter Food Item panel, type in the name of your first food item and click on the Search button.

7. Locate the best matching food item and click on the Add button; the item will appear in the right column. If no item is correct, try naming the food more generically and try again.

8. Repeat steps 6 and 7 until all the food items for the first day have been entered.

9. Click on the Select Quantity button in the right column.

10. For each item, select the serving size, and then select the number of servings.

11. Click on the Save and Analyze button to display a menu page.

12. Select the Nutrient Intakes link to display a table of the nutrients in the food you ate. Print this page.

13. If there are more days in your diet log, click on the Update Profile button at the top of the page.

14. Change the date to the next day of your log and repeat steps 5–13.

15. When you have completed each day in the log, click on the Calculate Nutrient History at the bottom of the nutrient table page.

16. The Healthy Eating History page opens displaying your energy (calorie) history.

17. Click on the 1 Week link at the top of the page to display a graph for this nutrient. Print this page.

18. Click on each of the nutrient type links at the left to display your eating history for each nutrient type. Print each page.

19. Write a report comparing your actual intake to the RDA for each vitamin and mineral. Be sure to determine whether you are getting enough or too much.

Review Your Learning

1 All of the following about fat-soluble vitamins and water-soluble vitamins are true *except*

A. water-soluble vitamins are soluble in water but not in fat.

B. water-soluble vitamins are stored in the body.

C. fat-soluble vitamins are soluble in fat but not in water.

D. fat-soluble vitamins are stored in the body.

2 The vitamin that is available only from meat and, therefore, should be supplemented in the diets of vegans is

A. vitamin A.   C. vitamin B_{12}.

B. vitamin C.   D. vitamin E.

3 The primary function of vitamin B_1 (thiamin), vitamin B_2 (riboflavin), and vitamin B_3 (niacin) is

A. to enable normal vision and normal cell development in the body.

B. as a coenzyme for energy metabolism.

C. as an antioxidant.

D. to enable blood clotting.

4 The primary function of vitamin C (ascorbic acid) is

A. to enable normal vision and normal cell development in the body.

B. as a coenzyme for energy metabolism.

C. as an antioxidant.

D. to enable blood clotting.

5 Good food sources for the mineral phosphorus are all of the following *except*

A. almonds.   C. eggs.

B. cereals.   D. meat.

6 A good food source for vitamin B_{12} is

A. leafy green vegetables.

B. rice.

C. milk.

D. meat.

7 The mineral calcium is used for all of the following body functions *except*

A. as an antioxidant.

B. for bone health.

C. to help maintain normal blood pressure.

D. to enable muscle contraction.

8 Water has all of the following functions in the body *except*

A. lubricating joints.

B. maintaining body temperature.

C. transporting nutrients.

D. as a coenzyme for energy metabolism.

9 To retain vitamin and mineral content during cooking you should

A. minimize cooking time.

B. bake food.

C. fry food.

D. soak food items in water before cooking.

10 The most common nutritional deficiency in the world is

A. osteoporosis.

B. iron-deficiency anemia.

C. obesity.

D. degeneration of the retina.

Notes

Food with Nutritional Appeal

8

Inside This Chapter

- Growing Nutritious Food
- Harvesting, Transporting, and Processing Nutritious Food
- Receiving, Storing, and Preparing Nutritious Food
- Cooking Nutritious Food

After completing this chapter, you should be able to:

- Explain how the steps in the food-processing system affect nutritional content.
- Distinguish between organic, certified organic, natural, local, and conventional produce.
- Define genetically modified and bioengineered food products.
- List and explain processing and cooking techniques that can help to retain nutrients in food.

Test Your Knowledge

1. **True or False:** Organic produce always has more nutrients than conventional produce. *(See p. 150.)*

2. **True or False:** Processed vegetables are of poorer nutritional quality than fresh vegetables. *(See p. 153.)*

3. **True or False:** Quickly cooking vegetables helps to retain important nutrients. *(See pp. 156–157.)*

4. **True or False:** Food products containing genetically modified organisms must indicate that fact on the label. *(See p. 151.)*

5. **True or False:** Genetically modified food products have been proven harmful for human consumption. *(See p. 151.)*

Key Terms

Antibiotic

Bioengineering

Biotechnology

Blanch

Certified organic food
    product

Chemical loss

Conventional food
    product

Crossbreeding

Food irradiation

Freeze-drying

Genetically modified
    organism (GMO)

Harvesting

Herbicide

Hybrid plant

In season

Local produce

Organic food product

Pan-steaming

Pesticide

Physical loss

Recombinant DNA
    technology

Seasonal produce

Selective breeding

Sous vide

Transgenic GMO

Think About It...

A customer enters your establishment and asks if your food products contain genetically modified organisms. How do you respond?

Introduction

Making healthy choices as a consumer and providing healthy menu items to guests is an important start in improving health. You have learned in previous chapters some factors that promote a healthy diet and food choices that are good for people. This chapter represents an important turning point in the text as you move from learning *about* these various food products to learning techniques of incorporating them into your profession. Some of these factors, like retaining nutrients when cooking vegetables or buying seasonal local produce, are within your realm of control as restaurant and foodservice professionals. Others, such as growing, shipping, storing,

Exhibit 8a

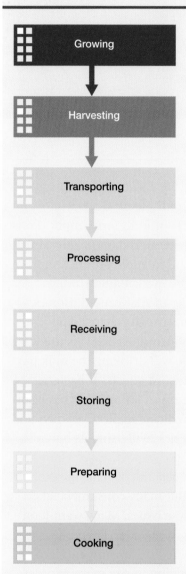

Stages of Food's Journey

- Growing
- Harvesting
- Transporting
- Processing
- Receiving
- Storing
- Preparing
- Cooking

and processing techniques, may be more challenging to control or even to understand. The central question then becomes: as a restaurant or foodservice operator, how do you know that the food that goes onto plates is wholesome and nutritious? And similarly, how can you *ensure* that the food you serve is wholesome and nutritious?

In this chapter you will consider eight key stages in the journey food takes from farm to fork: growing, harvesting, transporting, processing, receiving, storing, preparing, and cooking. (See *Exhibit 8a.*) In each stage you will explore some factors that can ensure that food reaches the consumer in a nutritious state. You will also explore one special case in food production, genetic modification, and its ethical and nutritional implications for you as a restaurant or foodservice professional.

Growing Nutritious Food

Some operators feel they have little control over agriculture and the nature of the food that arrives in the delivery trucks. While it is certainly a challenge to ensure high nutritional content of the food you serve, your ultimate responsibility as a restaurant or foodservice professional is to do as much as possible to ensure that the food you serve is wholesome and nutritious. To do so, it is important to be familiar with the food you are serving, even at its earliest stages. Decisions made by the farmer, fisherman, or other producer have implications for your guests' health in the weeks, months, or even years to follow.

As an extreme illustration, consider the cases of mercury poisoning in the fishing village of Minamata, Japan, in the 1960s. Pollution from a local factory caused infant mortality, birth defects, and brain damage to individuals who ate fish from Minamata Bay. Though the first known deaths and protests about the tainted bay began in 1956, dumping of mercury and other contaminants continued until 1968. How many restaurant and foodservice operators do you think unknowingly sold tainted fish from Minamata Bay during this time? What was the role and responsibility of the operator in this instance?

Ideally, the food you serve will be safe and wholesome, but guests still are concerned about the food that enters their bodies. Some agricultural tools of particular concern to consumers are: **pesticides** (chemicals that kill insects and other plant pests); **herbicides** (weed killers); hormones being injected into animals; **antibiotics** (medicines that prevent infection); **genetically modified organisms (GMOs)** (plants or animals whose genetic makeup has been altered),

Exhibit 8b

Genetically modified organisms   Hormones   Herbicides

Decisions made in growing food affect nutrients.

and feed made from animal products. (See *Exhibit 8b.*) Many guests worry that the presence or application of these products in producing food will have negative short- or long-term implications for their own health. For example, the chemical daminozide, also called Alar, was commonly used as an aid in apple production from 1963 to 1989. It was withdrawn from the market after studies showed that exposing mice to high doses of Alar caused tumors. Some of the products currently used in agriculture are being similarly questioned. If bovine growth hormone (BGH) is used to cause dairy cows to produce more milk, will drinking the milk pass the hormone to people's bodies and cause ill affects? If bacteria become resistant to antibiotics, will eating an animal that has been given an antibiotic render that same medicine ineffective when it is prescribed for humans? If an animal is sick, will using its bones in animal feed cause other animals to get the same disease? These are compelling questions to consumers. In general, conclusive research studies and clear-cut answers are few. But many consumers take a "better safe than sorry" approach to these issues. Many want food produced without the use of pesticides, herbicides, hormone injections, antibiotics, genetically modified organisms, and feed made from animal products, and are willing to pay more in order to eat these items.

As a restaurant or foodservice professional, you have some responsibility in providing good quality food for consumers, and the decisions you make can help your operation to serve healthier food and satisfy customers' wants.

Pesticides · Feed · Antibiotics

Organic Food Products

Many consumers and restaurant and foodservice operators are beginning to choose organic food products, and as a professional, it is important that you know what this means. It is crucial to make a distinction between conventional, natural, organic, and certified organic food products. **Conventional food products** are those grown using approved agricultural methods. In the United States, such methods are studied by the United States Department of Agriculture (USDA) and the Food and Drug Administration (FDA). The approved methods allow for the use of certain fertilizers, pesticides, hormones, and drugs that are recognized as safe. Most of the food in the supermarket and from foodservice purveyors comes from conventional producers. Natural food products, to many consumers, connote wholesome, healthy, or environmentally friendly images. While this may be true, the term "natural" is legally meaningless. Nearly any food can be called "natural." Similarly, an **organic food product** label implies that the food product is produced without pesticides or synthetic fertilizers, but this definition varies by country. **Certified organic food products** meet the requirements of a particular certifying agency, such as a government agency or an independent organization. These certifiers typically require that no pesticides or synthetic fertilizers be used and, in most cases, that the food has not been genetically modified. Each certifying body has slightly different requirements, and there is no universally accepted standard for certified organic food.

A common misperception about organic food products is that they contain more nutrients than conventionally grown food. Another is that organic food products are produced by small producers and conventional food products by large producers. Actually, both large and small producers grow organic and conventional food products, and the finished food products are quite similar nutritionally. Of concern to food professionals should be preserving these nutrients throughout the journey from farm to fork.

Genetically Modified Food

Genetically modified food organisms need a special mention in any discussion about contemporary agriculture. Genetically modified organisms (GMOs) are plants or animals whose genetic makeup has been altered using **recombinant DNA technology.** As the name suggests, this technology allows the DNA, the genetic code, of an organism to be combined with part of another DNA code, typically from another organism as shown in *Exhibit 8c.* This results in the genetic code of the receiving plant or animal being changed, with the change becoming permanent. Also, the change is transmitted to the offspring of the plant or animal. **Transgenic GMOs** are those where the DNA of one species is implanted in another.

There are a number of reasons a scientist or food producer may choose to genetically modify an organism. Genetically modified plants may be better able to resist pests like insects, weeds, or fungi; may have improved nutritional value; may be able to withstand extreme heat, cold, or drought; or, most commonly, may resist specific herbicides or pesticides. This last category is of special concern to consumers. If a plant, such as soybeans, is resistant to a specific herbicide, then the field may be sprayed with that herbicide to kill the weeds. However, this leaves the soybean plants intact but with herbicide on them. Consumer concern may lie as much with the spray used to kill the weeds that remain on the beans as with the modified soybeans.

It is important to distinguish genetically modified food products from the general categories of biotechnology and bioengineering in food, as well as from traditional crossbreeding or selective breeding methods. **Biotechnology** and **bioengineering** are simply the applications of technology to living organisms in order to produce something of use. This

Exhibit 8c

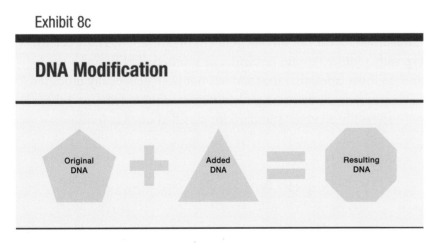

DNA Modification

Original DNA + Added DNA = Resulting DNA

definition includes not only genetic modification but also the use of biological organisms in the production of wine, cheese, and yogurt, for example. In a general sense, humans have been modifying the genetics of plants and animals for generations by using crossbreeding and selective breeding, which are considered natural methods of bioengineering. In **crossbreeding,** different varieties of plants or animals exhibiting favorable characteristics are bred together to produce offspring with the best qualities of each species. **Hybrid plants** are a common example of crossbreeding. **Selective breeding** occurs when the best plants of the harvest or the best animals of the herd are selected for reproduction. The difference between crossbreeding and selective breeding and GMOs are that genetic modifications are considered "forced" or artificial because:

- GMO modifications have been done by scientists on a cellular scale.

- The differences between the original and modified products can be both quick and dramatic with GMO.

From a nutritional standpoint, genetically modified food products are comparable to unmodified food products. In fact, some may have been modified to increase the presence of certain micronutrients. There is no conclusive evidence that genetically modified food products are harmful to people's health.

Consumer Concerns

Consumers have raised objections to the use of genetically modified organisms in food, and some countries do not allow GMOs in food at all. There are a number of reasons for these concerns. As a relatively new technology, consumers worry about the long-term environmental and health effects of eating these food products. Consumers are often concerned that a genetically modified organism could have a gene from another organism that they do not eat because of allergenic, moral, or other reasons. Consumers are further concerned that they do not know when they are eating GMOs. While the European Union and Japan require labeling of genetically modified food products or products containing GMOs, the United States, Canada, and many other nations do not.

Harvesting, Transporting, and Processing Nutritious Food

Harvesting is the process of gathering crops to bring them to market. Like growing, this stage of the food system is largely removed from the control of the typical chef or restaurant manager.

Exhibit 8d

Harvesting starts the deterioration of nutrients in food.

But decisions related to where and how food products are harvested, as well as which of these food products you use, can impact the nutrition of your guests.

As a general rule, a restaurant or foodservice manager should consider that harvested food products, such as a head of broccoli cut from the earth, are decaying tissue that has been separated from the rest of the plant. Similarly, fish, meat, and poultry are decaying once they are killed. (Various types of harvesting are shown in *Exhibit 8d.*) The challenge for the food processor and the restaurant or foodservice professional is to preserve the quality of this food before it becomes unsafe, unpalatable, or nutritionally poor. With each stage of processing, food experiences nutrient loss and in some cases, such as canned meat, fish, and vegetables, the addition of food additives like sodium, nitrites, and preservatives. This nutrient loss may be a **physical loss** (loss of nutrients due to peeling, trimming, processing, and other physical actions) as in the case of processors removing the tough but vitamin- and fiber-rich stems of broccoli when packaging frozen florets, or it may be a **chemical loss** (loss of nutrients due to destruction or transformation of the chemical composition of food) such as a reduced level of vitamin C in a frozen green bean when compared to its fresh counterpart. A good general rule for food like fresh fruit and vegetables is that the longer the food is allowed to grow and the sooner it is eaten after harvest, the more nutritious the item will be. One reason is that after harvest, micronutrients like vitamin C begin to deteriorate. Exposure to sunlight, heat, and long storage times further contribute to nutrient loss.

Transporting Food

Transportation is required to move the food products from where they are harvested to where they are used. Depending on how far apart these locations are, many different forms and steps of transportation may be required. For example, fresh raspberries from Chile in January might have been harvested in Chile's autumn and gone through many transportation steps to arrive in Chicago to be sold. The items might have been hand carried in the field, carried on a wagon to the farm's processing center, taken by truck to the nearest airfield, flown to Chicago, driven to a local distributor, and finally taken to the store or foodservice operation. This is a lot of handling, and during this time, the natural nutrients and sugars in the raspberries are undergoing changes, some good, some not so good.

Using Local Food

Using and serving **local produce** (produce grown near the place of use) is a good way to serve food products that experience little of this loss of quality or nutrients. Since the produce does not have to travel far to market, it can grow for a longer period of time and be quickly used and consumed without long periods of storage or transportation. Even in large cities, access to fresh food products harvested the same day are available to consumers and food professionals. Of course, this is only possible when the food is **in season** (the period when the food product is harvested), which is why **seasonal produce** (produce that is in season locally) is another means of serving nutritious food. In general, produce that is in season is cheaper, tastier, and more nutritious than produce that is not in season locally and needs to be trucked, shipped, or flown long distances to market. Of course, any source of food products must be safe, even locally grown food; be sure to use only food sources that are certified safe, such as those with a GAP (good agricultural practices) certification.

Food Processing

Of course, depending on the location of the operation, time of year, budget, and needs of the guest, fresh, local produce may prove challenging or impossible to serve. It is now possible to ship fresh food worldwide, and formerly inconceivable possibilities such as fresh raspberries in winter in Chicago are now available (though at a higher monetary and environmental cost). A number of alternatives to fresh produce are available, including frozen, canned, and dried food. From a nutritional perspective, these food products often are comparable to fresh food products.

In addition to the usual processing methods of freezing and canning, there are several special processing techniques in use. **Food irradiation,** treating food with ionizing radiation, can reduce or eliminate bacteria and parasites that cause foodborne illness. Irradiation also inhibits sprouting and mold growth. In addition, irradiation can sometimes be used in place of fumigation with chemicals to eliminate insect pests. Food irradiation does not change the nutritional value of the food nor does it make the food radioactive or dangerous to eat. Food that has been irradiated is stored, handled, and cooked in the same way as untreated food.

Another processing method is **freeze-drying.** This process removes all the moisture from food to prevent spoilage. In freeze-drying, a freeze-drying machine first freezes the food to turn the water in the food to ice. Then the air pressure within the machine is lowered so the ice changes directly into water vapor. When the food is sufficiently dry, it is packaged in water-proof pouches. Freeze-dried food retains its nutrients and can be stored for a long time. The food is restored to its original form with the addition of water.

Sous vide, French for "under vacuum," is another food-processing method that utilizes vacuum packaging. In this technique, fresh ingredients are used to create a dish. The food is vacuum-packed in a pouch, slowly cooked in a vacuum, and then chilled or flash-frozen. This method reduces food shrinkage and preserves nutrients and flavor. Because the food is fully cooked, *sous vide* food is ready to heat and serve.

Speaking in general terms, the more processing a food undergoes, the less nutritional value it contains. When preservatives like sodium and nitrates are added, as they are with preserved meat, this is definitely the case. But this generalization assumes that the fresh and processed food products are identical at the start. While it may sound odd that a canned tomato can have more nutrients than a fresh one, consider that many food processors locate their processing facilities close to where the food is grown. This means that a tomato harvested today may be canned today, which means that the fruit will be fully ripe and canned immediately after picking. Alternatively, a fresh tomato, especially in an out-of-season location, may have to be picked under-ripe, treated with ethylene gas to force-ripen it, and sent many miles over several days before reaching the consumer.

From a culinary perspective, various food products respond differently to processing, and many food items are able to retain excellent quality and flavor. In the kitchens of even the best restaurants are canned tomatoes and fish; frozen berries, corn, and peas; and dried mushrooms and beans.

Receiving, Storing, and Preparing Nutritious Food

The steps of receiving, storage, and preparation also affect the nutritional value of food products, mostly in a negative way. However, the use of proper procedures can minimize the loss of nutrients.

Receiving

Once the food enters the establishment, the role of the restaurant or foodservice professional in maintaining the nutritional value of the food is critical. Since long storage times and warm temperatures can compromise both the safety and the nutritional value of the food products, frozen products should be received frozen. Meat, fish and poultry must be received at 41°F (5°C) or lower. Food products like onions, potatoes, and dry goods can be received at room temperature and should be clean and dry. Fruit and vegetables should be free from insect infestation, mold, cuts, discoloration and dull appearance, and unpleasant odors and tastes. A general rule is that the produce should feel heavy for its size and be free from wilting and wrinkling.

Storage

Over time, the nutritional value and the safety of food deteriorate because the food can dry, become susceptible to rot, or grow mold or fungus. The best way to prevent such deterioration is to maintain a low inventory of food products that are susceptible to this and utilize a quick turnaround system. As a general rule, order only what you need in short term, and when possible, opt for frequent, smaller deliveries rather than large, infrequent orders. Also, it is critical that you maintain proper storage temperatures, a cool room temperature for dry goods, 41°F (5°C) for refrigeration, and 0°F (−18°C) temperatures suitable for keeping frozen food frozen.

Exhibit 8e

Food should be prepared as close to serving time as possible in order to retain the maximum amount of nutrients.

Preparation

Fresh fruit and vegetables should be prepared as close to service as possible in order to preserve quality and nutrition. (See *Exhibit 8e.*) Advance preparation can cause oxidation and reduce the amounts of important micronutrients such as vitamin C, which can leach out of the food. While it may be convenient to wash, cut, and **blanch** (boil lightly in advance) vegetables well before service, or to cut and wash salad ingredients and other vegetables, with each process and application of water, the nutritional quality of the food diminishes slightly.

Cooking Nutritious Food

Cooking is the area where a responsible cook or restaurant manager can make a tremendous difference in serving nutritionally sound or nutritionally poor food. Some food products, like rice, yucca, grains, and dry beans, must be cooked in order to make their nutrients available to the body. For example, when carbohydrates like the starch in these food items cook, they absorb water and gelatinize, making them palatable and also nutritious. Others, like fresh fruit and vegetables, are best eaten raw in order to obtain the maximum nutrients.

The key to cooking nutritious food is to manage time and temperature so that food is cooked only as much as necessary and is served as soon as possible. The longer the food sits on the stove or in the steam table, the less nutrition will be available to the guest. Multistage cooking such as precooking vegetables, shocking them in water, chilling until service, reheating at service, and storing in a steam table may be useful from a timing perspective, but it also causes the nutritional value of the food to decrease markedly.

Cooking Meat, Fish, and Poultry

Meat, fish, and poultry are at their best and most healthful when served close to the time they are cooked. Other ways to optimize the flavor and nutritive qualities in these food products are to grill, broil, steam, bake, poach, or sauté them, and then serve immediately. (See *Exhibit 8f.*) Tough cuts are best when slowly cooked by either braising or using in a soup or stew. They should be served with the broth, which is a good way to retain some of the nutrients lost in the cooking process. Cooking meat or vegetables in an iron pan can be additionally useful by adding iron to the diet.

When cooking meat, fish and poultry, the protein in the flesh coagulates when heat is applied. With tender food like fish, shellfish and chicken breasts, the protein coagulation as well as proper temperature indicates doneness. For tougher meat, the initial protein coagulation is only one step in the cooking process. When moisture is added, the tough connective tissue in the meat can break down to form gelatin. In addition, fat in the meat slowly melts, or renders, during the cooking process; this adds flavor and moistness. As you learned in Chapter 6, when adding fats to a dish, choose monounsaturated fats over saturated fats when possible and when consistent with the desired flavor of the dish. Avoid reusing cooking oil because the fat becomes rancid and unhealthy with overuse.

Exhibit 8f

Nutrient-Preserving Cooking Methods

Type of Food	Cooking Method
Fresh fruit, vegetables	None (serve raw); pan-steamed
Meat, fish, poultry	Quick cooking by grilling, broiling, steaming, baking, poaching, or sautéing and then serving immediately
Tough meat, poultry	Braising or in a soup or stew and served with the broth

Cooking Fruit and Vegetables

Fruit and vegetables should be served raw where appropriate. When cooking, cook quickly in minimal liquid and serve immediately with the cooking liquid where possible. Steaming in the microwave or on the stove by pan-steaming are ideal methods. **Pan-steaming** is done by placing the vegetable in a sauté pan with a bit of water or stock, then covering and cooking over high heat until the vegetable is tender but not soft.

Another way to maintain the maximum amount of nutrients is to season lightly. One common, but not advisable, practice is to add baking soda to enhance the color of green vegetables. While this works for color, it destroys the texture of the vegetable and the fragile vitamin C. Frying can be similarly damaging to vitamin C and other nutrients and of course, it adds fat to the dish.

Activity

Revise for Nutrition Effectiveness

Consider the Buffalo chicken salad menu item from Jon's Pub. Reading the description below, revise this dish and its preparation to make it safer and more nutritionally sound.

■ Three days before service: Food received from supplier.

■ Forty-eight hours before service: Lettuce washed and cut, stored in refrigerator. Tomatoes and cucumbers washed and cut, then stored in ice water in refrigerator.

■ Twenty-four hours before service: Chicken breaded and deep-fried, then chilled.

■ Twelve hours before service: Sauces made.

■ Six hours before service: Vegetables drained from ice water and placed on service counter.

■ Four hours before service: Chicken placed on service counter.

■ Three hours before service: Buffalo sauce and bleu cheese dressing placed on service counter.

■ Two hours before service: Salad (lettuce, cucumber, tomato) tossed with bleu cheese dressing.

■ At service: Chicken reheated briefly in deep-fryer. Salad assembled. Chicken taken from fryer basket to sauce, then put on top of salad and served.

_____

_____

_____

_____

_____

_____

_____

Summary

Consumers and food professionals are increasingly concerned with what goes into their food. Often their concerns have to do with how the food products are grown or harvested. They also relate to decisions made by restaurant and foodservice professionals such as sources of supply, types of food used, condition when received, and on-site storage and processing of food products.

Serving organic and local food products, buying seasonally, and if fresh is unavailable, using processed produce are ways to purchase food with good nutrition. Once in house, food should be stored under the appropriate conditions, prepared just before service, and cooked quickly with minimal holding to ensure nutritional quality.

Each point in the food system—growing, harvesting, processing, receiving, storing, preparing, and cooking—leaves the restaurant and foodservice professional with an opportunity to preserve the nutritional quality of the food at hand or cause it to deteriorate. Exposure to the air and to high temperatures, and natural decaying processes cause deterioration of the nutrients in food products. Minimizing all these factors is necessary for food products to arrive at the stove or table with the maximum amount of nutrients.

Review Your Learning

1 All of the following negatively affect the nutritional content of food *except*

A. growing food using pesticides and herbicides.

B. using fresh food products that are out of season.

C. letting newly received food sit on the receiving dock for a long time.

D. serving uncooked or minimally cooked food products.

2 Certified organic food products typically have all the following characteristics *except*

A. they are free from pesticides.

B. they are not genetically modified.

C. they are free from synthetic fertilizers.

D. they are higher in nutrients.

3 Which technique should Chef Emma use to prepare her green beans in the most nutritionally sound manner?

A. Blanch, shock, and reheat

B. Microwave, steam, and serve

C. Boil

D. Sauté

4 All of the following are advantages of using seasonal local produce *except*

A. cheaper.   C. organic.

B. more nutritious.   D. tastier.

5 Which is usually true of organic produce?

A. It is grown by small farmers.

B. It has more vitamins than conventional produce.

C. It is grown using natural fertilizer.

D. It is grown from pesticide-resistant crops.

6 Which is *not* a reason why genetically modified food products are being grown?

A. Consumer preference

B. Improved nutritional value

C. Frost resistance

D. Herbicide resistance

7 Which are reasons consumers are concerned about eating genetically modified food products?

A. Proven health risks

B. Potential allergic reaction

C. Lack of nutrients

D. All of the above

8 All of the following results in vitamin C deterioration *except*

A. frying.

B. cutting and storing in ice water.

C. growing.

D. storage.

9 All of the following cooking methods are appropriate for a tough cut of meat *except*

A. pan-steaming.   C. braising.

B. stewing.   D. soup.

10 All of the following are nutritionally sound serving techniques *except*

A. daily deliveries of fresh food products.

B. cooking vegetables until just tender.

C. serving raw fruit and vegetables.

D. cutting salad vegetables in advance.

159

Notes

Cooking and Eating More Healthfully

After completing this chapter, you should be able to:

- Explain techniques that can boost the flavor of food in a healthy way.

- Explain the importance of food's sensory appeal in promoting healthy eating.

- List and describe techniques for food preparation that preserve nutrients.

- Describe how common food preparations may be modified for improved nutrition.

- Explain techniques to lower the fat content of food.

Test Your Knowledge

1. **True or False:** A good way to reduce the calorie content of food is to substitute oil for butter. *(See p. 177.)*

2. **True or False:** Meat, fish, and poultry are the center-of-plate items around which a menu item must be based. *(See p. 170.)*

3. **True or False:** A plate featuring a variety of bright, colorful vegetables may be an indicator of a nutritious dish. *(See p. 171.)*

4. **True or False:** When baking, substitute prune purée or applesauce for fat to produce an identical product. *(See p. 179.)*

5. **True or False:** Many artificial sweeteners are sweeter than sugar. *(See p. 164.)*

Key Terms

Aspartame	Infused oil	Saccharin
Baking	*Jus*	Slurry
Barbecuing	Maillard reaction	Smoke-roasting
Braising	Mother sauce	Steaming
Broiling	Oven-frying	Stewing
Center-of-plate concept	Papillae	Stir-frying
Coulis	Poaching	Sucralose
Dry-sautéing	Purée	Sweat
Emulsion sauce	Reduction sauce	Umami
En papillote	Roasting	Wheat berry
Grilling	Roux	

Think About It...

Why can't you taste food when you have a stuffy nose from a head cold?

Introduction

As people become more health conscientious they demand more nutritious options at the dining table. In Chapter 8 you learned about steps you can take to ensure your operation is choosing and serving guests wholesome, nutritious food. Yet you also must recognize that if your operation does not serve nutritious menu items that taste good, your customers will begin to look elsewhere for their meals, regardless of your focus on healthy alternatives.

Exhibit 9a

Nutritious food should appeal to all the senses, not just be good for you.

It takes the combined skills of nutrition and cooking to make nutritious food that tastes good. The chefs in your operation must have a good understanding of healthful cooking techniques to provide your guests with tasty food that is lower in fat and salt. They must also understand the concepts of taste and aroma to tantalize the appetite. Plate presentation is equally important and must consider color, balance, texture, and architecture, as illustrated by the dish in *Exhibit 9a*.

In this chapter you will look more carefully at the actual food being cooked and served. You will learn:

- How people perceive taste

- Some tricks or techniques you can employ to make the food you cook and eat healthier

- Which of these changes have minimal affect on food quality and palatability

- Which of these changes will be unacceptable to consumers

- How you can lower fat, refined carbohydrates, and/or calories while increasing the flavor impact of a dish

By using more nutritious cooking techniques, a little food science, and flavor principles, any operation can be successful at meeting both the flavor and nutritional needs of its customers.

How People Taste Food

The perception of taste is a combination of aroma, genetics, emotions, traditions and culture, geography, and religious and philosophical beliefs. While some of these factors—traditions, culture, geography, and religious and philosophical beliefs—are not directly affected by the physical act of tasting, they do influence the willingness to try new food items and the liking or disliking of certain types of food.

In the mouth, there are at least ten thousand taste buds known as **papillae,** the Latin plural of papilla, meaning "on the tongue." These little organs also are found on the sides and roof of the mouth and at the back of the throat, letting people know if they like a particular taste or not. There are many small papillae at the tip and sides of the tongue, while the papillae towards the back of the tongue are larger and more tightly packed. The papillae send a stimulus to the brain identifying the food from a previous experience of eating the same item. This stimulus combined with the smell of the food creates the sensation of taste.

Exhibit 9b

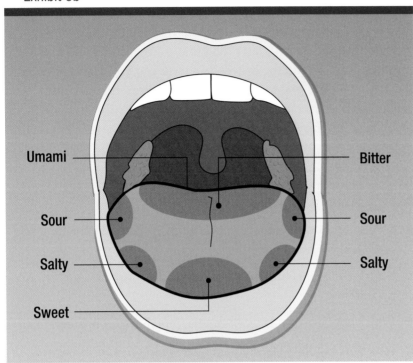

The taste buds on the tongue are somewhat regional.

Taste Buds and Taste

There are only five types of taste cells in the taste buds; the thousands of distinct tastes are distinguished by the combination of taste and aromas. These cells are designated to identify the following primary tastes:

- Sweet
- Salty
- Sour
- Bitter
- Umami

These tastes can be experienced throughout the tongue but are predominately tasted in the areas identified in *Exhibit 9b*.

Sweet

The sweet taste is inherently preferred by humans. It is perceived primarily at the tip of the tongue. A family of sugars from cane, beet, honey, and fructose are strongly experienced. The following chemicals also are identified in this area:

- **Saccharin**—Artificial sweetener containing only one-eighth of a calorie per teaspoon; three hundred times sweeter than sugar. This sweetener sometimes produces a bitter aftertaste, especially when it is used in food items that are heated.

- **Aspartame**—Artificial sweetener made from amino acids; two hundred times sweeter than sugar. This sweetener is best used in cold dishes because it breaks down when heated.

- **Sucralose**—Artificial sweetener that is six hundred times sweeter than sugar. This sweetener is appropriate for use in a wide range of food items and beverages.

The sweet taste is affected by temperature; the colder the temperature, the less the sweet taste is perceived. One example is ice cream. Ice-cream mixes are extremely sweet when first mixed, but as they are frozen, the sweetness is much less noticeable.

Salty

Salt, a seasoning, enhances the flavor of food. It is predominately tasted on the lower sides and lower center of the tongue. Sodium chloride, sodium benzoate, sodium fluoride, and other salt compounds give the impression of salty taste. People can condition their preference for salt to either high or low amounts.

Two common things affect the perceived saltiness of food:

■ **Smoking**—Smokers tend to taste salt less vividly and, therefore, tend to salt food more heavily. Thus, cooks who smoke should be wary of oversalting food.

■ **Temperature**—The temperature of food is a factor in the perception of saltiness; the hotter the food, the less the salt is tasted. A classic example is oversalting soup. The soup is salted when hot; as it cools, the salty taste becomes more predominant. The best temperature range to taste food that is served hot is between 70°F and 105°F (21°C and 41°C); this gives the truest taste of the food.

Sour

Sour (acid) taste is detected on the sides of the tongue toward the back. Food such as citrus, wines, oxalic acids from spinach, rhubarb, and other leafy greens, and vinegars give that sharp sensation called sour. The skilled chef will learn to use sour to balance and enhance flavor. The use of acid in recipes can trick the tongue into thinking there is more salt than is actually present—so before reaching for the salt shaker, try a squeeze of lemon or lime juice.

Bitter

Nature has provided humans with a safety net against ingesting food poisons: the taste of bitter. Poisonous alkaloidal food is most associated with the bitter taste. The human taste-sensory system has evolved to alert people to this taste. The many bitter-sensing papillae are large in order to detect poisonous alkaloids and to stop people from swallowing food that is unsafe to eat.

Food items and components such as Brussels sprouts, spinach, chocolate, caffeine, saccharin, and quinine contain alkaloid compounds, giving a bitter astringent taste. These types of food items also have chemical compounds that are antioxidants. There has been discussion of genetically modifying these types of food to remove the bitter taste, but this would also remove the antioxidants.

Umami

Umami, recently recognized as the fifth taste sensation, is the savory taste experienced all over the tongue. It can enhance other flavors. It originated in the Japanese vocabulary as "wonderful taste" because it is prevalent in many Japanese dishes. The amino acid, glutamate, is associated with this flavor profile. Food associated with umami are monosodium glutamate, mushrooms, seaweed, soy products such as soy sauce and miso, meat, corn, peas, fish, tomatoes, and cheese. By using this taste, cooks can create many savory, delicious food items with little or no salt.

Piquant

The taste of spicy, hot food is not a taste exactly but rather a response to an acid-like chemical irritation to the tongue. The trigeminal nerve centered in the tongue picks up this response and sends it to the brain as a pain response. A person can condition this response over time by increasing the spiciness of the food eaten. On the other hand, overuse of these types of food can "burn the palate" and desensitize the ability to taste other food. Sources of piquant are chiles, peppercorns, horseradish, and mustard.

Exhibit 9c

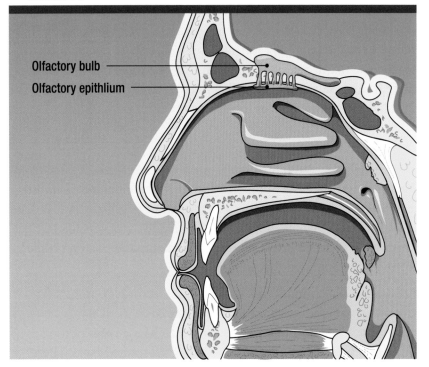

Olfactory bulb

Olfactory epithlium

Olfactory sensors in the nasal cavity react to food's aroma.

The Nose and Food Aroma

The basic taste of food is only part of the definition of flavor. Smell plays a significant role in sending messages to the brain for food identity and emotional response. Smell (olfactory response) gives food complexity and dimension. The "nose" actually refers to the olfactory receptors inside the nasal cavity, as shown in *Exhibit 9c,* which react to different aromas. Food aroma can reach these sensors by being inhaled through the nose and by traveling from the mouth via the opening near the back of the mouth.

As a food—for example, a baked potato—comes close to the nose, the nose detects its aroma and sends messages to the brain. Over time, the brain learns to recognize the food as a potato. At the same time, the brain collects the sensory stimuli associated with eating the food and decides whether the overall sensation is pleasurable or painful. Later, when the same taste and aroma combination is received, the brain recognizes this food as something liked or disliked. Over time, a person builds a palate or a memory stamp of food flavor profiles.

The same response can occur when a person chews food. As food is chewed and swallowed, the gases are received by the nose by way of the opening at the back of the throat, triggering the same response to the recognition of the food. Thus, the nose is the primary source for taste perception. That is why a person with a cold cannot taste things well.

As people age, the senses of smell and taste diminish. Starting at around forty years of age, people experience a loss of taste perception each decade until there is a total loss of up to 70 percent by age seventy. This loss can have significant consequences on a person's nutritional state because there is an increasing tendency to choose food that is heavily salted or fried or that contains either high fat or high sweetness in an attempt to maintain the sensation of taste. These types of food do not contribute much to a healthy diet. The complete loss of smell is called anosmia, which can be extremely dangerous for older adults living alone. With this condition, the appetite usually diminishes, possibly resulting in malnutrition.

Experiencing Flavor

Flavor is perceived through all the senses. People see, smell, feel, and hear flavor in the ways shown in *Exhibit 9d* on the next page.

Building Flavor

Skilled chefs with nutritional sensitivities build flavor through layers using fat-free marinades, dry rubs, infused oils, salsas, vinaigrettes, citrus, reductions, smoking, and infusions. Building flavor means using a balance of taste and smells that complement each other. Part of this is knowing which flavors naturally complement each other. Asian and Latin American cuisines have been balancing flavors for a long time. Examples of popular flavor combinations are:

■ **Sweet and sour**—Chicken with pineapple and tomatoes

■ **Hot and sour**—Asian hot and sour soup

Exhibit 9d

Perceiving Flavor

Aspects of the Flavor Experience

Seeing flavor	■ Color
	■ Visual texture
	■ Consistency (lumpiness)
	■ Visible steam
Smelling flavor	■ Greatest sensitivity to taste comes from breathing out with the mouth closed
	■ About 4,300 flavor compounds have been identified
	■ Typically, cooked food contains 300–800 compounds
	■ Wine tasting has a narrow taste spectrum and a broad smell spectrum
Feeling flavor	■ Mouth feel
	■ Texture
	■ Temperature—greatest flavor sensation between 70°F and 105°F (21°C and 41°C)
Tasting flavor	■ Taste receptors
	■ **Maillard reaction** (the interaction between an amino acid and a sugar to form browning and a variety of flavors)
Hearing flavor	■ Sounds of preparation, cooking, and eating—snap, pop, crunch, sizzle

- **Acid and fat**—Salmon with lemon sauce

- **Acid, fat, and piquant**—Chipotle BBQ pork

- **Acid, fat, piquant, and sweet**—Chipotle honey BBQ pork

When food is swallowed, the flavor of it should feel as if it is descending all the way to the stomach, not simply ending at the tongue. Each bite should be an enjoyment not easily forgotten. By using all the tastes of sweet, sour, salt, bitter, and umami, you will provide a meal with a lasting affect that makes the food delicious. The diner should receive the message that what was experienced was a wonderfully delicious meal and, subliminally, that it was nutritionally good as well.

Cooking More Healthfully

Once you have nutritious ingredients to work with (as explained in Chapter 8), you can consider how to cook this food in ways that are both appealing to the consumer and nutritionally sound. As some general guidelines, consider the following tactics for designing more healthful menus and recipes:

- Serve smaller portions.

- Increase the amounts of fruit, vegetables, and whole grains on the plate, which also creates aesthetic appeal.

- Reduce the amounts of meat, rich sauces, and refined grains on the plate.

- Replace pan-fried and deep-fried food with food cooked by other methods.

■ Increase the use of healthful seasonings, such as herbs, spices, fruit and vegetable **purées,** thick liquids made from finely ground food, and **reduction sauces,** sauces made by reducing a liquid until it is the consistency of a glaze.

■ Replace saturated fats with monounsaturated or unsaturated fats where possible.

The remainder of this section will provide some specific ways to cook more healthfully.

Exhibit 9e

A nutritious, healthful meal must start with healthy ingredients.

Ingredients

The first step in cooking more healthfully is to start with high-quality, flavorful, healthy ingredients, like those shown in *Exhibit 9e.* No amount of skillful cooking can make an unhealthy or poor-quality food delicious and healthy. Use a variety of fresh, flavorful ingredients, emphasizing the use of whole grains, fruit and vegetables, lean meat, poultry, fish, and seafood. When choosing fats, select small quantities of flavorful vegetable fats such as olive oil and nut oils over saturated fats such as butter or lard. The start of a healthy dish is healthy ingredients.

Portion-Control Principles and Meal Proportions

In designing a healthy menu item it may become necessary to rethink the center-of-plate concept commonly taught in culinary and hospitality schools and used by chefs worldwide. The **center-of-plate concept** is that the main element of a meal is focused on an expensive centerpiece item, usually a protein-rich food such as meat, poultry, or fish, and that the rest of the components are mere accompaniments. So, a traditional center-of-plate menu offering may be a fourteen-ounce strip steak (the center-of-plate item) accompanied by French fries and a little vegetable, as shown in *Exhibit 9f* on the next page.

While this menu item may appeal to customers, it is at odds with the U.S. Department of Agriculture's (USDA) recommendation of a three-ounce portion for meat, poultry, or fish, and it is low in fresh fruit, vegetables, and whole grains. A three-ounce portion of meat is

Exhibit 9f

The center-of-the-plate concept focuses on the protein item to the detriment of the rest of the meal.

Exhibit 9g

The whole-plate concept results in a more nutritionally balanced meal.

about the size of a deck of cards. It is tempting, as a restaurant professional, to dismiss this portion size as unrealistic. Who would pay for such a small steak? How could you compete with operators who serve traditionally sized cuts?

As a restaurant professional, it is necessary for you to rethink the center-of-plate concept and to use various portion-control principles in order to provide your customers with good nutrition. For example, the same basic ingredients in the steak, potato, and spinach dish could be reconfigured to be a spinach and wheat-berry salad (a **wheat berry** is a whole, unprocessed wheat grain) topped with six half-ounce slices of seared sirloin and Southwest-spiced, roasted potato-skin croutons, as shown in *Exhibit 9g*. In this menu item, the protein is in the three- to four-ounce range and the menu item has been completed with more vegetables and grains.

Other portion-control principles to consider include the following:

- Plan menu items to mirror the percentage of carbohydrates, protein, and fat that were discussed in Chapter 3 as recommended for a nutritionally balanced diet. Following these percentages will promote the use of more vegetables, fruit, and grains and less protein and will allow a restaurant or foodservice operation to satisfy customers' appetites without adding excess calories.

- People tend to judge the size of food portions by how much of the plate the food covers. Food that covers most of the plate is typically judged as a normal-sized portion; food that covers very little of the plate is typically judged as a skimpy portion. To help customers appropriately judge the amount of food they are eating, use plates and bowls of appropriate size. In addition, certain presentation techniques will help a customer judge the portion size. For example, a three-ounce chicken breast that is sliced and fanned out on the plate will cover more of the plate than will a three-ounce chicken breast presented in its usual form. Food-presentation techniques that add height to a menu item can also be used.

- For all menu items, set and follow portion standards. Menu descriptions and pictures of menu items ensure that employees plate the correct portion of food.

- Require the use of portion-control devices, such as scoops, ladles, and scales, to ensure the correct portions are placed on each plate.

Regardless of which portion-control principles are used, the focus must be to control the overall quantity of food served to a customer as a portion of that customer's total daily intake.

Activity

Alternative Dish

Think about the appeal and nutritional value of the steak salad described on page 170 (spinach and wheat-berry salad topped with six half-ounce slices of seared sirloin).

1 Would the steak salad appeal to consumers? Why or why not?

_____

_____

_____

2 In what ways is the nutritional profile of the dish improved over that of the traditional fourteen-ounce strip steak accompanied by French fries, creamed spinach, and a dinner roll?

_____

_____

_____

2 How does the food cost of the steak salad compare to the cost of the traditional steak dish?

_____

_____

_____

Think About It...

One of the serious eating problems in the United States is large portions. What can you, as a restaurant professional, do to reduce the sizes of portions but still keep your customers satisfied?

Appearance

The adage that people eat with their eyes is nowhere more important than in healthful cooking. Fortunately, healthy food can be very visually appealing. What could be more enticing than a whole grilled fish stuffed with herbs, lightly steamed pencil asparagus, or a fanned ripe half pear? As a general rule, colorful food is nutritious food. A colorful array of fresh fruit and vegetables, rich brown grains, and pink or pale lean meats are not only visually attractive but indicative of fresh wholesome ingredients, proper cooking techniques, and valuable nutrient content. Making healthy food appealing goes a long way toward encouraging guests to eat more healthfully.

Adapting Recipes for Good Nutrition

An easy way to prepare healthful meals is to start with wholesome, healthy ingredients and prepare them simply. Stir-fried vegetables and tofu with brown rice, poached salmon with steamed asparagus, or a fresh fruit platter need little in the way of modification to be healthy and delicious menu items. These simple recipes, however, are not sufficient to cover all cooking requirements. Barbecued ribs with potato salad, coleslaw, and hushpuppies, for example, require creative adaptation by a nutritionist, food scientist, or chef before they can constitute a healthful menu selection.

It is often necessary to take existing recipes and modify the cooking techniques used so that a more balanced and nutritious meal can be prepared. A number of techniques can be employed to modify or adapt recipes for nutritional purposes:

- Changing cooking techniques

- Reducing some ingredients

- Replacing some ingredients

- Adding some ingredients

A Little Food Science

In making recipe and cooking changes, it is important to remember food-science principles. For example, when reducing fat in a brownie recipe, you need to think about what functions that fat is serving in the recipe. It is likely providing moisture, conveying flavor, and providing color, richness, body, and mouth feel. It is not sufficient simply to remove the fat from the recipe; it must be replaced by a substitute that can provide reasonably well the functions that the fat provided to the dish.

Recipe modification requires some analysis before changes are made. The recipe modifier must understand the purpose of the ingredient being changed. Here are some possibilities:

- **The ingredient is for leavening.** Steam or captured gases generated by chemical reaction of sodium bicarbonate (baking soda) and acid (buttermilk) increase volume. Yeast and carbohydrates ferment to produce carbon dioxide. Air is captured by whipping.

- **The ingredient is for tenderizing.** Fat is used for many reasons in cooking, whether it is from butter or oil. Fat transfers heat; it also tenderizes and flavors. Sugar tenderizes, sweetens, and gives color to a crust. Milk sweetens, tenderizes, and provides acid. Eggs yolks are used for tenderizing, color, and structure.

- **The ingredient is for flavoring.** Butter, sugar, eggs, fruit, fruit purées, and artificial flavorings all provide flavor. Salt rounds out flavors. Citrus and vinegars intensify flavor and the salty taste.

- **The ingredient is for structure.** Egg whites are used to provide body and volume. Egg albumen gives strong structure to cells that capture air during baking. Starches such as potato starch, cornstarch, arrowroot, rice, flours, grains, and cereals have properties that thicken liquids.

Exhibit 9h

Stir-frying uses very little fat.

Modification by Changing Cooking Techniques

An easy technique to employ in modifying recipes is to use alternate cooking techniques. Methods that result in significant fat absorption, like deep-frying and pan-frying, can be replaced with those that allow the fat to cook the food and then drip away like stir-frying, as shown in *Exhibit 9h*, or those that avoid fat altogether. As an illustration, consider the popular dish of Buffalo chicken wings. Wings are traditionally dredged in flour, deep-fried, and tossed in a mixture of butter and hot sauce. By roasting them in a hot oven rather than deep-frying them, a similar but lower-fat result can be obtained. *Exhibit 9i* on pages 174–175 lists more low-fat cooking methods that can be used in preparing healthy meals.

Here are some additional points to remember related to these cooking methods:

- With all these methods, except *sous vide*, carry-over cooking is important to remember. You must bring the food to five degrees below the desired temperature, remove it from the heat source, and then cover it and let it rest. This allows the food to reabsorb some of its juices, becoming more tender and succulent.

- Some of these techniques, such as grilling, broiling, and roasting, produce Maillard-reaction browning, which results in an additional way to heighten the flavor impact of the dish.

- Trimming visible surface fat from meat or poultry is an additional step you can take to reduce the overall fat content of the dish.

Exhibit 9i

Low-Fat Cooking Methods

Method	Description
Baking	Same as roasting but for nonmeat items. Food is placed directly in a baking dish and cooked in the oven. High heat creates the Maillard reaction of browning.
Barbecuing	Food is cooked on a grate over indirect heat. Dry barbecuing has dry herbs and spices applied to the exterior of the meat. Wet barbecuing has basting with a barbecue sauce.
Braising	This slow and flavorful method of cooking is used with tougher or less fatty cuts of meat and with fruit and vegetables. It can be made lower in fat by choosing a leaner meat or trimming excess fat. The meat is seared using the dry-sauté method, and then a flavorful liquid with aromatic vegetables is added when cooking the meat. The whole food item is used, half submerged in the braising liquid, covered, and allowed to cook very gently for a long period of time until tender. When cooking is completed, the meat is removed and the braising liquid is degreased to remove excess fat, or the liquid can be left overnight to chill and the hardened fat layer removed. If there are vegetables in the sauce, they can be puréed and used as the thickener for the sauce.
Broiling	Food is cooked on a perforated pan over a catch pan with high direct heat from above in a broiler. Classically, fat is used when broiling lean poultry and fish to aid in browning, but it drips off prior to serving. Used on tender cuts of meat trimmed of visible fat, vegetables, fruit, and pizza. The high heat and quick cooking retains vitamins and minerals.
Dry-sautéing	Food is cooked at high heat in a nonstick sauté pan with very little or no fat. The pan is prepared by heating the pan to a high heat, wiping the surface with oil, removing excess, and repeating the procedure until the pan is glazed. Meat, fish, and eggs do well with this method, but starchy food and tofu do not. Afterwards, the pan is deglazed with stock, wine, or water. The pan is not washed with soap but rubbed with salt and rinsed to retain the nonstick surface. If necessary, pan spray or oil in a spray bottle (atomized oil) can be used to touch up the surface.
En papillote	Food baked and steamed in a greased paper or parchment bag is named for the French term for "in parchment." The dish, usually both meat and vegetables, is cooked and often served in the bag. Because the greased bag retains the moisture and reduces the harsh heat of the oven, the dish is aromatic, moist, and flavorful.
Grilling	Food is cooked on a grate over direct or indirect heat. (Sometimes "grilling" is mistakenly used to refer to cooking in oil on a flat surface also called a grill.)
Oven-frying	Oven-frying food can be done to lower fat but get the crispy crust of fried food. The food is breaded and then baked or broiled at high heat.
Pan-steaming	Food is cooked in a pan on the range or in a microwave dish with a small amount of boiling liquid.

Method	Description
Poaching	Food is cooked gently, just below a simmer, in liquid such as stock, wine, juice, or water. Often used to cook fruit, meat, or fish. This is a gentle cooking method that keeps food tender and moist. The poaching liquid often is reduced and used as a sauce. The related shallow-poaching method uses less liquid and is for single servings of tender cuts of meat or fish.
Roasting	Same as baking but for roasting meat, vegetables, and poultry. Food is placed on a rack over a catch pan and cooked in the oven. The high heat and quick cooking retains vitamins and minerals and also creates the Maillard reaction of browning.
Smoke-roasting	Also known as pan-smoking. Aromatics like woods, teas, and herbs impart great flavor to food. The food is smoked on the range, then finished in the oven. The advantage of this method is little or no salt is required for seasoning to achieve good taste. To give more flavor before smoking, the items can be marinated.
Sous vide	*Sous vide* is French for "under vacuum." This method involves slow cooking of food in vacuum-sealed plastic bags. It requires special equipment to vacuum seal the bag and cool the packaged food properly. The packaged food is cooked slowly in a controlled temperature water bath or steam to the desired temperature. It can be held at that temperature until service or cooled quickly and reheated at a later date. The advantage of this cooking method is that the food is extremely flavorful, tender, has little waste and weight loss, and has maximum vitamin and mineral retention. A significant advantage for restaurant operations is that the food cannot overcook, which is extremely important for reducing food waste. Banquet chefs find this method helpful when preparing meals for large crowds because the food can be made ahead and reheated for service. *Sous vide* also can be used to marinate single-service food items to be cooked quickly at a later time. Under correct conditions, vacuum sealing extends the shelf life of the product.
Steaming	Food is cooked in a perforated basket over boiling water with no fat. This method is especially good for vegetables, and it avoids the problem of leaching out the vitamins and minerals when vegetables are boiled.
Stewing	Identical to braising except the meat, vegetables, or fruit are cut into pieces and the pieces are fully immersed in the flavorful liquid.
Stir-frying	Food is cooked over extremely high heat with a small amount of fat in a wok or sauté pan and stirred constantly. Using a round-bottom wok is superior to using a flat-bottom sauté pan because the round bottom uses much less fat. If the wok is seasoned, even less oil is needed.
Sweat	Food items, particularly vegetables, are cooked in a small amount of fat over low heat. The food is covered with a piece of foil or parchment paper and the pot is covered to allow the food to cook in its own juices.

Modification by Reducing Select Ingredients

By now you know which food items cause nutritional problems when used in excess—salt (sodium), fat, and refined carbohydrates, including sugar. A good way to modify a dish for health purposes is to reduce these ingredients. Often, significantly reducing the levels of salt, fat, or sugar in a dish has a minor impact on the finished dish and may even improve it. For example, using canned black beans to make a black-bean soup adds a lot of sodium to the dish before it is even seasoned by the chef. Substituting dried beans for canned beans can result in a soup with more flavor and lower sodium and one that guests prefer. It also saves money.

At other times, reducing or removing salt, fat, or sugar from a recipe creates a finished product with poor flavor. In general, consumers like the taste of salt, fat, and sugar, which is why they are so prevalent in the food people cook. When modifying recipes, it is of the utmost importance that the modified recipe taste good. If a guest chooses a healthy menu item that does not taste good, that guest is likely to think negatively about your operation, your chefs, and healthy eating in general.

Exhibit 9j

Recipe Substitutions to Lower Fat

Traditional Food Item	Possible Alternative Food Item (if it meets the recipe's needs)
Whole milk	2-percent or skim milk
Eggs, whole or yolks	Egg whites or a commercial egg substitute, fruit or vegetable purée
Butter	Trans-fat-free margarine, olive oil, nut oils, avocado
Coconut and palm oil	Canola oil, soybean oil, safflower oil, grapeseed oil, applesauce, low-fat plain yogurt
Cheese	Low-fat varieties
Yogurt	Low or no fat
Bacon	Turkey bacon
Sausage	Turkey sausage, seasoned ground turkey, soy crumbles
Ground beef	Ground sirloin, ground turkey breast, ground soy
Chocolate	Cocoa
Cream	Canned evaporated skim milk

Reducing the Amount of Fat

There are a variety of techniques for reducing the fat content of various preparations, including baked goods, sauces, main dishes, and other preparations. One technique is to use a nonfat substitute. For example, whole milk is approximately 4 percent milk fat. By switching to skim milk, which has a fat content close to 0 percent milk fat, this fat is practically eliminated. If the results of this substitution are unpalatable, replacing only half of the milk with skim milk or switching to milk with 1 percent milk fat should be tried. *Exhibit 9j* lists some additional useful ways to lower the amount of fat in a dish.

If none of these work for the recipe, search for a new food product that does work. New food products and applications are developed regularly.

As a restaurant professional it is your responsibility to keep abreast of these developments and to contribute to them yourself by experimenting with various modifications.

Exhibit 9k

Common Ingredient Substitutions	
Item	**Substitute**
Salt	Herbs, spices, and acid items
Refined sugar	Commercially available sugar substitutes, fruit juices, purées, and dried fruit
Fat	Fruit purées in baked goods, liquid in savory preparations, strained yogurt, starch, and commercially available gels and gums

Modification by Replacing Select Ingredients

Another way to modify recipes with positive results is to replace some of the ingredients rather than eliminating them. Sometimes this replacement can result in a similar product that appeals to consumers; at other times the results are awful. The best strategy is to use recipes or formulas from a trusted source and to experiment with different combinations. *Exhibit 9k* identifies some common substitutions for ingredients that are often reduced or eliminated from recipes. Not all substitutions result in a healthier product. For example, using honey in place of refined table sugar simply results in the substitution of one sugar for another. Nutritionally, they are quite similar. Similarly, substitutions do not always work on a one-to-one ratio. For example, saccharin, like most artificial sweeteners, is many times sweeter than sugar. If one cup of saccharin were substituted for one cup of sugar in a cookie recipe, the end result would be unpalatable.

There are different ways to substitute one or several recipe ingredients for another. Since this guide is about nutrition and not food science, it is not appropriate to list and explain all the principles and facts of food science here. What you must remember is that food substitutions must be done in such a way that all of the functions of the replaced food item are fulfilled. To illustrate this point, examples of food substitutions are given in a later section.

Replacing "Bad" Fats

Saturated fats (butter, lard, tropical oils), hydrogenated fats (margarine, shortening), and trans fats can be reduced by using less, replacing them with substitute fats, or using food-science principles to mimic the properties of fats (although this does not typically affect calorie content). For example, margarine made with saturated fats can be replaced by margarine made with monounsaturated fats, such as canola oil. Vegetable shortening can be used in place of animal-fat shortening. Fats are typically found in high amounts in food such as meat, full-fat dairy products, sauces, nuts, oils, and salad dressings.

Using high-quality lean meat is a good strategy for replacing the large amounts of fat found in prime cuts. For example, USDA Choice can be used in place of USDA Prime beef. Although USDA Choice is a leaner grade of beef because it has less fat marbling than USDA Prime, it is still of high quality and sufficiently juicy to broil or grill. USDA Select beef is lean because it has the least fat marbling. It must be prepared by using a moist method of cooking to ensure tenderness. Moisture in lean meat can be maintained by cooking in parchment, foil, or vegetable leaves. Basting lean meat with stock will also prevent it from drying out when cooking and will keep the fat content of the resulting dish low. When sautéing, brushing a little oil on the meat and cooking in a nonstick pan is a healthier cooking technique than placing the meat into a puddle of oil.

Finally, when making substitutions to reduce fat in a dish, remember why the fat is in the dish in the first place. Butter, rendered bacon, duck fat, and goose fat have flavors that are appealing to consumers and cooking properties that are difficult to imitate. A pie crust can be easily made with lard or shortening; when substituting vegetable oil for shortening, it is considerably more difficult to obtain a comparable result. When making substitutions, remember the purpose for the substitution and the functions that fat are playing in the food item. Not all fats can be reduced, removed, or replaced.

Modification by Adding Select Ingredients

Many people think healthy cooking needs only to be about removing less desirable ingredients from a menu item. Healthy cooking also can be about adding healthful ingredients. Most people in developed countries do not get sufficient fiber from their diet. Adding fresh fruit and vegetables, whole grains, and legumes to dishes is a good way to make food that is nutritionally sound, contains more fiber, saves money (these types of food are usually cheaper per pound than meat, fish, poultry, cheeses, and other ingredients), and interests your guests from a culinary perspective. For example, adding an interesting preparation of amaranth, quinoa, or millet to your menu will accomplish these goals. Also, using these and other nutritious but nonstandard ingredients can expand your creativity as a chef.

A good adaptation can yield a dish that is not only acceptable but potentially delicious. Herbs, spices, stocks, reductions of stock, wine, vinegar, juices, infused vinegar, purées of vegetables, fruit, or legumes, and whole grains are all delicious food. Using them sensibly and artistically can result in tasty fare that guests love.

A good frame of mind is to think of healthy cooking as simply good cooking with good ingredients rather than as an unwelcome adaptation of classical cooking.

Applesauce can replace fat in baked food.

Examples of Recipe Modification

Once the purpose of ingredients is understood, you can begin to modify recipes to be lower in fat, sugar, and salt. This section provides some specific examples.

Modifications in Baking

- The fat in many recipes can be lowered by using fruit purées such as applesauce in place of butter or oil, as shown in *Exhibit 9l*. This will result in a moist, denser cake, and the crumb will still be tender.

- To lower cholesterol, an egg substitute can be used in place of an egg. The rule of thumb is one-quarter cup of egg substitute equals one egg. Egg substitutes are egg whites with a small amount of vegetable oil added to replace the egg yolk. Yellow food coloring is usually added for color.

- To lower sugar, replace it with a sugar substitute following the manufacturer's directions.

Modifications in Soups, Sauces, and Gravies

Much culinary creativity and experimentation comes in the soup, sauce, and gravy categories. Classic sauces are flavorful but tend to be loaded with fat. Many are thickened with **roux,** a cooked mixture of fat and flour. Others are **emulsion sauces,** such as Hollandaise and mayonnaise, that consist of egg yolk and butter or oil. The result is a sauce made predominantly of fat.

There are several ways to reduce the fat content of soups, sauces, and gravies:

- Use a reduction of stock. Start with a stock made from vegetables, meat, poultry, or fish and simmer until it is about one-third of the original volume. Stock and broth are nearly fat free, because the fat rises to the top and can be skimmed off. In the process of reduction, the stock will develop body and its flavors will intensify. Then, less thickener is needed.

- Use a slurry. In place of a traditional flour-and-fat roux, a **slurry**—a thin paste made from water or stock mixed with starch, such as cornstarch—can be a thickening alternative. To use a slurry, dissolve starch in cold water and incorporate it into the hot sauce.

Exhibit 9m

Chutney is a good alternative to gravy with meat.

- Use skimmed stock. Rather than using a premade **mother sauce,** a classic sauce from which other sauces are made, make a sauce of pan drippings, wine, broth, or stock from which the fat has been skimmed from the top.

- Use less oil in salad dressings by replacing bland salad oils with intensely flavored nut oils, olive oils, or **infused oils**—oils that have been heated with seasonings for flavor. Also, replace 25 percent of the oil with slightly thickened stock.

- Dilute cream-based sauces, dips, and dressings with broth, juice, or skim milk.

- To mimic a creamy sauce for macaroni and cheese, for example, blend cottage cheese and strained yogurt, using corn starch as a thickener if heating.

- In place of heavy cream, canned evaporated skimmed milk will give the body of cream.

- In a braise or soup, puréeing the vegetables in the cooking liquid will thicken the sauce, retaining all the nutrients.

- In place of gravy, fruit **coulis**—a thick puréed sauce—salsas, and chutneys, like the one shown in *Exhibit 9m,* make excellent sauces for meats.

- In béchamel sauce, use skim milk and trans-fat-free margarine.

- Two teaspoons of sour cream or plain yogurt can be added as a garnish on low-fat cream soup to give it the mouth feel of full-fat cream soup.

- Vegetable *jus,* the French term for juice, and consommé make great sauces.

Modifications for Meat

Exhibit 9n

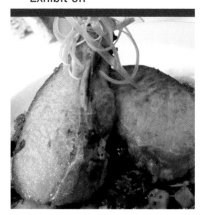

Reduce fat by using low-fat meat.

- Choose low-fat meat such as beef or pork tenderloin (shown in *Exhibit 9n*), beef eye of round, beef flank steak, beef sirloin steak, pork loin chops, turkey breast, ostrich, buffalo, venison, or rabbit.

- Trim visible fat, and cook the meat using a low-fat cooking technique such as dry-sautéing, stir-frying, grilling, broiling, pan-smoking, or roasting.

- For poultry, select white-meat chicken instead of the legs and thighs, which have a higher fat content.

- When cooking chicken, leave the skin on and remove it just before serving.

- If using a marinade, boneless, skinless chicken breast will work fine.

Exhibit 9o

Tuna is a good source of omega-3 fatty acids.

Exhibit 9p

Sweating vegetables with stock, instead of sautéing them reduces the use of oil.

Exhibit 9q

A strudel is a low-fat dessert because it lacks the high-fat crust of a pie.

Modifications for Seafood

- Care should be taken not to overcook fish and seafood, thus ruining their delicate flavors.

- Dry-sautéing, grilling, and poaching are the best cooking methods.

- Using swordfish, mackerel, salmon, and tuna (see *Exhibit 9o*) provides customers with omega-3 fatty acids.

- Shellfish, such as shrimp, lobster, and crawfish, have high cholesterol but no saturated fat, so they are nutritious choices.

Modifications for Vegetables

- Instead of sautéing vegetables in oil, sweat them in a little stock, as shown in *Exhibit 9p;* this extracts flavor from the vegetables and is a good foundation for the rest of the dish.

- To finish a vegetable, a small amount of butter or flavored nut oil can be added.

- If you use fat, use it at the end, so its flavor still can be perceived.

Modifications for Desserts

It is important to know the function of a dessert's ingredients. If an ingredient substitute will change the integrity of the dessert, then do not make the substitution, as in pie crust.

- Use low-fat and fat-free cottage cheese, ricotta cheese, yogurt, or cream cheese. If fat-free items are used, it is important to use some type of starch to protect the proteins from heat when baking, or they will curdle.

- The fat in a pie crust is there to make it flaky. To reduce or change the fat, it would be necessary to change the nature of the dessert from a pie to a strudel or a cobbler. (See *Exhibit 9q*.) If making a strudel, phyllo (also spelled *filo*) dough can be used as the pastry by spraying it with atomized oil before baking to reduce the fat significantly. If making a cobbler, little or no fat is needed.

Modifications for Garnishes

- Instead of using small pieces of fried items such as shallots or potatoes, use thinly sliced pieces of vegetables.

Reducing Salt

■ To decrease salt use but add a salty flavor, increase the use of herbs and spices. Use citrus and vinegars to season before adding salt.

■ To add more flavor along with the salt, use small amounts of prosciutto, olives, capers, anchovies, Parmesan cheese, or soy sauce instead of salt.

When making modifications, remember to keep flavor in mind at all times. If fat is the contributing factor to flavor, then a strong flavor alternative must be substituted. Be creative, and use modifications as an opportunity to make food memorable.

Activity

Menu Item Modification

Listed below are food items in a dinner that is too high in fat. Using the principles in this chapter, suggest five modifications to improve this meal's nutritional value.

Menu Item

Butter-roasted half-chicken with pan gravy, cheddar mashed potatoes, and a fried shallot garnish

1 _____

2 _____

3 _____

4 _____

5 _____

Summary

As a restaurant or foodservice professional, you can employ many techniques to improve the healthfulness of the meals you serve. Substituting cooking methods, selecting healthy ingredients, adding healthy ingredients, and reducing levels of unhealthy ingredients are all techniques that will make a dish healthier.

When modifying food for nutrition, it is important to remember that the food needs to taste good and be attractively presented. When making specific substitutions, consider the function of the ingredient in the food and make the substitution accordingly. Incorporate healthy food with high flavor impact.

Activity

Improving Beef Pot Roast

Locate a recipe for a traditional beef pot roast. Review this recipe for ways to lower the fat by answering these questions.

1 What cooking method is used to prepare this dish? Can the method of cooking be modified to decrease fat? If so, how?

_____

_____

_____

2 What cut of meat is used? What different meat cut could be used to lower the fat content?

_____

_____

_____

3 What other food items typically accompany this dish? How can you change these to increase the fiber content of the meal?

_____

_____

_____

4 Traditionally, the sauce for the pot roast is thickened with a roux. Can the sauce be made an alternative way? If so, what way?

_____

_____

_____

_____

Review Your Learning

1 **For healthful food to be accepted by diners, it must be**

   A. as flavorful as regular food.

   B. quicker to obtain than regular food.

   C. cheaper than regular food.

   D. All of the above

2 **Which cooking technique should *not* be used in healthy cooking?**

   A. Stir-frying

   B. Pan-steaming

   C. Broiling

   D. Deep-frying

3 **Which is *not* an acceptable technique for lowering the sugar content of a food?**

   A. Substituting honey for sugar

   B. Using an artificial sweetener

   C. Replacing some of the sugar with a sweet fruit purée

   D. Using less sugar in the recipe

4 **Which is a good reason to use processed food?**

   A. It is available when a high-quality fresh version is not.

   B. It is more nutritious than fresh food because it does not travel as far.

   C. It is free of pesticides and harmful fertilizers.

   D. It is tastier than fresh food.

5 **Which technique is appropriate for reducing the fat content of a sauce?**

   A. Using a reduction sauce

   B. Using an emulsion sauce

   C. Using a roux-thickened sauce

   D. Using a fat-free oil

6 **All of the following techniques are appropriate for adding fiber to a dish *except***

   A. substituting a vegetable purée for egg yolks in a soufflé.

   B. replacing potatoes, white rice, or pasta with whole grains.

   C. adding beans.

   D. replacing butter with margarine.

7 **Which is a good reason to use a flavorful nut oil in a dish?**

   A. Nut oils are inexpensive.

   B. Nut oils have fewer calories than other oils.

   C. You need less oil to convey a strong flavor.

   D. All of the above

8 **Which type of food does *not* represent a healthful way to add flavor to a dish?**

   A. Infused vinegar   C. Herbs

   B. Compound butter   D. Toasted spices

9 **Which is *not* a way to modify a dish for improved nutrition?**

   A. Adding ingredients that are more nutritious

   B. Reducing overly fattening ingredients

   C. Changing the cooking method

   D. Replacing whole grains with enriched grains

10 **Which is *not* true about cooking healthfully?**

   A. Consumers reject healthy food because it does not taste good.

   B. Cooking healthfully takes more skill than not cooking healthfully.

   C. Healthy food can be more attractive than regular food.

   D. Healthy cooking is almost always vegetarian or macrobiotic.

Eating in the United States

10

Inside This Chapter

- A Healthy Diet

- The American Diet

- Special Diets

- Popular Fad Diets

- Herbs and Herbal Supplements

- Relationship of Diet and Exercise

- Weight-Loss Diets

- Health Risks of American Diets

- Food Additives—Their Role and Impact

- Allergens in Food Items

After completing this chapter, you should be able to:

- Describe a healthy diet.

- Define the various types of vegetarian diets.

- Characterize diets related to ethnic/cultural, religious, and philosophical positions.

- Describe the nature and effects of various diets found in the United States.

- Describe sports diets and popular fad diets and their effects on the body.

- Characterize the impact and role of food additives and supplements in diets.

- Explain how to deal with allergens in food items.

Test Your Knowledge

1 **True or False:** Not every food fits into a healthy diet. *(See p. 189.)*

2 **True or False:** Beef Stroganoff is a good example of a kosher entrée. *(See p. 196.)*

3 **True or False:** Food additives are artificial substances made by food manufacturers. *(See p. 208.)*

4 **True or False:** Restaurant and foodservice professionals are not responsible for knowing if allergens are present in menu items. *(See p. 211.)*

5 **True or False:** Low-carbohydrate nutrition bars are usually a reduced-calorie dining option. *(See p. 199.)*

Key Terms

Benzoate

Body mass index (BMI)

Carbohydrate loading

Carotene

Colorant

Complementary and alternative medicine

Culture

Emulsifier

Fad

Food additive

Gum

Kosher

Lacto-ovo-vegetarian

Lacto-vegetarian

Low carbohydrate

Macrobiotic diet

Macrobiotics

Mannitol

Meal replacement product

Meat replacement product

Monosodium glutamate (MSG)

Morbidity

Mortality

Nitrate

Nitrite

Obese

Obesity

Overweight

Pareve

Phosphate

Sorbitol

Sports diet

Stabilizer

Thickener

Trend

Vegan

Vegetarian

Introduction

Food is a very strong symbol of hospitality. It can convey that a person cares about and is attentive to others, like the scene shown in *Exhibit 10a.* The serving and enjoyment of food helps cement social bonds, smooth over rough times, and celebrate momentous occasions. These are important factors to remember when running a restaurant or foodservice operation. Obviously, another important factor is the food being served. In most operations, guests can choose only food that is on the menu, which is why the menu is so

Exhibit 10a

Food and hospitality are natural partners; this influences what food people choose.

important. The goal of this guide has been to educate restaurant and foodservice professionals in nutrition so they can plan a balanced menu and prepare food that gives people the choices they need to have healthful and tasty food in their diets.

A wide variety of diets is present in the United States, from the mainstream to the less popular. Some of them are nutritionally sound, while some require modifications to achieve acceptable nutritional levels. The food choices someone habitually makes, which comprise that person's diet, is called an eating pattern. An eating pattern is formed through relationships with others, as well as the many other factors described in Chapter 1. It is dynamic, in response to changes in the economic, social, and technological environment, and for some people, a nontechnical understanding of nutrition. But these are not the only determinants. Eating patterns also differ from one culture to another and even within the same culture—the way of life within a social group in which there are common customs among members. Other important influences in eating patterns can be religious beliefs and preferences, as well as the food associated with security, home, and family. In this chapter, you will learn about some of the eating patterns and diets found in the United States and how you can incorporate this knowledge into menu planning.

Also important to the planning of menus is an understanding of food additives and food allergens: topics that many consumers and food professionals are concerned about. This chapter will discuss generally what additives are and why they are used. Finally, you will learn about food allergens, a vital issue for some people, and what your responsibilities are to your customers with allergies.

A Healthy Diet

Throughout this guide, you have been presented with facts about nutrition and diets. You have likely concluded that a healthy diet is one that meets the needs of a healthy body. A healthy body is one that is not too fat or too lean, with good muscle tone, strength, and stamina. It is the body of a person who is physically fit, but not necessarily an athlete. Although a healthy body may temporarily suffer from a viral, bacterial, or other type of disease, it returns to being disease free in a normal amount of time. A healthy body certainly does not suffer from a nutrition-deficiency disease.

Exhibit 10b

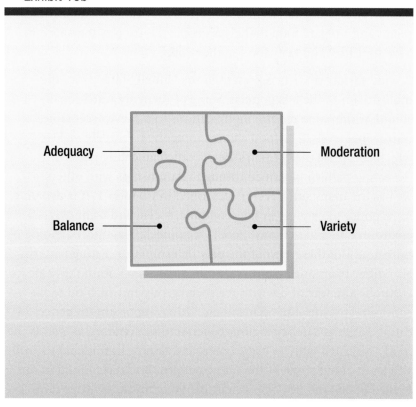

A healthy diet has four components.

To meet all the needs of a healthy body and keep it that way, a healthy diet has certain characteristics, which fit together like a jigsaw puzzle to form a complete diet and maintain health, as shown in *Exhibit 10b*. The four parts of a healthy diet are:

- **Adequacy**—Carbohydrate, protein, and fat are consumed in the recommended amounts for the level of exercise the body receives

- **Balance**—Carbohydrate, fat, and protein are consumed through food in the recommended proportions:

  ☐ 45 to 65 percent of total calories from carbohydrates

  ☐ 20 to 35 percent of total calories from fat

  ☐ 10 to 35 percent of total calories from protein

- **Moderation**—Only enough food and nutrients are consumed for the needs of the body, and empty-calorie food is consumed in very small amounts.

- **Variety**—A variety of food types and items are consumed so all nutrients, especially vitamins, minerals, water, fiber, and phytochemicals, are obtained

This does not sound so difficult. Why, then, do so many Americans have trouble achieving a healthy diet?

The American Diet

There is no single diet that can be called the typical American diet; there are too many variations in food choice due to environment, tradition, economics, agriculture, and technology. However, if all these differences were averaged together, the diet of the majority of Americans can be said to have these problems:

- Too much fat

- Too much protein

- Too many empty calories like sugars and alcohol

- Not enough whole-grain carbohydrates (fruit and vegetables)

- Not enough water

- Too much food overall (coming from larger portions, eating more, and snacking)

There has been a lot of publicity in recent years about these problems. As a consequence, more people in the United States are increasingly aware of what they eat and how it might affect their health. Concerns about food safety and nutrition are growing, but are Americans eating healthier? A closer look at American eating trends reveals that parts of the typical U.S. diet still are lacking in nutrient content. Although there is much demand for healthier options, Americans continue to make poor choices when eating in and dining out. Compared to the recommendations in the *Dietary Guidelines for Americans 2005* (see *Exhibit 10c*), Americans are neglecting some nutritional recommendations.

- Fruit and vegetable intake is still below the recommended nine servings per day. On average, Americans eat only 1.5 servings of vegetables and one serving of fruit per day.

- Meat, poultry, and fish intake has climbed dramatically.

- Grain and cereal consumption has risen, but not enough to meet recommended levels.

- Vegetable fats are used more often than animal fats, which is good, but total fat consumption is higher than recommended.

- Fiber intake is insufficient.

Because many people skip breakfast, between-meal eating contributes significantly to the nutrient intakes of Americans. This also is a problem because the choices of "snack" food tend toward empty calories instead of healthy food items. Wise snack choices can be part of good dietary habits if snacks are nutritionally balanced, but most Americans do not snack wisely.

Bad Food, or Bad Diets?

Nutritionists agree that all food items can play a role in healthy diets, and that there are no "bad" food items, as long as moderation is used. However, there are "bad" diets. Many factors contribute to less-than-ideal diets.

Exhibit 10c

Dietary Guidelines
for Americans
2005

The U.S. Department of Agriculture's *Dietary Guidelines for Americans 2005* provides recommendations for eating in the United States.

Exhibit 10d

Making good food choices is up to each individual.

For example:

■ **Large portion sizes**—Consumers can and should modify their eating behaviors to account for larger portions that are sometimes served at restaurant and foodservice operations. For example, when eating out, diners can request that their server present only half the meal with the other half wrapped to take home. At home, measuring portions using standard household measuring utensils is helpful in controlling portion size.

■ **Poor food choices**—Failure to eat a balanced diet and eating too many high-calorie and empty-calorie food items can result in weight gain and nutrition-deficiency diseases.

Ultimately, each person is responsible for making food choices that supply the nutrients needed, and for keeping portion size and the total amount of food consumed within actual bodily needs. This must be done both at home and when dining out. (See *Exhibit 10d*.) This means that high-fat and high-sugar items are fine choices some of the time, just not all of the time. Restaurants and foodservice operations are making this easier by providing menu items that help people achieve a balanced diet.

Sometimes, food choices are influenced by economics, and it becomes important to get the most value from one's food dollar. But if that results in obesity, it is a poor value because obesity can result in higher healthcare costs. Even taking small steps such as substituting low-calorie salad dressing can have a great impact. Eating on the run also impacts food choices because healthful options may not be as available in these situations.

Despite jam-packed schedules, economic situations, and other demands, people still should consider obtaining food that results in a healthy diet to be important. Everyone should try to eat three healthy and nutritionally balanced meals every day, appropriate to their activity levels. As a restaurant and foodservice professional, you are in a position to help your customers to attain healthy diets.

Variants in U.S. Diets

Cultural and regional diversity is a factor in American eating, but not as much as one would think. In the near past, there were distinct regional variations, but most have disappeared or at least weakened. A few regional and cultural favorites persist, such as the ones shown in *Exhibit 10e* and listed below:

■ **New England**—Boiled root vegetables and meat

■ **Southwest**—Food with a heavy Mexican influence

■ **Western states**—Food items like barbecued meat

- **South**—Collard greens (a relative of cabbage), southern fried chicken, grits, and chitterlings (food made from the small intestines of a pig)

- **California**—Health-food items like avocado and bean-sprout sandwiches

Exhibit 10e

Regional Food

A few food items remain representative of different regions in the United States.

In addition, there are various ethnically influenced food categories, such as African-American "soul food," Mexican food, and Asian food.

Today, much of what Americans eat every day is fairly uniform and has little to do with people's local environments. In fact, regional specialties and ethnic food items are available in most places in the United States. This is due to several things:

- Food production changes

- Farming changes

- Homogenizing of cultures

- National advertising

Food production today tends to be globally dispersed, and most food items are likely to have been grown and processed far from

191

their points of consumption. Also, the current food system in the United States is centralized, in the sense that any given agricultural product is grown in a decreasing number of farms. This makes for larger crops and herds and, consequently, fewer food choices.

Also, the greater distance that food can be quickly transported is causing a decline in local farming, especially in areas where year-round, open-air food production is not an option. Despite population growth in the northeastern United States, for example, the number of farms in that region and total land area farmed have declined steadily.

So, even though there is no typical American diet, the average diets of the majority of Americans are more homogeneous and less nutritious than they should be. In addition, there are a number of diets in the United States that are followed for special reasons.

Special Diets

Some people adhere to special diets due to philosophical, health, or religious reasons. Restaurant and foodservice professionals should accommodate these people and provide food that fits their needs. These special diets are described below.

Vegetarian Diets

A **vegetarian** is someone who does not eat meat, fish, or fowl or products containing these food items. (See *Exhibit 10f*.) Within this broad definition, vegetarians can vary widely in their eating patterns. People choose vegetarian diets for several reasons, including health, the environment, animal welfare, economic and ethical considerations, world hunger issues, and religious beliefs. According to the Vegetarian Resource Group, there are about 5.7 million non-institutionalized vegetarian adults in the United States.[1] Because this number of potential customers is too large to ignore, every restaurant and foodservice professional should attempt to understand vegetarians' dietary needs. In fact, the National Restaurant Association reports that eight out of ten restaurant and foodservice operations in the United States with table service offer vegetarian entrées.

"It is the position of the American Dietetic Association (ADA) and of Dietitians of Canada (DC) that appropriately planned vegetarian diets are nutritionally adequate and provide health benefits in the prevention and treatment of certain diseases."[2] There are three types of vegetarians:

Exhibit 10f

Vegetarians do not consume meat; instead, they get their protein from vegetable sources.

---

[1] Vegetarian Resource Group Web site. *www.vrg.org/journal/vj2003issue3/vj2003issue3poll.htm.* 6/22/06.

[2] Journal of American Dietetic Association, volume 103, pp. 748–765, 2003.

- The **lacto-ovo-vegetarian** eating pattern is based on grains, vegetables, fruit, legumes, seeds, nuts, dairy products, and eggs; it excludes meat, fish, and fowl.

- The **lacto-vegetarian** excludes eggs as well as meat, fish, and fowl.

- The eating pattern of the **vegan,** or total vegetarian, is similar to the lacto-ovo vegetarian pattern except for the additional exclusion of dairy and other animal products.

Effects of Vegetarian Diets

If vegetarians do not eat complementary proteins and a wide variety of food types and perhaps supplement their diets, they may develop the deficiency diseases described in previous chapters. Research suggests that vegetarians may have low blood levels of vitamin B_{12}, and supplementation may be necessary for vegetarians who avoid or limit animal food items. Vegan diets also may lack vitamin D because fortified cow's milk is its most common dietary source. However, vegan food items supplemented with vitamin D, such as soy milk and some cereals, are available to fill this gap. Exposure to sunlight is also a factor affecting vitamin D status, since the body can produce its own vitamin D if an adequate amount of sunlight reaches the skin. Also, vegetarians may have lower levels of zinc.

The level of iron intake recommended for vegetarians is higher than that of nonvegetarians because iron is not as available from a vegetarian diet. Although vegetarian diets are higher in total iron content than nonvegetarian diets, the amount of iron stored in the body is lower in vegetarians because the iron from plant food items is more poorly absorbed. Although vegetarian diets are lower in total protein, protein in lacto-ovo-vegetarians, lacto-vegetarians, and vegans appears to be adequate.

Vegetarian Food Items

Vegetarian food items, widely available in today's markets, make it easy to follow a vegetarian diet and for restaurant and foodservice operations to cater to vegetarians. Fortified food items such as soy milk, meat analogs, juice, and breakfast cereal can add variety as well as needed nutrients.

An assortment of plant food items eaten over the course of a day can provide all essential amino acids if done correctly by eating complementary proteins. The consumption of complementary proteins—incomplete proteins that, when eaten together, supply the necessary amino acids—should be a continual practice for vegetarians. Complementary proteins need not be eaten at the same meal but should be eaten in the same day. An example of a complementary protein combination is rice and beans.

Meat replacement products also help vegetarians obtain the needed amounts of protein and other nutrients that are found in meat, fish, and fowl. Examples of **meat replacement products** for vegetarian diets include soy-protein products such as soy burgers, sausages, and chicken products. See *Exhibit 10g* for a list of food items that provide nutrients normally provided by eating animal flesh.

Exhibit 10g

Replacement for Animal Sources of Nutrients

Supplied Nutrient	Source
Protein	Tofu and other soy-based products, legumes, seeds, nuts, grains, and vegetables
Zinc	Whole grains, whole-wheat bread, legumes, nuts, and tofu
Iron	Legumes, tofu, green leafy vegetables, dried fruit, whole grains, and iron-fortified cereals and breads
Calcium	Tofu processed with calcium, broccoli, seeds, nuts, kale, legumes, lime-processed tortillas, soy beverages, and calcium-enriched orange juice
Vitamin D	Fortified soy beverages and sunlight
Vitamin B$_{12}$	Fortified soy beverages and cereals

Macrobiotic Diet

Macrobiotics is a philosophy of life directed toward improving its quality and length through improved quality of food. Adherents believe that consuming food that is less processed, more natural, and prepared with more traditional cooking methods will do this. Consequently, macrobiotic adherents emphasize locally grown food, whole-grain cereals, legumes, other vegetables, fruit, seaweed, and fermented soy products. They prepare food from these ingredients using the principle of balance between opposites instead of scientific dietary guidelines. They also consume large amounts of rice and other cereals because they are considered naturally balanced. Very sweet food items and dairy products are avoided, as are very salty food items and red meat.

As a result, the macrobiotic diet has the following makeup:

■ 50 to 60 percent whole cereals

■ 25 to 30 percent vegetables

- 10 percent beans

- 5 to 10 percent soup

- 5 percent seaweed

- Less than 5 percent of a combination of whitefish, seeds, nuts, oil, sea salt, other spices, and desserts

People choosing macrobiotic diets are often identified as following a vegetarian diet because the diets are similar although for different reasons. The same health risks are present.

Religion-Influenced Diets

Religious restrictions on food choices vary widely and impact an individual's food choices. These restrictions may be mild (discouraged) or severe (prohibited). Although there is a wide range of food restrictions among religions, fasting is a practice that is observed in many religions. In this section, some religion-influenced diets are discussed. Religion-influenced diets rarely result in health problems, but they may require changes in the menu, recipes, and practices of restaurant and foodservice operations.

Kosher Diet

A significant part of Orthodox and Conservative Jewish observance is associated with food and dietary laws. For these people, nonkosher food is considered to reduce spiritual sensitivity. Kosher dietary laws impact all meals, whether at home, at work, or when eating out; thus, restaurant and foodservice professionals should understand them. Also, kosher is a religion-defined diet, not a style of cooking; there is no such thing as "kosher-style" food.

Meat, fruit, seeds, and vegetables are all allowed in a kosher diet. However, one may not eat any animal that eats other animals. Also, individuals may only eat animals killed by a professional slaughterer in the most merciful way. Birds of prey are forbidden, as are pork, rabbit, and horsemeat. Additionally, meat must be inspected for disease and certain parts of the animal—hindquarters and the fat below the abdomen—cannot be eaten. Meat must be free from blood out of respect for living creatures, and kosher diners may not eat swordfish, octopus, squid, monkfish, or any other sea creature lacking fins or removable scales. All shellfish is forbidden, including lobster, crab, mussels, and oysters, as is meat from animals with cloven hooves, such as pigs.

Additionally, certain food items must always be separated from other food items. For example, meat items and dairy items must never be mixed together or eaten in the same meal. (See *Exhibit 10h.*) The items may not be prepared together, cooked together, stored

Exhibit 10h

This is not a kosher meal. Meat and dairy cannot be mixed.

together, washed together, or eaten with the same utensils or off of the same dishes. Beef Stroganoff, for example, could never be kosher, since it is a combination of milk and meat. Eggs, acceptable seafood, vegetables, and fruit may be eaten with both meat and milk. Such food items are called **pareve** because they are neither meat nor dairy food items. These dietary rules must be followed under rabbinical supervision for a restaurant or foodservice operation to be considered kosher.

Hindu Diet

Hindus do not eat food items thought to retard spiritual or physical growth. The eating of meat is not prohibited, but pork, fowl, duck, snail, crab, and camel are avoided. Cows are considered sacred and may not be eaten or harmed. Although many Hindus are strict vegetarians, those who eat meat are forbidden from eating beef. Other products from the cow, however, such as milk, yogurt, and butter are considered "pure" and may be eaten.

Muslim Diet

Muslims have diet restrictions that impact restaurant and foodservice operations. They cannot eat pork, ham, bacon, or any other part of a pig. They cannot drink alcohol. Meat must be slaughtered following halal rules.

Fasting and Other Religious Restrictions

There are some additional food-related religious restrictions affecting restaurant and foodservice operations:

■ Fasting is observed in many religious groups worldwide, usually as a form of discipline or to atone for sins. Fasting may last for a certain period of time or at a certain time of day. For example, Christians fast during Lenten season and Mormons fast on the first Sunday of the month.

■ Seventh-Day Adventists advocate a lacto-ovo vegetarian diet and avoid meat, fish, fowl, coffee, tea, and alcoholic beverages.

■ Caffeine-containing food items and beverages are either prohibited or restricted by many religions, as caffeine is considered a stimulant that may have unhealthy or addictive consequences.

■ Members of the Church of Jesus Christ of Latter Day Saints (commonly called Mormons) voluntarily do not consume wine and alcoholic drinks because they are believed to be stimulants.

- During the month of Ramadan, devout Muslims fast from sunup to sundown and eat only before or after these times. (Ramadan is the ninth month of the Islamic calendar—a lunar calendar; because of this, it varies from mid-September to early December.) The act of fasting is said to redirect the heart away from worldly activities; its purpose being to cleanse the inner soul and free it from harm. Fasting during Ramadan is not obligatory for people for whom it would cause problems: children, people with an illness or medical condition (including the elderly), diabetics, nursing or pregnant women, and travelers who intend to spend fewer than five days away from home.

- Many Christians observe Lent for the forty-six day period before Easter. Since Easter is based on a lunar calendar, Lent falls somewhere between mid-February and mid-April. During Lent, observant Christians restrict the quantity and types of food they eat. Fasting and abstinence were more severe in the past; today, the most noticeable effect is not eating meat on Friday, which typically causes an increase in the consumption of fish on that day.

Accommodating Religious Diets

Restaurant and foodservice operations can accommodate religious eating patterns or at least provide information that allows guests to make informed decisions. Consider these points:

- Menu items cooked in wine might not be selected although alcohol is believed to evaporate during cooking.

- Nonmeat eaters may select meat substitutes or vegetarian options.

- Prepared kosher items may be sourced from suppliers, which not only eases preparation and labor, but also provides ingredient information on the product label for guests to see.

Popular Fad Diets

Unlike the diets previously described, fad diets are based on a limited understanding of nutrition, how the body processes and uses food, and other factors, such as social pressure. Many of these diets are directed toward specific bodily changes such as weight loss, weight gain, more energy, longer life, joint health, and so on.

Exhibit 10i

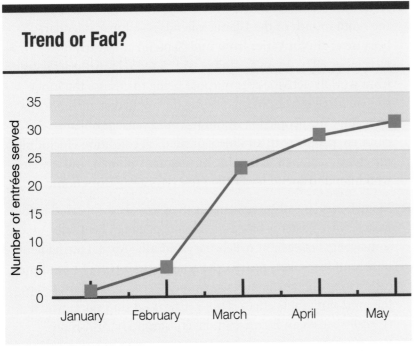

Trend or Fad?

There is not enough information to decide if interest in this entrée is a trend or a fad.

A fad is not a trend. A **trend** is a long-term increase or decrease in some factor like popularity, weight, a belief or idea, or income level. A **fad** is a short-term increase or decrease in popularity of an idea, a belief, a practice, or a product, and fads can come and go. It is difficult to distinguish a fad from a trend early on, as you can see from examining the graph in *Exhibit 10i;* only time will tell which is which. As a restaurant or foodservice professional, you must make your best guess as to which to adapt your recipes and menu to, and which to ride out. This section talks about some popular fad diets that might impact your operation.

The Problem with Fad Diets

Food and nutrition misinformation can have harmful effects on the health of consumers. Diet books are routine best sellers, promise quick fixes, and often encourage consumers to rely on a single research study on which its recommendations are based. They also contradict recommendations made by reputable health organizations such as the U.S. Food and Drug Administration (FDA), the National Academy of Sciences, and the American Dietetic Association. Food fads involve exaggerated claims that food items or supplements may cure disease or offer quick weight loss. Consumers are bombarded with an overwhelming amount of food and nutrition misinformation, most of it related to fad diets.

Unfortunately, knowing how to distinguish nutrition facts from nutrition misinformation is not always clear. Nutrition facts are the result of the repeated application of the scientific method and expert review. Nutrition misinformation does not meet these standards. Food and nutrition misinformation can be a barrier to public health by giving consumers a false sense of security and causing the delay

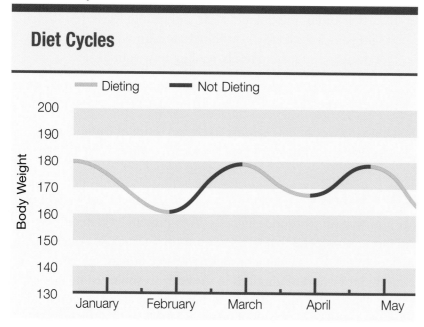

Diet Cycles

Cycles of dieting and normal eating are often found with fad dieting.

of appropriate healthcare. And usually, they simply are not effective.

Another problem with fad diets and other diets that are not nutritionally balanced is what happens when the dieter ends the diet. Typically, the dieter returns to the original weight, or worse, an even higher weight. Then, the dieter typically goes on another diet to get back to the lower weight. The net result is a series of high- and low-weight cycles with no long-term weight reduction, as shown in *Exhibit 10j.* Besides being disappointing, this stresses the dieter's body.

Low-Carbohydrate Diet

There is no legal definition for the term "low carbohydrate." The FDA, which regulates health claims on food labels in the United States, has not defined what *low carbohydrate* means, and its use on food labels is not approved by any government authorities. "Low carbohydrate," and its variants "low-carb" and "lo-carb," are actually a designation used by marketers to attract consumers to food items and have no legal definition.

The assumption that low-carbohydrate food is healthier food is not necessarily true. Low-carbohydrate food actually may be high in fat and calories. For example, manufacturers of low-carbohydrate candy bars often replace carbohydrates with substances such as the sweeteners **sorbitol** and **mannitol** (sugar alcohols). When eaten in large quantities, sorbitol and mannitol can act as laxatives and may cause diarrhea, cramping, or other discomforts. A single low-carbohydrate nutrition bar, for example, may contain five grams of saturated fat (25 percent of a person's daily recommended maximum intake) and hundreds of calories, a large proportion of them from saturated fat.

The logic of the low-carbohydrate diet is as follows:

1 If carbohydrates raise blood sugar and insulin levels, resulting in weight gain, a decrease in carbohydrates should result in lower blood sugar and insulin levels, leading to weight loss.

2 If one does not eat carbohydrates, the body breaks down fat for the energy it needs.

Actually, any weight loss is more likely the result of eating fewer calories, whether the calories are from carbohydrates, fat, or protein.

High-Fat Diet

Misinformation surrounds high-fat, high-protein food items. Some fad diets recommend that large amounts of fat, such as a quarter stick of butter, be eaten at a meal for a variety of reasons, from increased transport of vitamins in the body to enhanced metabolic effects. The truth is that there is nothing special about certain food items or combinations of food items. A calorie is a calorie no matter when or how it is consumed. Nutrition experts consistently recommend a balanced diet with only the needed number of calories.

High-Protein, Low-Carbohydrate Diet

The high-protein, low-carbohydrate diet, really a variation of the low-carbohydrate diet, emphasizes consumption of food high in protein like meat, fish, fowl, beans, and eggs and the minimization or avoidance of cereals and other starchy carbohydrates like potatoes, bread, and pasta. Eating fruit also is minimized or avoided because of the high sugar levels it can contain. Whether other carbohydrate sources, like greens and green and yellow vegetables, are included depends on the exact variant of this type of diet.

The long-term effects of a high-protein, low-carbohydrate diet are unknown. However, obtaining most of one's calories from high-protein food items is not a balanced diet because the other nutrients provided by cereals, starches, and some carbohydrates are lacking. Anyone on this diet must replace these essential nutrients through daily supplements. Also, meat, especially certain red meat, is high in fat and cholesterol, and individuals who follow this diet may be consuming too much of these substances.

Actually, high-protein, low-carbohydrate diets are often low in calories because they limit food choices and quantities. That is the primary reason they cause short-term weight loss.

Exhibit 10k

No vitamin or mineral supplements are needed by most athletes.

Sports Diets

A **sports diet** is some combination of higher than normal amounts of protein, sports-diet supplements, electrolyte replacement, and carbohydrate loading, which are done to enhance athletic ability, strength, agility, and endurance. The exact combination depends on the sport and the beliefs of the athlete and coach.

There is no doubt that what an athlete eats and drinks affects his or her health, body composition, and athletic performance especially for endurance sports like the marathon shown in *Exhibit 10k*. As sports nutrition has increased in popularity, so has the sale of energy aids, assorted supplements, and herbal and diet aids aimed at improving sports performance. Unsubstantiated claims entice athletes to use these products to optimize performance; non-athletes also buy these products. In general, no vitamin or mineral supplements are needed if an athlete is getting enough calories from a variety of food items to maintain body weight. No single nutrient supplement should be used without a specific medical or nutritional reason; an example of a legitimate use of a supplement is an iron supplement used to help with anemia.

Carbohydrate Loading

Carbohydrates are important for maintenance of blood-glucose levels during exercise and to replace muscle glycogen. **Carbohydrate loading** is a method used by some athletes to maximize the storage of glycogen in the muscles. This involves consuming high proportions—even excesses—of carbohydrates prior to an athletic competition. Muscles normally store only small amounts of glycogen. Usually, this does not present a problem. But if an individual exercises intensely, and continues for an hour or more, muscles will run out of glycogen, and stamina (as well as performance) will be greatly reduced. Carbohydrate loading is not for every athlete. But if an athlete wants to improve performance, carbohydrate loading can help. Researchers are studying the best way to increase stores of glycogen in the muscles of endurance athletes.

Drinking sports beverages that contain carbohydrates and electrolytes during exercise provides fuel for muscles, helps maintain blood glucose, and decreases the risk of dehydration. Also, supplements may be needed by athletes who use severe weight-loss practices, eliminate one or more food groups from their diets, or consume high-carbohydrate diets with low nutrient density.

Exhibit 10l

The wheat grass in this photograph is an example of an herbal supplement.

Herbs and Herbal Supplements

In addition to the variety of diets found in the United States, many people believe that supplementing their diet with herbs will help them lead a healthier and longer life. This section examines whether herbs and herbal supplements, like those shown in *Exhibit 10l,* should play a role in a healthy diet.

The Center for Complementary and Alternative Medicine (NCCAM) describes **complementary and alternative medicine** as "a group of diverse medical and health care systems, practices and products that are not presently considered to be part of conventional medicine."[3] These alternative health systems tend to make regular use of herbs and other products that are often taken as dietary supplements. Echinacea, ginkgo, ginseng, and other herbal supplements are among the most popular herbs used today.

Herbal supplements are derived from natural plant sources such as flowers, roots, and leaves, but "natural" does not always mean "harmless." Questions still remain about many herbal supplements' effectiveness, benefits, side effects, dosages, value over time, and other safety issues. Under current U.S. law, herbal supplements can be made available without being tested or regulated like food items or drugs. Because of this, herbal supplements have become a regular part of the diet for many people for a variety of reasons and are a significant portion of the U.S. economy.

Just because a product may be sold does not guarantee that it works or is safe. Products that claim to be "natural" or "herbal" are not usually scientifically tested to prove either of these things, and there have been some outstanding examples of dangerous herbal remedies. For example, herbal products containing ephedra (now banned by the U.S. government) have caused serious health problems and even death. Before taking any herbs or herbal supplements, consumers should consult their physicians, dietitians, or nutritionists.

Impact on Restaurants and Foodservice Operations

Herbs and herbal supplements are part of an ever-growing category of ingredients often considered "alternative." The attraction is their assumed, yet controversial, health benefits. Operators should not overemphasize the health benefits or importance of these products for this reason. Also, since supplements are loosely regulated, legal problems could arise with customers who were negatively affected by taking them. In general, it is best to refrain from making herbal health claims on menus. When asked about a menu item containing

---

[3] National Center for Complementary and Alternative Medicine Web site. Health Information page. *www.nccam.nih.gov/health/whatiscam.* 6/22/06.

herbs or an herbal product, make supplier information available, but allow guests to decide for themselves.

Relationship of Diet and Exercise

To successfully lose weight and keep it off, individuals must balance caloric intake with exercise. Ideally, dieting should be done by eating a nutritionally balanced, low-calorie diet and increasing one's level of physical activity.

Although many weight-loss programs advertise various ways to help individuals lose weight, the only proven long-term and safe method is to burn more calories than are consumed, namely, eating less food or healthier food, or by exercising more. In addition, behavior-modification techniques such as eating smaller portions can help control eating habits.

One pound of fat contains approximately 3,500 calories, so to lose one pound a week, a person should eat 3,500 fewer calories per week. This can be done by reducing one's daily intake by 500 calories per day (500 for seven days will reduce calories by 3,500 a week). Physical activity also contributes significantly to weight loss.

Helpful tips for weight loss:

- Activity can be increased by taking the stairs rather than the elevator, or walking instead of driving when possible.

- Reducing food intake gradually can help make new eating habits lifelong habits.

- Reducing fat intake on a daily basis, as well as reducing intake of other high-calorie food is effective, as fats contain nine calories per gram and carbohydrates and proteins contain four calories per gram.

- Habits that make a person eat more can be changed or modified. For example, if someone tends to snack while watching television, then taking a walk instead of watching television or drinking a calorie-free beverage instead of snacking will help.

- Calorie watchers should learn about the caloric content of food through the Nutrition Facts panel on food packages as well as know the calorie expenditure of various physical activities.

- Calorie counting is not the only way to lose weight. Eating smaller amounts of a variety of food and increasing activity level will usually lead to slow but steady weight loss. This slower change of pace also allows people to become used to the new diet, with the changes becoming a normal part of their lives.

Weight-Loss Diets

Consumers are often attracted to diets that promise magical, no-stress weight loss. The truth is that most weight-loss diets:

■ Do not work at all or work only for a relatively short time.

■ Are nutritionally unbalanced.

■ Tend to result in eating binges, especially when the diet is terminated.

■ Result in a reduction of body water, or sometimes muscle, instead of fat.

■ Result in weight loss that is often short-lived and followed by a return to the previous weight.

Many approaches to modifying caloric intake have been tried. One way to classify them is in terms of the total caloric intake—as starvation, fasting, very low calorie, or low calorie. Another way to classify them is in terms of what food they recommend or prohibit. Most fad diets, for example, are for the purpose of weight loss and have the shortcomings already discussed.

Exhibit 10m

Liquid meal replacements reduce calories drastically.

Meal Replacement Diets

Meal replacement products implement a type of calorie-controlled diet. Under these diet plans, individuals replace a meal with a liquid drink containing approximately two hundred calories, like the one shown in *Exhibit 10m*. Caloric intake is controlled, sensory stimulation of eating is reduced, and the need to make decisions about portion size is drastically lessened. Individuals must be extremely motivated to stay on a premeasured meal plan on a long-term basis, and many find this to be difficult.

Obviously, meal replacement diets conflict with the goals of restaurant and foodservice enterprises because they cause dieters to bypass these operations. To attract dieters, many restaurant and foodservice operations have added reduced-calorie items to their menus.

Health Risks of American Diets

Major causes of **morbidity** (disease rate) and **mortality** (death rate) in the United States are related to poor diet and a sedentary lifestyle. These conditions include cardiovascular disease, hypertension, type 2 diabetes, obesity, osteoporosis, iron-deficiency anemia, oral disease, malnutrition, and some cancers. Restaurant and foodservice operations can help by providing healthy, nutritious food that is low

Exhibit 10n

Interpreting BMI

BMI	Weight Status
Below 18.5	Underweight
18.5–24.9	Normal
25.0–29.9	Overweight
30 and above	Obese

U.S. Centers for Disease Control and Prevention

in excess fat, sugar, and other empty calories, and by providing sufficient choices for their customers.

Food items provide an array of nutrients that may have beneficial effects on health, and supplements cannot replace a healthful diet. Individuals already consuming the recommended amount of a nutrient in food will not achieve any additional health benefit if they also take that nutrient as a supplement. Moreover, in some cases, supplements may cause intakes to exceed safe levels of vitamins and minerals; see Chapter 7 for a discussion of Tolerable Upper Intake Levels.

Obesity in U.S. Adults

The health problem most able to be overcome by an improved diet in the United States is overweight and obesity. A person who is overweight or obese has a weight that is greater than what is generally considered healthy. These terms also identify ranges of weight that have been shown to increase the likelihood of certain diseases and other health problems.

According to the Centers for Disease Control and Prevention (CDC) of the U.S. Department of Health and Human Services' National Health and Nutrition Examination Survey for 1999–2002, the following percentages of U.S. adults are overweight or obese:

- An estimated 65 percent of U.S. adults aged twenty years and older are either overweight or obese.

- An estimated 30 percent of U.S. adults aged twenty years and older—over sixty million people—are obese.

Overweight and obesity ranges are determined by using weight and height to calculate a number called the **body mass index** (BMI). BMI is used because, for most people, it correlates with their amount of body fat. The definitions of overweight and obese are in terms of BMI, listed in *Exhibit 10n*. It is important to remember that, although BMI correlates with the amount of body fat, BMI does not directly measure body fat. As a result, some people, such as athletes, may have a BMI that identifies them as overweight even though they do not have excess body fat.

The formula for BMI is:

$$\text{BMI} = \left(\text{Weight (lb)} \div \text{Height (in)}^2 \right) \times 703$$

Eating highly caloric food and too much food combined with a sedentary lifestyle is the main cause of obesity in the United States. The human body adapted over the millennia to the amount and nature of food eaten and the amount of activity undertaken. Activity levels have declined over shorter time periods, but the human body's capabilities and needs have not changed.

Most diet and nutrition experts believe that the key to a healthy diet is balance, moderation, and physical activity. If this is correct, then obesity is the result of many interrelated factors that are affecting these three dimensions. These factors must be managed so that the number of calories taken in is matched to the number of calories needed by the body according to the lifestyle practiced by each person. Generally, this means that the caloric intake must be reduced or the amount of physical activity increased, or both. Only when these two are balanced and become part of one's daily routine will weight control be achieved.

Activity

Your BMI

Calculate your own BMI using the BMI formula. Then, if you are over twenty years of age, check your work by going to the CDC's online BMI calculator for adults at *www.cdc.gov/nccdphp/dnpa/bmi/adult_BMI/english_bmi_calculator/ bmi_calculator.htm*. (If you are twenty years old or younger, see the next section.)

Obesity in U.S. Teens and Children

Not only is adult obesity a problem, but teen and childhood obesity is growing at an alarming rate. About 16 percent of U.S. children and teens, aged six to nineteen, are overweight according to the U.S. Centers for Disease Control and Prevention (CDC).[4]

Although calculating BMI for teens and children uses the same formula for adults, interpreting the BMI for teens and children is more complicated since their bodies are growing. For children and teens, the CDC interprets BMI using percentiles on age-specific and gender-specific growth charts for two reasons:

■ The amount of body fat changes with age.

■ The amount of body fat differs between girls and boys.

Because of these factors, the interpretation of BMI is both age-specific and gender-specific for children and teens. The BMI-for-age growth charts take into account these differences and allow translation of a BMI number into a percentile for a child's gender and age.

After BMI is calculated for children and teens, the BMI number is plotted on the CDC BMI-for-age growth charts (for either girls or boys) to obtain a percentile ranking. (Percentiles are the most

---

[4] U.S. Centers for Disease Control and Prevention Web site. *www.cdc.gov/nccdphp/dnpa/obesity/*. 6/22/06.

Exhibit 10o

Interpreting BMI Percentiles for Teens and Children

Percentile Range	Weight Status Category
Less than the 5th percentile	Underweight
5th percentile up to the 85th percentile	Healthy weight
85th to less than the 95th percentile	At risk of overweight
Equal to or greater than the 95th percentile	Overweight

U.S. Centers for Disease Control and Prevention

commonly used indicator to assess the size and growth patterns of individual children in the United States.) The percentile indicates the relative position of the child's BMI number among children of the same gender and age. The growth charts show the weight status categories used with children and teens (underweight, healthy weight, at risk of overweight, and overweight). BMI-for-age weight status categories and the corresponding percentiles are shown in *Exhibit 10o*.

Because of the dependence on the CDC growth charts, the best way to determine the weight status category for teens and children is to use the CDC's online BMI calculator.

Several causes of childhood obesity are known:

- **Poverty and scarcity of food**—In these situations, children tend to be given high-calorie food items, which add calories, instead of fruit and vegetables.

- **Low self-esteem**—Children with low self-esteem sometimes turn to food to compensate, and the food items they choose tend to be high-calorie items instead of fruit and vegetables.

- **Lack of physical activity**—Lack of physical activity for children in today's U.S. lifestyle also contributes to obesity because the excess calories consumed are not burned off.

With childhood obesity, parents can be important change agents. Parents must find a way to teach their children how to eat healthily and should focus on the quality of the diet rather than the quantity of calories. Schools and other institutions responsible for the diets of teens and children should do the same. At least they should not make it easy to have an unhealthy diet.

Activity

Teen or Child BMI

Determine the BMI of one or more teens or children using the CDC's online BMI calculator for them at *http://apps.nccd. cdc.gov/dnpabmi/calculator.aspx*

Restaurant and Foodservice Professionals Can Help

Restaurant and foodservice operations have promoted healthy lifestyles for many years through nutrition information and education, as well as physical-activity education. In addition, the restaurant and foodservice industry has provided many options and menu items from which consumers may choose. Most quick-service operations have voluntarily provided nutrition information to guests. The restaurant and foodservice industry also is involved with programs to help fight obesity.

Food Additives— Their Role and Impact

A **food additive** is a substance or combination of substances that is present in food as a result of processing, production, or packaging. An additive is a chemical just as nutrients are chemicals. Many additives are naturally occurring or are extracted from food. For example, **carotene** (the precursor of vitamin A), which is used as a yellow food coloring, contains orange or red crystalline pigments found in plants. Other additives are chemically identical to natural substances—for example, ascorbic acid (vitamin C), which is used as an antioxidant. (The function of antioxidants is provided in *Exhibit 10p.*)

Technically, food additives include familiar ingredients such as salt, baking soda, vanilla, and yeast. However, most people tend to think only of other chemicals added to food items as additives. All food additives are carefully regulated by federal authorities.

Functions and Impacts of Food Additives

Food additives perform many functions in food, such as improving flavor, color, and texture, retaining nutritional value, preventing spoilage, and extending shelf life. Some of these additives perform functions that are often taken for granted. Since most people no longer live on farms, additives help keep food wholesome and appealing while it is transported to markets. Without additives, many food items would be less attractive, less flavorful, less nutritious, more likely to spoil, and more costly. Without them, people would not enjoy a variety of safe and tasty food items year-round, and many convenience food items would not be possible. *Exhibit 10p* on the next page lists the different types of additives and their functions. The Center for Science in the Public Interest lists food additives and their effects on the body at *www.cspinet.org/reports/chemcuisine.htm.*

Allergens in Food Items

Allergens are substances that can cause an allergic reaction. For some people, their immune system recognizes allergens as "foreign" or "dangerous." These same substances cause no response for most other people. Allergens can be present in food. Currently, there is no cure for food allergies, so food-allergic consumers must avoid the food items to which they are allergic.

Exhibit 10p

Food Additives and Their Functions

Additive	Function
Antioxidants	Antioxidants slow the oxidation process that turns fats rancid. Some fats, especially vegetable oils, do not become rancid as quickly because they contain naturally occurring antioxidants, such as tocopherol.
Benzoates	Benzoates are used as preservatives in acidic food items such as fruit juices and syrups, pie fillings, pickles, pickled vegetables, and sauces. Benzoates occur naturally in cranberries.
Colorants	Food colors (or colorants) fall into three groups; natural pigments extracted from plant materials, inorganic pigments and lakes (metals combined with organic colors), and synthetic coal-tar dyes.
Emulsifiers	Emulsifiers enable the formation of water-fat mixtures; they are a common ingredient in baked items because they help integrate the fat. Examples of some emulsifiers are gums, egg yolks, albumin, casein, and lecithin. All these substances help disperse oil in water uniformly. Emulsifiers also interact with fats to modify their crystal structure, which reduces viscosity or increases aeration (as in whipped cream). Emulsifiers interact with starch to reduce stickiness and to slow the staling of bread. They interact with gluten and thereby improve the baking quality of wheat flour, resulting in better texture and volume in packed goods.
Gums	Gums are substances that form a sticky mass in water. Gums help to keep emulsions from separating into constituent parts and are widely used in salad dressings, processed cheese, and confections.
Monosodium glutamate (MSG)	MSG is probably one of the best known and widely used flavor enhancers. MSG occurs naturally in food items and is often added to canned soups and meats. MSG gives some people headaches.
Nitrates	Nitrates are natural constituents of plants and, together with nitrites, are used in the pickling of meats. Nitrate is converted into nitrite in the process.
Nitrites	Used in canned meats, nitrite is the essential agent in preserving meat by pickling. It inhibits the growth of *Clostridium botulinum* and therefore prevents botulism. Nitrites also preserve the desirable color and flavor of these products.
Phosphates	Phosphates are used widely within food processing and have several applications. For baked goods, phosphates are used as leavening agents. Phosphates are also used in the tenderizing of meats and in the processing of meats and seafood to improve texture.
Stabilizers	Stabilizers help maintain the structure of emulsions. They are often used in meringues and marshmallows to produce body and mouth feel.
Thickeners	Thickeners add body to a food product without imparting flavor. Modified starches are used as thickeners in commercial baking, as they work well with acidic ingredients, tolerate high temperatures, and do not cause pie fillings to "weep" during storage.

Exhibit 10q

Eight Recognized Allergens

Milk and dairy products

Eggs and egg products

Fish

Shellfish (e.g., crab, lobster, shrimp)

Tree nuts (e.g., almonds, Brazil nuts, cashews, chestnuts, hazelnuts, hickory nuts, macadamia nuts, pecans, pine nuts, pistachios, and walnuts)

Peanuts

Wheat

Soy and soy products

Common Food Allergens

More than 160 food items have been identified to cause food allergies in sensitive individuals. However, there are eight major food allergens identified by the Food Allergen Labeling and Consumer Protection Act (FALCPA) of 2004. These eight allergens account for over 90 percent of all documented food allergies in the United States and represent the food items most likely to result in severe or life-threatening reactions. These food allergens are listed in *Exhibit 10q*.

Impact of Food Allergens

FALCPA states that 2 percent of adults and about 5 percent of infants and young children in the United States suffer from food allergies.

Approximately 30,000 consumers require emergency-room treatment, and 150 Americans die each year because of allergic reactions to food. People with food allergies experience reactions in which the immune system overreacts to what is harmless for most people. These reactions include chemicals that are released in the body, causing the skin to become red, itchy, and swollen, blood vessels to widen, and internal muscles to contract.

Avoiding Allergen Problems with Guests

FALCPA requires that the label of a food containing an ingredient that is or contains a "major food allergen" declare the presence of the allergen. FALCPA applies to food products that are labeled on or after January 1, 2006, for domestically manufactured and imported packaged food items that are subject to FDA regulations. FALCPA labeling requirements extend to retail and foodservice establishments such as bakeries, food kiosks at malls, and carryout operations.

Exhibit 10r

For a person allergic to nuts, removing these nuts is not enough; the banana split will still be dangerous because it still will have some nut residue.

Although FALCPA only applies to packaged FDA-regulated food items, the FDA advises consumers who are allergic to particular food items to ask questions about ingredients and preparation when eating out. This implies that servers should be able to answer customers' questions about the food allergens in the food they serve. Obviously, it is management's responsibility to make this effective by holding regular training on allergens in the food being served.

Because even one bite of allergenic food could lead to a serious reaction or death, people with food allergies must avoid allergenic food items completely. Therefore, it is important that restaurants ensure that a guest with an allergy is not served an item that he or she is allergic to. Servers must listen carefully when a guest says he or she has a food allergy and must be able to respond accurately. For example, if a customer asks whether an egg roll was fried in peanut oil, the server should be able to answer; moreover, the server should then ask whether the diner is allergic to all peanut products.

Communicating Allergens in Menu Items

Servers should be able to describe a menu item and its ingredients upon request. Staff members should know what ingredients are in an item or where to find the information. In some cases, it may be helpful to show guests the product label of the ordered food so they can assess the situation for themselves.

If a server does not know whether a menu item is free of a potentially dangerous food substance, the server should say so and refer the guest to a manager. Ideally, there should be a designated point person on staff during each shift to answer questions about ingredients. If no one knows for sure if an allergen is present in an item, say so and recommend that the guest order another item.

Front-of-the-House and Back-of-the-House Partnering

Cross-contaminating food items with potentially allergenic food items should be avoided. Food for allergy sufferers should be prepared and served without any contact with allergens. Kitchen staff should be trained to use a prep table that has not been exposed to the allergen and to clean all cooking utensils after working with potentially allergenic food items.

Chefs should be trained so they can prepare allergen-free versions of items upon request. Allergens should never be included in creating a "chef's surprise" dish. Furthermore, all menu items should be clearly described; this will go a long way to alleviating problems with food allergens. Food manufacturers may make changes to product formulas, so read labels carefully. Just because a product was safe last month does not mean that it is safe today.

Additionally, think about allergens before making product substitutions. For example, if you have always used vegetable oil, do not suddenly substitute peanut oil. It may not occur to a regular guest with a food allergy to ask if a dish he or she enjoyed for years has now changed, and even a trace of the allergen can set off a severe allergic reaction. If a guest is allergic to peanuts, simply removing them from the banana split you are serving (shown in *Exhibit 10r* on the previous page.) is not enough to prevent a possible life-threatening episode, because trace amounts may be left behind. It is necessary to prepare a new banana split with equipment and ingredients that have not come in contact with peanuts.

Servers should call for emergency help if a guest is in need of help. Emergency numbers should be posted at all phones and have the name, address, and phone number of your restaurant or foodservice operation near each phone so this information can be given to the emergency squad.

Activity

Healthy Dining in Your Neighborhood

Visit several different types of eating establishments (coffee shop, national chain, fine dining) and ask for a menu to take; if one is not available, ask permission to copy one, even if it is on the wall. Review all the menus for:

- Healthy choices (described on the menu as such)

- Allergens (specified within menu-item descriptions)

- Healthy-preparation options (grilled fish instead of fried)

Following your review, rate each menu on the basis of offering healthy-choice options, declaration of allergens where appropriate, and flexibility of food-preparation methods.

Summary

A healthy American diet has adequate carbohydrate, protein, and fat in the correct proportions for the level of activity the body receives, contains few empty calories, and has variety to ensure the proper intake of vitamins and minerals. However, the majority of Americans do not follow a healthy diet. Many factors, including large portion sizes and poor food choices, contribute to less-than-ideal diets.

A variety of diets are found in the United States. Some people adhere to special diets for philosophical, health, or religious reasons. For example, people following a vegetarian diet do not eat meat, fish, or fowl or products containing these items. Religion-influenced diets, such as those followed by Jewish or Hindu people, restrict various food items and may restrict the way food is prepared and served.

There are also a number of fad diets. Fad diets often offer quick fixes and contradict recommendations made by reputable health organizations. For example, low-carbohydrate, high-fat, and high-protein diets are not balanced diets and may lack essential nutrients. The long-term effects of these diets are not known.

Major causes of disease and death in the United States are related to poor diet and a sedentary lifestyle. These conditions include cardiovascular disease, hypertension, type 2 diabetes, obesity, osteoporosis, iron-deficiency anemia, oral disease, malnutrition, and some cancers. The health problem most able to be overcome by an improved diet in the United States is overweight and obesity. Not only is adult obesity a problem, but teen and childhood obesity is growing at an alarming rate. Too many calories combined with a sedentary lifestyle is the main cause of obesity in the United States. Restaurant and foodservice operations can help by providing healthy, nutritious food that is low in excess fat, sugar, and other empty calories, and by providing sufficient choices for their customers.

Food items provide an array of nutrients that may have beneficial effects on health. However, for people with food allergies, some food items must be avoided. Although there are more than 160 food items that have been identified to cause food allergies in sensitive people, eight major allergens have been identified—milk and dairy products, eggs and egg products, fish, shellfish, tree nuts, peanuts, wheat, and soy and soy products. Restaurant and foodservice operations are responsible for ensuring that all servers, chefs, and kitchen staff are able to answer customers' questions about food allergens in the food they serve. In addition, restaurant and foodservice professionals have a responsibility to manage their menus so guests can make informed dining choices that help them maintain a balanced diet over a period of time.

Review Your Learning

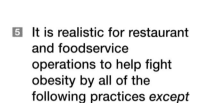

1 All the following terms are types of vegetarians *except*

A. lacto-ovo.

B. lacto.

C. vegan.

D. macrobiotic.

2 The kosher diet can include

A. beef, fruit, seeds, and vegetables.

B. lobster and other shellfish.

C. game meat like rabbit and quail.

D. pork.

3 Which statement is true about low-carbohydrate diets?

A. The FDA has not defined what "low-carbohydrate" means.

B. Low-carbohydrate food items are low in calories.

C. The long-term effects of low-carbohydrate diets are well known.

D. Carbohydrates are not an important part of a healthy diet, so low-carbohydrate intake is not a problem.

4 All of the following statements are true about herbal supplements *except*

A. they are derived from natural plant sources.

B. they can enter the market without testing or regulation.

C. products containing ephedra have been banned by the U.S. government.

D. they are harmless as long as they are "natural."

5 It is realistic for restaurant and foodservice operations to help fight obesity by all of the following practices *except*

A. offering a variety of menu choices.

B. offering detailed nutrition information.

C. offering nutrition education.

D. offering only nutritionally balanced meals of the correct size.

6 All of the following statements are true about allergens *except*

A. there are eight major allergens identified by the FALCPA.

B. substituting menu ingredients will probably not cause any harm.

C. allergens should be declared in menu descriptions.

D. restaurateurs must guard against cross-contamination in preparation areas.

7 All of the following statements are true about additives *except*

A. many additives are naturally occurring or extracted from food items.

B. additives are regulated by the government.

C. additives are often nutrients.

D. additives are typically unnecessary.

8 All of the following statements are true about obesity *except*

A. many lifestyle factors contribute to obesity.

B. a sedentary lifestyle contributes to obesity.

C. obesity may also cause other disease states such as diabetes and heart disease.

D. obesity can be managed by omitting meat from the diet.

9 All of the following statements are true about replacing animal sources of nutrients *except*

A. fortified soy beverages and sunlight can supply vitamin D.

B. whole-grain bread and brown rice can supply vitamin B$_{12}$.

C. tofu and other soy-based products can supply protein.

D. legumes, tofu, and green leafy vegetables can supply iron.

10 A healthy diet includes all of the following *except*

A. all the necessary vitamins and minerals.

B. sixty-four ounces of water and twenty-five grams of fiber per day.

C. at least 3,000 calories per day for the average person.

D. nutritional balance of carbohydrate, fat, and protein.

Notes

Field Project

Real-World Analysis

This field practicum will reinforce the concepts of this guide by showing how nutrition is used in the restaurant and foodservice industry to provide healthier food. It will help you to develop the analytical skills you need to be successful.

Assignment

One effective way to exercise your nutritional knowledge is to apply it to a real-case scenario at an actual restaurant, and the activities below provide you with an opportunity to learn from practitioners in the restaurant and foodservice industry. By understanding the constraints and requirements of an actual operation, you will enhance and sharpen your applicable knowledge of nutrition and sharpen your recipe refining and healthy cooking skills.

1 Select a restaurant that has a full menu.

2 Get permission from the manager and the chef to review some of their menu items.

- ☐ Explain that you are doing a research project to review menu items for healthy options and that you would like to provide feedback about some of their recipes, to show how they could be made healthier by using low-fat cooking methods and reducing amounts of fat and salt.

3 Select five menu items to review—two appetizers, two entrées, and one dessert. Choose menu items that:

- ☐ Are high in fat

- ☐ Could incorporate the use of whole grains or whole-grain flour

- ☐ Could include more vegetables or carbohydrates

4 Calculate the nutritional content of each menu item.

- ☐ Look for the amount of carbohydrate, protein, fat, sodium, cholesterol, and vitamins and minerals.

- ☐ Look at all the ingredients; you may have to review food labels to determine nutritional content for the ingredients.

- ☐ Look at the types of fats used—polyunsaturated, monounsaturated, saturated, or trans fat— and document that information.

- ☐ You may use nutritional analysis software if you have it available.

5 Assume that the five items you chose make up one person's diet for one day.

- ☐ Determine if the nutritional content of that day's food falls within the USDA dietary guidelines and percentages.

- ☐ Identify the dietary categories that are within and outside the guidelines.

continued on next page

Real-World Analysis *continued from the previous page*

6 Review and document the preparation and cooking methods used for each menu item.

☐ Can you improve them to make the food lower in fat?

☐ Provide a cooking technique for preparing the item in an alternative manner that retains the integrity of the dish.

7 Rewrite the recipe to improve the nutritional balance of the menu items.

☐ Look for opportunities to use low-fat alternative ingredients and cooking methods, use whole grains, and increase the amounts of vegetables or carbohydrates.

☐ Is there a way to decrease trans fat and saturated fat in the recipe?

☐ Give suggestions to decrease salt and yet increase flavor.

☐ Keep in mind that the recipe must retain its tastiness and flavor.

8 Recalculate the nutritional content of each revised menu item. Show how your changes to the recipe lowered the fat and salt content and improved nutritional balance but maintained the recipe.

9 Discuss your results with the chef and determine if your changes are acceptable and reasonable.

10 Write an in-depth report explaining all of your actions and discoveries from start to finish.

☐ Provide the chef and your instructor with a copy.

Index